Modern Day Slavery
Human Trafficking Revealed

Modern Day Slavery

◆

Human Trafficking Revealed

Catherine Paris, Founder
Women In Need Network

Claddagh Ltd.
Florida

Modern Day Slavery
Human Trafficking Revealed

Claddagh Ltd. Publishing House

For information address:
Claddagh Ltd.
P.O. Box 773134
Ocala, FL 34477-3134
www.CladdaghPublishing.com

ISBN: 978-0-9795213-0-0

Printed in the United States of America

Contents

Preface..vii

Modern Slave Trade..8

Child Victims of Trafficking...18

    Communicating with Child Victims...............................19

    Understanding Child Victims of Trafficking.................21

    Child Camel Jockeys..23

    Child Sexual Exploitation..29

    Child Prostitution..32

    Child Sex Tourism...33

    Child Soldiers..39

    Panhandling...43

    Child Labor..44

    Child Labor Victims..45

    Agriculture..47

    Fisheries..50

    Domestic Servitude...51

    Tanzanite Mines..56

Child Labor in Mines and Quarries..............................58

Forced Labor..60

United States Response to Human Trafficking....................73

States with Human Trafficking Laws...............................85

Florida Responds to Trafficking....................................102

Global Response to Human Trafficking............................114

United Nations..134

Interpol...141

Human Trafficking Cases...144

Rescue and Restore..177

Resource Guide...180

Appendix...183

- Emancipation Proclamation.................................183
- Thirteenth Amendment 186
- The Mann Act...188
- The Hobbs Act..194
- Model State Anti-Trafficking Criminal Statute............196
   o Appendix A...216
   o Appendix B...219
- TVPA Minimum Standards...................................220
- PROTECT Act 2003...225
- Palermo Protocol...319

Glossary of Acronyms..336

Afterword..338

Preface

On January 1, 1863, as the nation approached its third year of bloody civil war, President Abraham Lincoln issued the *Emancipation Proclamation*. This proclamation declared "that all persons held as slaves" within the rebellious states "are, and henceforward shall be free."

Our nation along with the entire world is battling an evil too tragic to imagine, let alone think about on a daily basis. Unfortunately, the time has come to wake up and take a cold hard look around us. Human trafficking is taking place from one end of the globe to the other. The reality is that *"human trafficking"* is just a polite way of saying *"modern day slavery"*. We can no longer keep our heads buried in the sand while pretending this blight on humanity does not exist.

What can we do about human trafficking? For one thing we can educate ourselves. We can discover how to recognize victims of trafficking, we can learn how to protect ourselves from becoming victims of human trafficking, and we can help those who have been victimized by the perpetrators of trafficking in persons. You have already taken the first step, just by picking up this book. It is important to read the information contained within these pages, learn from it, and to share that knowledge with those around you. The next step is to continue to learn about human trafficking and to stay ionformed. New information comes forward every day. Throughout the course of this book you will learn what is being done around the world and here in America.

When I organized my first training conference on human trafficking, I was surprised to discover how many people did not know what human trafficking was. The most common misconception I have came across was that many people confused trafficking with smuggling. There is a great difference between the two, the most primal difference being that trafficking victims are not willing participants. I will go into greater detail on this matter, in the section covering smuggling versus trafficking.

This book also discusses the various laws, agencies, countries, and protocols dealing with human trafficking. Case studies have been included, along with pertinent news items, and the latest information available from our government. There are local, national, and global campaigns being waged to fight modern day slavery. United States statutes, legislation, and international laws referenced in this book contain the actual language of those laws. Passages appearing in italics are excerpts and / or quotes;6 their origins are identified. If you are interested in becoming involved in any of the campaigns listed in this book, you will find contact information in the resource guide. If you decide that you are unable to become involved, you can always send a donation to one of the many nonprofit non-governmental organizations (NGO's) waging war on human trafficking. They need your support in order to continue their worthwhile efforts on behalf of victims. Public education is extremely important. You can help by spreading the word and sharing your knowledge with those around you. Talk about human trafficking to your family, your friends, and your co-workers. By bringing this topic into the light, more people will be aware of this plague spreading throughout the world; making it easier to detect possible victims of trafficking.

Dedication

This book is dedicated in loving memory, to my brother, Rob.

Modern Slave Trade

Modern slave trade? Human trafficking? Sounds like something Hollywood would make up, just to sell movie tickets. Regrettably, this is a real issue and it is occurring globally. That includes our great nation, the United States of America. So, the big question is: *What is human trafficking?* Human trafficking is just a polite way of saying "modern day slavery". While I was promoting a training seminar entitled *Human Trafficking: How Much Do You Know?*, I discovered most of the people I came in contact with confused trafficking with smuggling. There is a big difference between the two.

Smuggling

Smuggling is a criminal act in which the person being smuggled is an active and willing participant. The purpose of engaging in smuggling is to enable individuals to enter a country illegally, without authorization or documentation. There are at least two persons engaging in this criminal activity, the smuggler and the person being smuggled. Below is the legal definition of the smuggling of people:

"The procurement, in order to obtain, directly or indirectly a financial or other material benefit, of the illegal entry of a person into a State Party of which the person is not a national or permanent resident."

- Protocol Against the Smuggling of Migrants by Land, Sea and Air

Smuggled persons are free to come and go as they please, they can change jobs or leave without fear, and there is no actual or implied coercion. Smuggling always involves the crossing or attempt to cross international borders, it facilitates the illegal entry of a person into another country, and it is a willing act on the part of the illegal alien to gain entry. Finally, the relationship between the smuggler and the illegal alien ends, once the party has crossed an international border. A key component of smuggling is that the relationship ends at the conclusion of this criminal enterprise.

Human Trafficking

Human trafficking is a criminal act in which the person being trafficked is not an active or willing participant. The purpose of engaging in human trafficking is to make a profit off the sale and / or services of the victim. In cases of human trafficking, the person being trafficked is a victim and the party or parties engaging in this enterprise are the criminals. The United Nations created the following definition of human trafficking; which has been adopted by the United States:

"The recruitment, transportation, transfer, harboring or receipt of persons, by means of threat, or use of force or other forms of coercion,

of abduction, of fraud, of deception, of the abuse of power or of
position of vulnerability or of the giving or receiving payments or
benefits to achieve the consent of a person having control over
another person, for the purpose of exploitation."

- The UN Protocol to Prevent, Suppress and Punish
Trafficking in Persons, Especially Women and Children

Victims of human trafficking are enslaved, subjected to limited movement, or isolation, or had their documents confiscated. The person must be involved in labor, services, or commercial sex acts. The trafficked person does not have to cross international or national (state) borders; the actual moving of the victim, if any, can be contained to a small region. The trafficking of persons must contain an element of force, fraud, or coercion (perceived or implied), unless the victim is a minor involved in commercial sex acts. This crime contains forced labor and / or exploitation of the victim. It is important to remember that a person who is trafficked is the victim of a crime. Who are these victims? They are men, women, and children. Where do they come from? They come from impoverished regions; they are homeless persons picked up off the streets; they are runaways tricked into forced prostitution; they are women and children kidnapped of the streets and sold into slavery.

There are three elements of human trafficking. They are the process, means, and end. The "process" of human trafficking is the recruiting, harboring, moving, or obtaining of a person. The "means" of human trafficking is by force, fraud, or coercion. The "end" of human trafficking is for the purpose of involuntary servitude, debt bondage, slavery, or sex trade. The three elements can be broken down further by looking deeper into each component.

Process

The process, solicits recruitment through deceit. One popular example of deceit is through misleading advertisements for employment overseas. These ads are written for the sole purpose of convincing women to accept positions with businesses that are not legitimate. A typical advertisement can read something like this:

"Go work abroad, housing will be provided. No work permit required, you will meet new and interesting people, nice co-workers. Your own comfortable work space, excellent salary, good benefits. Are you interested?"

Let's take a closer look at what that particular advertisement means. "Go work abroad" means you will be leaving your native country and the laws which protect you. "Housing will be provided" can be translated into you having your own room or portion of a room in a brothel. "No work permit required" means you will be working illegally in a foreign country. "You will meet new and interesting people" can mean that you will be forced to have sexual relations with up to thirty men per night in any number of varying degrees of perversion and degradation. "Nice co-workers" usually means that you will be held captive in a brothel with other women who had also been tricked into believing that they were accepting good positions in a reputable business. "Your own comfortable work space" can be translated into your own cot, if you're lucky, in your own room, or it can also mean that you are forced to dance and perform sexually explicit acts in a glass cubicle for men who pay to watch you. "Excellent salary" means that your trafficker will make money off of you. "Good benefits" can mean many things, including forced drug use, beatings, rapes, mutilations, sexually transmitted diseases, HIV/AIDS, and most likely death once you have outlived your usefulness. "Are you interested"? I truly hope not. There is an old expression, perhaps you are familiar with it, "if it sounds too good to be true, it probably is too good to be true". On the surface, that advertisement for employment sounds great, however, you need to ask yourself one question: *"If the job is so good and the company is reputable, why are they advertising for employees in other countries?"* One would think that such a fantastic offer would be grabbed up by people in their own country; people who actually speak the language and who are familiar with the local customs and laws.

Another form of recruitment that is popular with traffickers of persons is to deceive friends and / or family members. For example, a recruiter has a brother who lives in a poor village in Mexico. This brother is the father of twelve children, the oldest of whom is eleven years old. The recruiter pays a visit to the brother, coming all the way from New York City. The sister shows up looking wealthy, wearing a beautiful suit, talking about her great life in America. She brags about how much money she makes more than enough to support her brother's family. She convinces her brother to send his eleven year old daughter back to America with her. She promises to be able to get her niece a job working in the house of a wealthy American woman. She tells her brother that his daughter will make enough money to send home to take care of the rest of the family. She also promises that her niece will receive a good education in an American school. The brother decides to agree to his sister's proposition; after all, if you can't trust your own sister with your child, who can you trust? Weeks later, the sister sends a letter to her brother, informing him of the terrible accident they got into when upon their arrival in New York. She writes explaining how her niece had died, filling the letter with her broken hearted sorrow over this senseless tragedy. In reality, the sister (a.k.a. the recruiter) brought her niece to New York and sold her into child prostitution. The recruiter made money and the child was forced into a life of degradation. In order to prevent the child from trying to escape, she has been beaten, raped and told that her family will die if she doesn't do what she is told. She may have been told that her family was already killed and that she would be next. Traffickers use threats, force and fear to control their victims. Forced drug use is another control tactic used by human traffickers.

Kidnapping is another process used to gain victims and slaves. Victims are grabbed off the streets here in America, in major cities throughout the world, through raids on poor unprotected villages, and from shelters helping displaced persons, usually seeking assistance in the aftermath of natural disasters. Young women are often kidnapped from nightclubs and resorts. The recruiters commonly spike their drinks with a drug which prevents them from defending themselves or fleeing. Women have been snatched out of their vehicles while sitting alone at a traffic light late at night. Teen runaways are highly susceptible to human traffickers, as are drug users and prostitutes. Men have been grabbed from remote villages and forced into labor camps. Children have been rounded up and forced to work as soldiers. Kidnapping involves force and usually violence or the threat of violence. Many who resist the kidnappers are either killed or forced to watch their loved ones slaughtered before their eyes.

Means

"Means" is one of the three elements of human trafficking and contains an element of force, fraud, or coercion. Force is when extraneous circumstances cause the victim to make a decision they would not normally make of their own free will. A victim agrees not to flee because they believe they will be killed as a result of their attempt at freedom. Fraud is described as deception deliberately practiced to secure unfair or unlawful gain. Fraud is a means used by traffickers to procure a benefit from a person who is being trafficked. Agreeing to smuggle a person into another country, usually charging that person a fee for this service, deliberately deceiving this person into believing that they will be free to go on their way once they arrive at their destination is an example of fraud being used to secure a victim of human trafficking. However, once this person crosses the border, the smuggler turns them over to another recruiter or a "coyote", and collects money for this service from the trafficker. The smuggler has sold the victim into slavery having been paid twice to transport someone across the border. The smuggler was paid by the victim and the coyote. The trafficker informs the person who was just smuggled across the border that they owe an additional payment for travelling into the country. They are charged an extremely high fee, which they are unable to pay. It is at this point they are told they must work off their debt and cannot leave until it is paid in full. There is the threat of violence and a fear that they will be turned over to the authorities if they attempt to escape. Coercion is defined as compulsion by force or threat. A perfect example of this is when a young woman is kidnapped and then driven around by her abductors who drive past her home showing her that they know where her family lives. They drive past her school to show where she and her siblings attend, past her parents' place of employment to show they know how to get to her loved ones whenever they want. They threaten to kill her family and prove to her they are capable of carrying out such a threat.

End

This element is very simple to describe. The end result is modern day slavery. In order for a charge of human trafficking to be prosecuted and / or proven, at least one of the three elements must be met.

Traffickers

Trafficking organizations can range from individuals who are involved in the recruitment, transportation and exploitation of an individual victim, to networks providing isolated services and linking together to expand coverage, to numerous people who provide the entire range of services in highly sophisticated, structured networks. Organized criminal networks are also involved in the trafficking of persons for profit and gain. Traffickers use coercive tactics including deception, fraud, intimidation, isolation, threat and use of physical force, and/or debt bondage to control their victims. Victims are nothing more than a commodity to these slave traders; they are often referred to as "merchandise". Traffickers choose their victims based on a need to meet a particular demand; the principal of supply and demand applies here. They understand the process of moving victims to desired locations, all the while exerting control over every aspect of the trafficking victim's life and environment. Victims are deprived of their personal freedom and become virtual hostages in their trafficking roles. Traffickers are adept at making profits through various levels of procurement and sales; victims can be accessed at little or no cost, in Mexico people can be purchased for as little as fifty dollars. Once a trafficker has procured their victim, they begin making money immediately, whether it is through forced labor or commercial sexual exploitation. Once a trafficker no longer needs a particular victim, they exercise one of two options; they either kill their victim or they sell their victim to another trafficker. Either way it is a cost effective decision; terminating a victim's life means the trafficker no longer has to spend money on food for the victim, while reselling a trafficking victim brings one last source of income from that particular victim. Human trafficking is a multi-billion dollar enterprise ranked as the number two illicit industry in the world. It has surpassed the drug trade and now ranks second, behind arms dealing.

The Cost of Human Trafficking

Victims of human trafficking pay a horrible price due to the psychological and physical harm they suffer from their enslavement. This includes disease and stunted growth, which often have permanent effects. Victims forced into the commercial sex trade are often controlled with extreme violence and force drug use. Sex slaves suffer from extreme psychological torture, food deprivation, sleep deficiency, exposure to sexually transmitted diseases, including HIV/AIDS, and violent sexual activity. Many victims suffer from reproductive damage, and in many cases death.

Anxiety, insomnia, depression, and post-traumatic stress disorder are common psychological manifestations among trafficked victims. Unsanitary and overcrowded living conditions, coupled with poor nutrition, cultivate a host of adverse health conditions such as scabies, tuberculosis, and other communicable diseases. Children who are trafficked suffer from many of the same effects listed above, as well as malnutrition, poor growth; arrested development, illiteracy, lack of social skills and growth, and are denied a future. Street children use drugs to escape the pain of sexual exploitation, hunger, and violence. Children as young as seven and eight years of age have been seen sniffing or snorting toxic substances, and using drugs such as marijuana and heroin.

Child Victims of Trafficking

Children suffer tremendously at the hands of these monsters that make a living from their suffering. Children are used for labor in sweatshops, landscaping and migrant farming, construction, factories, fisheries, panhandling, janitorial jobs, hotel or tourist industries, restaurant services, domestic servitude, child camel jockeys, child soldiers, and child sexual exploitation.

Identifying Child Victims of Human Trafficking

Children who are victimized by human traffickers are often mistaken for prostitutes, runaways, migrant farm workers, or domestic servants. It can be difficult to pick up the subtle signals, however, if you look closely and ask the right questions, you may uncover children who are being exploited. Children who are exploited for labor are usually hungry or malnourished to the extent that they are poorly developed and may never reach their full height or development. Children who are forced into the commercial sex trade may show signs of having sexually transmitted diseases, including HIV/AIDS, kidney problems, and urinary tract infections. They may also show outward signs of physical abuse.

Forced into a life of slavery, these child victims of human traffickers will have special needs. These needs will most likely include treatment for physical ailments or disabilities associated with forced labor and the effects it has on developing bodies. The children are exposed to physical abuse which can leave scars and untreated broken bones; never healing properly, causing lifelong physical pain and disabilities. The children can also suffer from hearing loss, headaches, respiratory problems, cardiovascular problems, and loss of limbs. Many of the children also develop chronic back problems and visual problems often associated with forced labor in the agriculture, construction, or manufacturing industries.

Children who are victims of trafficking can also be identified by a variety of environmental factors. These factors can include whether or not the child is living at the workplace or with an employer, living with multiple people in a cramped space, does not attend school, or has sporadic school attendance with a significant gap of schooling here in the United States.

Child victims of human trafficking also suffer psychological effects caused by their exploitation. These effects include shame, helplessness, humiliation, shock, denial, disbelief, disorientation, confusion, post traumatic stress disorder (PTSD), phobias, panic attacks, and depression. Recognizing these signs is the first step to helping child victims of human trafficking. Communication is often the next step.

Communicating with Child Victims

It is particularly important to remember that victims of human trafficking are extremely vulnerable, have suffered incredible degradation, and may have cultural and language barriers that make communication difficult. When dealing with children who have been victimized, this process can become especially difficult. The children have special needs and are likely to believe that what has happened to them is their own fault. Young victims of human trafficking may not be able to establish trust with the person who is trying to help them. This is due to the horrendous experiences inflicted upon them by their traffickers. Often times, the child has been coached by the trafficker to respond to questions in a certain way. This is a tactic used by the trafficker to cover up their crime. Once the child has been rescued and is in a safe environment, it is best to have a child welfare specialist ask the victim questions regarding their experiences. Specialists have experience on how to interact with child victims, especially those children who have been sexually exploited. What type of questions should be asked of the child? Depending upon the child's place of origin, these questions may vary slightly to include international concerns.

> Why did you come to the U.S.?
> What did you expect when you came?
> What were you promised?
> Were you scared?
> Do you have papers?
> Who has them?
> Do you go to school?
> Do you work?
> Are you allowed to leave anytime you want?
> Where do you live?
> Who else lives there?

Are you afraid to leave?
Have you ever been threatened?
Told you couldn't leave?
Has anyone touched you or hurt you?
Do you get moved around a lot?
Do you know where your family is?
Have you seen a doctor?
Are you in any pain?
Are you hungry?
When was the last time you had anything to eat?

While these questions present you with an opportunity to open a dialogue with the child victim of human trafficking, it is important to remember that you may not receive any answers to your questions. You may also receive conflicting answers, which may indicate that the child has been coached by the trafficker. Also remember that it is a slow and delicate process to establishing a trusting relationship with any victim of human trafficking, especially child victims. As you begin to develop a trusting relationship and a dialogue, please remember to be patient. It is a slow and tedious process. Your patience will eventually be rewarded. It is vital to remember that the child be approached in a manner that reflects his or her age, development, culture, language, and what is known about the nature of his or her experience.

Understanding Child Victims of Trafficking

It is extremely important to understand the mindset of child human trafficking victims in order to help them restore their lives. Child victims of human trafficking face significant problems. They are often physically and sexually abused, they have distinctive medical needs, psychological needs, all of which should be addressed before they advance into adulthood. They have been taught by their traffickers not to trust government officials. They have been taught to fear figures of authority representing various government agencies, especially law enforcement and immigration officers. The children are typically distrustful of the system – the very system that is working to help them. It is crucial to remember that child trafficking victims need to be handled delicately. It is only natural to become impatient and frustrated while working with victims. Often, feelings of frustration can evolve into anger towards the victim. This happens because t is so difficult to break through their defense barriers and to sift through the lies they have been taught to tell.

There are many reasons why these children have come to the United States. Not all children have been abducted from their homes. Some children are sent to this country by their families, even worse sold by their families to traffickers who smuggle them into this country. Children succumb to exploitation under the guise of opportunity. Many believe they are going to live with family members, to work in legitimate jobs, or to attend school.

Children have the most impressionable minds and the road to recovery is a long one, fraught with difficult hurdles that must be overcome. Understanding their mindset and building trust through open and honest conversation is the first step in helping them recover from the horrors they have endured. The children have more than likely experienced intense psychological abuse through intimidation or threats of physical harm to either themselves or to their families. These children have endured experiences that most people cannot even begin to imagine. It is essential to remember how fragile they are and should be treated accordingly. They have special needs that must be addressed immediately. These needs include food, shelter, specialized foster care, health care, immigration assistance, and legal assistance. They desperately need to feel safe and secure.

Child Camel Jockeys

Children are trafficked to the Gulf States and are forced to race camels for the entertainment of the elite. They are either abducted from their families or sold by them; many of the children come from the Indian subcontinent. They are brought in from countries such as Pakistan, Bangladesh, Nepal, Sri Lanka, and Sudan. These countries are poor and can't afford the basic necessities. Boys who are bought from their parents are purchased for as little as five hundred dollars. One rescued boy claims his father sold him for alcohol. One mother sold her first three sons in hope of work and money. The boys are kept in prison-like conditions where they are deliberately underfed to keep them light so the camels run faster. The camps they live in are surrounded by barb wire fences. The children race at speeds of up to 50km an hour (30 mph); this sport is popular among the wealthy in the United Arab Emirate (UAE). Children as young as a year and a half are forced to race camels. They are strapped on to the camels with Velcro™; strips of Velcro™ are sewn to the legs of their pants and attached to the saddles used on the camels. This is how the very young camel jockeys are kept on the camels. The children are so frightened that they scream in sheer terror. The result of their screaming makes the camels run faster, therefore screaming is not discouraged. The faster the camels run, the more likely it is for the Velcro™ to separate, causing the boys to fall from the camels. The horrific results are death, disfigurement, mutilation, and maiming. Many of the boys have their limbs ripped from their small and fragile bodies. Human rights activists claim that there are more than 40,000 children living in the most inhumane circumstances. The child camel jockeys are said to be living in overcrowded iron tents, without electricity or furniture, while temperatures soar above one hundred degrees Fahrenheit. Some children have reported that they were forced to sleep outside on the sand. The rescued boys said they were required to wear metal helmets, even when the temperatures soared above one hundred degrees Fahrenheit.

Camel jockeys are purposely underfed in an effort to keep their weight down. Anyone considered to have become too heavy would have weights tied to their backs and be made to run under the hot desert sun. Serial offenders would be hung by their wrists from chains. The children live on small amounts of food that is both dirty and unhygienic. An average day's meal consists of brackish water and a half of loaf of bread. If they complain, they are beaten by their captors. The children are forced to work eighteen hour days. When they are not training or racing the camels, the boys are forced to care for the camels. The children are required to feed the camels, but they are beaten if they try to eat the animals' "good" food. The camels are considered to be more valuable than the children. Many thoroughbred camels have been bought for two million dollars; they are well fed, well cared for, and receive medical attention; unlike the enslaved boys who care for them, feed, train, and ride them. They are awakened at three o'clock in the morning, usually by being beaten with sticks. They live as slaves, working continuously without any rest, seven days a week all year long. The boys do all of the work, they must prepare dinner and tea for their masters and they must do it properly or face the consequences. While training and racing the camels, the children often fall down and are badly injured or crushed to death. Rescued jockeys have had their limbs ripped from their fragile young bodies; the result of being trampled by racing camels. The children generally range in age from a year and a half to six years old. Since it is illegal to keep underage jockeys, these boys never receive medical attention and some of them die very painful and agonizing deaths.

Years of abuse have caused the children to suffer from permanent physical injuries, such as having the flesh on their upper legs rubbed away; their bones have been damaged as well as their body structures. They have even suffered from sexual abuse by the men running the camps. Many boys have reported being repeatedly and violently raped during their time as camel jockeys. The child jockeys have suffered permanent sexual dysfunction as a result of years of racing on the camels. The years of abuse have left their sexual organs damaged to the point that they will be unable to procreate.

Camel racing is entrenched in hundreds of years of tradition. The children are a commodity with little or no value. Countless children have been left to die in the hot desert sun. It is unknown how many forgotten souls have been buried in the desert.

Mustafa's Story

Mustafa is a seven year old rescued camel jockey from Pakistan. He was rescued and taken to a safe haven where he received help until they were able to locate his parents. It took six months before he was returned to his family. Like many other children he had been kidnapped and taken into the United Arab Emirate (UAE) for the purpose of entertaining the elite.

This is what Mustafa had to say about his experience:

"I was playing outside my friend's house when I was taken away. I was sleeping with other children in a very hot shed made of iron. We were only given food as dirty half loaf of bread once a day. A lot of children had blood coming out of their noses."

Shakheel's Story

Barely five years old, Shakheel tells his story and how he has already learnt the harsh reality of life as a camel jockey in the UAE. He has a deep scar running up his abdomen from a fall he suffered in one race. His leg was broken in another incident when he was knocked off his mount during a race. He spoke from a sheltered safe house in a military base and he spoke haltingly in his native language Urdu. He described his wretched life in an ousbah (a simple desert settlement). An ousbah is where the boys live as prisoners with their camels and their trainers.

"They used to wake us at two or three in the morning. If we didn't get up or if they thought we were lazy, they would beat us with sticks. We had to clean up the camel dung with our hands."

Zulfiqar's Story

This child has reported that he has seen several riders break their arms, necks, and even die from injuries caused by racing the camels. Zulfiqar said that when there is a choice between tending to a thoroughbred camel or to a boy, the animals always get priority. The camels are worth more to the trainers than the children.

Hope

In July 2005, the UAE government formally introduced a law prohibiting camel jockeys under the age of sixteen. Under this new legislation, offenders face up to three years in prison and /or a fine of nearly $14,000. In May of 2005, representatives of UNICEF and the governments of Sudan, Bangladesh, Pakistan, and the UAE agreed to establish a program to help rehabilitate and reintegrate the boys who had been forced to work as camel jockeys. This plan required the UAE to list all the children currently working in the country as camel jockeys. This agreement also required the UAE to return all camel jockeys to their countries of origin and to contribute financially to the rehabilitation program. So far, 150 children have been returned to Sudan from the UAE.

Once the camel jockeys are returned to their home countries, the road to recovery begins. It is a long and arduous journey before they can obtain some semblance of their former selves. The road to recovery is difficult due to the fact that many of the children were so young when they left their homeland, and have forgotten their native language. It makes it impossible for them to communicate with their families. Children who survived the ordeal are emotionally scarred and ill equipped to return to their families. Rehabilitation includes medical care for physical injuries, as well as psychiatric care and counseling to help the boys deal with their traumatic experiences. The children receive an education with the emphasis on bringing them up to speed with other children their age. The boys have to be taught how to sleep, how to take a bath, how to go to the toilet, and how to eat. The children don't know how to sleep on beds. These are all new experiences for them, and while they are good experiences, it is also frustrating for them. They are embarrassed by their lack of social skills.

Establishing the identity of the children is a difficult task. Many parents are afraid of coming forward for fear of being implicated in their trafficking. Many children were sold or kidnapped at a very young age and do not know who they are or who their parents are; too many of them do not know where they come from. It is a daunting task; however organizations like Ansar Burney Welfare Trust International and UNICEF are committed to reuniting these children with their families. DNA testing is being used to identify the families of the camel jockeys. In cases where the children cannot be reunited with their families they are being provided with an education and vocational training, to help prepare them for their return to society.

October 2005 brought new hope to the plight of child camel jockeys. Kuwait and other Gulf states held an experimental race using robot camel jockeys. The remote operated robots are shaped like small boys. The experiment was successful and in February 2006, Kuwait held its first race using robot camel jockeys. Teams from the six Gulf Arab states participated in the race which was held on the dusty track of a racing club outside the capital Kuwait City. It is the hope of all interested parties that the participants of camel racing will be satisfied with the robot jockeys, therefore eliminating the need to exploit young boys.

Child Sexual Exploitation

There are an estimated two million children, ranging in ages of five years to eighteen years of age who are enslaved in the global commercial sex trade. The commercial sex trade includes child sex tourism and child pornography; it is not limited to the sexual exploitation of adults. Child sex tourism is the practice of traveling to another country for the purpose of having sex with children. Child sex tourists encompass pedophiles, as well as sexual opportunists. A pedophile is someone who prefers to engage in sexual activity with children, while a sexual opportunist is someone who is presented with the opportunity and takes advantage of the situation. The fear of contracting HIV/AIDS increases the demand for young victims; based on the misconception that the child sex worker will not have HIV/AIDS. It is estimated that twenty-five percent of child sex tourists are Americans.

The term commercial sexual exploitation of children, also referred to as CSEC, is used to explain the diverse exploitations of children for sexual purposes. Child sexual exploitation uses children as a commodity for child sex tourism, child prostitution, child pornography, and child sex slaves.

Child sex industries have evolved into large and well organized schemes in many poor nations. These industries have come to light in Asia, Africa, Eastern Europe, Latin America, Indo-

China, and the Pacific region. Contributing factors include adverse poverty, lack of education, inferior socio-economic advantages, and lack of law enforcement. Offenders are continually seeking out new destinations for child sex tourism; using the Internet to exchange information, distribute pornography, and plan new adventures. Children are being trafficked to a greater variety of locations in an on-going effort to feed the escalating demand for the commercial sexual exploitation of children. Unfortunately, there are homeless children, who are unable to defend themselves or even to fend for themselves; leaving many to exchange sexual activities as a means of survival. While the primary demand is for young girls, boys are also victims of child sexual exploitation.

Many children involved in child exploitation come from poor rural families; some of the families will opt to sell their children as a means of survival. Children have been abducted from their homes, in the street, and from schoolyards and forced into the child sex industry.

Poverty is a contributing factor of child sexual exploitation; the majority of children involved come from poor and marginalized families. Impoverished children have been forced, sold, duped, lured, and kidnapped for the purposes of child sexual exploitation. Extreme poverty can be a contributing factor for child prostitution; child sexual exploitation may be the only means of income for some families.

Globalization of the world economy has contributed to the growth of poverty in many developing and underdeveloped countries. International free trade has led to the demise of local and national producers, causing companies and small businesses to close operations, leaving the populace unemployed and unable to provide for their families.

Organized crime plays a major role in the commercial sexual exploitation of children. Child sex industries continue to thrive and develop due to the large profit margin and increasing demand for children. Child pornography, child sex tourism, child prostitution, and child sex slaves net organized crime networks billions of dollars each year.

Many underdeveloped countries suffer from corruption in their government and within their local law enforcement agencies. Authorities who ignore crime or who profit from it, enable offenders to escape prosecution. It is not uncommon for child sex tourists to pay off local officials in order to flee from their jurisdiction.

The breakdown of family can be another contributing factor to CSEC. Abuse within the family can cause a child to runaway in order to escape ongoing abuse, leaving them defenseless to sexual exploitation. Broken homes may force a child to become the breadwinner of the family, leading them into the commercial sex trade. In many societies, female children are perceived to be undesirable; viewed as being a burden instead of an asset. Male children are viewed as having the potential to be good income earners for the family. Female children are often deprived of an education, forcing them to seek employment in non-traditional sectors, such as the commercial sex trade. Alarming reports are beginning to surface leading many to believe that the rural attitudes have changed; having a girl child is now more desirable because she can generate a good income for the family through the commercial sex trade. This does not bode well for the future well being of female children. They will be forced to endure physical and psychological problems, as well as a potentially life threatening lifestyle for the economic benefit of their families.

Child Prostitution

The word prostitution means *"the act of engaging in sexual intercourse or performing other sex acts in exchange for money, or of offering another person for such purposes."* The word "prostitution" has become increasingly undesirable; many prefer to use the expression "sex work"; sex work is used as a common expression to describe adults who participate or work in the mainstream sex industry. By referring to prostitution as sex work, we are legitimizing the sex industry; a disturbing trend leading to the further decay of the moral fibers of mainstream society. Many children and young adults forced to participate in child prostitution are now being referred to as child sex workers; this is unacceptable. "Sex worker" implies that the participant has entered into an agreement of employment. Children and young adults (under the age of eighteen) cannot legally make this decision; therefore "child sex worker" relays a false impression leading others to believe that a child is capable of choosing this particular career path. This is just another tactic sexual deviants are using to create validation and justification for their criminal and immoral activities.

Victims of child sexual abuse suffer in many ways. They are exposed to physical abuse and physical ailments such as exhaustion, infections, malnutrition, tuberculosis, and venereal disease, including HIV/AIDS. They rarely receive medical attention. Some children will get to see a doctor once they have become critically ill, but in most cases that is unlikely. These children are a commodity. Once they outlive their usefulness they are easily replaced with another victim. Living conditions are extremely poor for child prostitutes; they are forced to live in filth and are provided meals that are inadequate and irregular. Many children suffer from brutal beatings and starvation when they fail to produce enough money for their masters. A sad fact of the child sex tourism industry is that drug use and suicide is a very common part of life for these victims of sexual exploitation. These children live in constant fear. They are afraid of being beaten by their pimps, they are afraid of being arrested by the local law enforcement authorities, and they are afraid of having to suffer from further sadistic acts by the men who pay to abuse them. Studies have shown that child prostitutes are forced to service between two and thirty customers per week. That adds up to anywhere between one hundred and fifteen hundred men per year. These appalling statistics explain why the children suffer from depression, low self-esteem, and feelings of helplessness.

Child Sex Tourism

"There's a special evil in the abuse and exploitation of the most innocent and vulnerable. The victims of sex trade see little of life before they see the very worst of life — an underground of brutality and lonely fear."
— President George W. Bush before the UN General Assembly, September 2003

Child sex tourism is a very lucrative industry which spans the globe. This industry makes its profits from the exploitation of children in poor developing countries. In 1998, it was calculated by the International Labor Organization that two to fourteen percent of the gross domestic product of Indonesia, Malaysia, the Philippines, and Thailand is the result of child sex tourism. Asian countries, including Thailand, India, and the Philippines, have long been the prime destinations for child sex tourists; however recent findings have shown that Mexico and Central America have been added to the list of popular child sex tourism locations. These countries are believed to be prime sex tourist spots because of a popular misconception that the laws are less restricting in these regions.

Who are these tourists and where do they come from? Research has shown that most of the child sex tourists are male and come for all income brackets. Many of these perpetrators come from Western European countries and North America. United States citizens account for an estimated twenty-five percent of the child sex tourists around the world. Child sex tourists come from all walks of life. Married, single, homosexual, heterosexual, business men, maybe even your neighbors are participating in child sex tourism. It is commonly believed that most child sex tourists are pedophiles seeking relationships with children for the sole purpose of satisfying their sexual desires, however many authorities disagree with this common misconception. Most child sex tourists are described as being "situational abusers". These are individuals who occasionally engage in sexual acts with children only when the opportunity presents itself. Situational abusers do not commonly seek out children as sexual partners, they just take advantage of any opportunity that arises and presents itself to the abuser. Some of these perpetrators deal in rationalization techniques. They have convinced themselves that they are actually helping these children by providing them with the financial opportunity to better their living conditions. They pretend to believe that by participating in child prostitution they are enabling both the child and its family to evolve out of their economic hardship. This distorted rationalization is one of several commonly used by child sex tourists in their own defense. Another popular justification of child sex tourists is that many foreign countries are more sexually liberated than America, therefore having sexual relations with children is not necessarily taboo in these countries. They like to believe that it is socially acceptable to participate in sexual activity with child prostitutes. Some child sex tourists are drawn to these foreign countries and engage in this activity because they feel safe in the anonymity afforded to them by being so far from home. This provides them with the freedom from the moral constraints that limit their activity in their own country. Many child sex tourists believe they can discard their moral values, evade accountability, and avoid legal repercussions by traveling to third world countries to end engage in child sexual abuse. Another appalling rationalization is that the men do not value these children or see any problem with their behavior based on their own racist beliefs and delusions of superiority. They do not see helpless children when they engage in child sex tourism; they see a commodity and an outlet for their own sexual gratification.

Efforts to combat child sex tourism and child exploitation are frustrating due to the conflict with foreign governments trying to encourage their tourism industry. Many countries have rampant police corruption. In countries such as the Philippines and Thailand, the police have been known to give protection to the brothels. It has been reported that many of the police officers help recruit children for the brothels. It is not uncommon for the police to be involved in sexual crimes against children in many countries where child sex tourism exists. Child sex tourists travel to countries such as Cambodia, Thailand, Costa Rica, Mexico, and Brazil expecting low cost prostitution, anonymity, and easy access to children. They do not fear prosecution for their crimes against children. The United States is committed to eliminating child sex tourism. In 1994, Congress passed legislation aimed at prosecution of child sex tourists. Congress established 18 U.S.C. § 2423(b) criminalizes traveling abroad for the purpose of engaging in illegal sexual activity with a minor. Millions of children suffer from the consequences of child sex tourism and the United States is committed to eliminating this horrific industry. Under the PROTECT Act of 2003, any United States citizen or resident convicted of engaging in sexual activity with a child under the age of eighteen while abroad, faces up to thirty years in prison.

Combating child sex tourism is a daunting task. Organizations such as World Vision, Campaign Against Child Exploitation (CACE), Coalition Against Trafficking of Women (CATW), and ECPAT (End Child Prostitution, Child Pornography, and Trafficking of Children for Sexual Purpose), just to name a few are working diligently to help these children. They work with the U.S. Immigration and Customs Enforcement, otherwise known as ICE, to bring the perpetrators of child sex tourism to justice. A major media campaign has been launched to discourage child sex tourism. Billboards have been placed in United States airports, outside foreign airports; advertisements have been placed on television, airline in-flight videos, magazines, and on the internet. These messages make it clear that anyone caught engaging in child sex tourism will go to jail. Child sex tourism causes damage to the child with lifelong residual effects. The abuser was able to get away this crime, until recently, that is. CACE has taken action to ensure that the child sex tourist is held accountable for his actions. CACE's primary objective is to take direct action against the abuser, while working in cooperation with other organizations in the host country. CACE takes direct action against the abuser in his hometown. There are three basic components used in the CACE model.

1. Investigate and Identify – the goal of the investigation is to gather evidence of the crime and identify the abuser.

2. Take Action in the Abuser's Hometown – victims of crime have the right to file a civil action and to seek compensation from their abuser. The victim does not have to wait for the perpetrator to be prosecuted or convicted of the crime in order for the victim to seek compensation. Federal statute permits the victim to file a direct action in the federal court in the abuser's hometown. CACE facilitates this process on behalf of the victims. They work with the victim and victim groups in the host country to locate attorneys in the abusers hometown who are willing to assist in the action.

3. Expose the Abuser in his Hometown Media – CACE employs a fulltime media consultant as part of their ongoing effort to expose the criminal actions of the perpetrator in his

hometown. They will not allow this culprit to go back to his life as if nothing has happened, as if he never committed heinous acts against children in other countries. The media consultant supplies information to the hometown newspapers and television. The direct civil action is the catalyst to exposing the abusers crimes to their home community.

Operation Predator, which is a nationwide ICE campaign to protect children from sexual predators, including child sex tourists, Internet child pornographers, criminal alien sex offenders, and child sex traffickers, was launched in July 2003. Through Operation Predator, ICE agents have arrested more than 7000 individuals, including 460 in New York. ICE encourages the reporting of suspected child predators, along with any suspicious activity. They have a 24 hour toll-free hotline which is staffed by investigators. The toll-free hotline number is 1-866-DHS-2ICE (1-866-347-2423).

United States vs. Seljan

October 2003 - An 85year old man was arrested as he attempted to board a flight to the Philippines, where he allegedly intended to have sex with two Philippine girls ages nine and twelve.

Immigration & Customs Enforcement (ICE) agents arrested John W. Seljan in Los Angeles before he was able to get on the plane to the Philippines to engage in sex acts with minors. Agents discovered pornographic materials, sexual aids, and nearly one hundred pounds of chocolates in his luggage. The ICE investigation began in Aug. 2003 after border inspectors intercepted correspondence to the Philippine girls indicating that he planned to have sex with the girls there. On March 28, 2005, John W. Seljan was sentenced to twenty years in prison for six counts related to child sex tourism. In addition, Seljan will be required to register as a sex offender and must remain under court supervision for the rest of his life, should he ever see the light of day. Seljan will be 105 years old at the end of his sentence.

United States vs. Clark

This case represents the first child sex tourism case in the nation brought under the PROTECT Act. A federal grand jury in Seattle charged Michael Lewis Clark with child sex tourism violations of the Protect Act in September 2003. Clark was arrested in Cambodia by local authorities for engaging in illegal sexual activity with two boys ages ten and thirteen. Subsequent investigation by ICE and the Cambodian authorities determined Clark may have molested as many as fifty children in Cambodia. The Cambodian authorities had him removed from their country and flown to the United States where he was charged. Clark pled guilty of engaging in and attempting to engage in sexual acts with minors. In 2004, Clark was sentenced to ninety-seven months in jail.

Child Soldiers

Child soldiers are a harsh reality of life for many children in numerous countries. Children are forced from their homes and villages by the very barbarians they are forced to serve and depend upon for their own survival. The use of children as soldiers has been universally condemned, yet in the past ten years hundreds of thousands of children have fought and died in combat around the world. Children are often killed or maimed in battles or while they are performing other tasks. They are forced to participate in extremely hazardous duties such as laying mine fields and using weapons. Child soldiers live under harsh conditions. They lack medical care, proper nutrition, and inadequate amounts of food. Most child soldiers are beaten, treated brutally, and subjected to humiliation. They are punished severely if they try to escape, punishment ranges anywhere between harsh and brutal beatings to death. Girl soldiers suffer from many forms of sexual abuse, ranging between harassment to continuous sexual assault. Many girls are assigned to a commander for sexual purposes, while others endure frequent gang rapes. One former girl soldier reported that at night, men and boy soldiers would come into the tents and rape them. If they cried afterwards, they were beaten with hosepipes. These rapes occurred each night, in the dark, making it impossible for them to identify their attackers. The girl stated that they were too afraid to report the rapes. The youngest girl in the group was eleven years old. Girls who are given to the commanders carry out many duties. They are soldiers by day and "wives" by night. Girls who become impregnated by the commanders are forced to strap the babies on their backs and continue in their duties as soldiers.

Child soldiers have been found in various Asian countries, in parts of Latin America, Europe, the Middle East, and Africa. In 2004, it was estimated that approximately 100,000 children, some as young as nine, were engaged in armed conflicts in Africa. The majority of child soldiers are involved in a variety of armed political groups, including government backed paramilitary groups, militias, and self defense units operating in combat zones. The rest of the child soldiers can be found in armed groups who are opposed to their central government rule, clan-based or factional groups fighting governments and each other in the defense of their territory and resources; as well as groups comprised of ethnic religious and other minorities fighting against their government.

While we have discussed children who have been abducted and coerced into service, there are child soldiers who voluntarily enlist. Having said that, let's take a look at the root of their voluntary enlistment. Research shows that these children enlist as soldiers due to a variety of reasons, such as, a means to survive in worn-torn regions amid social and economic collapse. Some have seen their family members tortured and killed by government forces or armed groups, lack of work or educational opportunities, and poverty, are other motivating factors to enlisting as child soldiers. Female soldiers who voluntarily enlisted did so as an escape from domestic servitude, violence, and sexual assault.

Demobilization, disarmament and reintegration (DDR) programs have been established in many countries. These programs are aimed at child soldiers. DDR programs have helped former child soldiers to acquire new skills and return to their communities. Girl soldiers are often overlooked and have been excluded from the DDR programs. These programs need to be sensitively designed to include female soldiers who have suffered from frequent rapes and various other forms of sexual violence. DDR programs are currently suffering from inadequate funding and resources, putting the programs at risk. Without sustained long-term financial commitment to DDR programs, child soldiers will continue to suffer from the effects their life of violence. Rehabilitation of child soldiers is a long and difficult process. The children have been brutalized and have carried out numerous killings. Many of the children have been forced to kill friends and family in the course of their service. They have wielded life-and-death power over adults, often in their own communities. They are forced to commit these atrocities as a way of breaking family and community bonds. The backlash of slaughtering people in their own village prevents the child soldiers from returning home. Many former child soldiers have returned to their regiments; they return for a variety of reasons, the most common ones being social and economic.

Former Child Soldier:

Quoted in an interview in 2002: *"Being new, I couldn't perform the very difficult exercises properly and so I was beaten every morning. Two of my friends in the camp died because of the beatings. The soldiers buried them in the latrines. I am still thinking about them."*

Former Child Soldier, age 13:

"Early on when my brothers and I were captured, we were told that all five brothers could not serve in the Army because we would not perform well. So they tied up my two youngest brothers and invited us to watch. Then they beat them with sticks until two of them died. They told us it would give us strength to fight. My youngest brother was nine years old."

Why use children as soldiers? They are cheaper to keep because they eat less, plus they are easier to manipulate. Children are often less demanding than adult soldiers. Children are also used as slave laborers. They carry army supplies and are used in government construction projects. In war, they are said to be fearless. The most common belief is that their unpredictability makes them better fighters. The smallest child soldiers are placed closest to the enemy. Some of them have been sent into battle high on drugs to give them the courage they need to fight. The development of lighter weapons means that boys as young as eight can be armed.

Panhandling

Child victims of human trafficking are also used for panhandling. They are forced into the streets as beggars – beggars with quotas to fill. If the children fail to reach their quota they are punished; they suffer from systematic violence, poor living conditions and poor health. Small children are often forced to work as beggars by family members or have been contracted out by their family. In exchange for allowing traffickers to use their children as panhandlers, families receive a percentage of what their children take in each week. One Roma child who talks about her life as a beggar in Greece says she has been going to Greece since she was four years old. She said that her mother sold her thirteen year old sister for prostitution in Italy. This child also mentioned a baby that her mother sold, however she did not identify the child's gender. The protectors take these children on foot from Albania into Greece for the purpose of begging, with the younger children working as panhandlers and the older children washing car windows for money. The protectors can be very cruel, often cutting children with knives and hurting them in order to make them work harder. Everyone is afraid of the protectors, who have shown a propensity for violence and cruelty. They threaten to kill these children and their families if they try to escape. Failure to earn the mandated amount of money set forth by the protector brings physical abuse upon the children.

Child Labor

There are an estimated 246 million children engaged in child labor worldwide. Of that 246 million child slaves, approximately three-quarters work in hazardous situations, including working in mines, with chemicals, or dangerous machinery. As difficult as it is to imagine 246 million children living as slaves, the harsh reality of this fact is that these children remain invisible. They work as domestic servants in homes, they are hidden from view on plantations and farms, and they labor behind the walls of factories and sweatshops. Millions of girls work as domestic servants, working twelve to seventeen hours per day for little or no money. The girls are extremely vulnerable, often times they are physically and sexually abused.

Research shows that the largest number of child workers are found in the Asian and Pacific regions. Children range in age from five to fourteen. The estimated total of child workers in this region is 127.3 million. The Sub-Saharan Africa has an estimated forty-eight million child workers. Latin America and the Caribbean have approximately seventeen and a half million child workers.

It is important for us to distinguish the difference between child labor and children working. Children who work while engaging in economic activities, such as providing income for and with their family is acceptable under international guidelines, providing the children are twelve years old or older, working under healthy conditions, and being paid for their services. Poverty has made it necessary for many families to send their children to work. Many child workers who have been interviewed openly stated that they work to help their family survive. As long as the children are not being exploited, are working under safe conditions, and being paid a fair wage, organizations, such as UNICEF does not oppose these children from engaging in economic activities.

Child Labor Victims

A six year old child in El Salvador spends twelve hours a day bagging and selling charcoal. He suffers from respiratory problems due to this work. Working twelve hours a day prevents this six year old from attending school. His lack of education condemns him to a harsh and impoverished life.

An eight year old girl works in an ironsmith's shop with her brother in Afghanistan. Her father will not send her to school because he says it is too costly and too far away. She is more valuable to him as a worker.

A twelve year old girl in Irvine, California was enslaved by a couple, forced to live in their garage, and made to work as a domestic servant for their family of seven. The couple arranged to bring her to America under fraudulent conditions, concealed her presence from immigration authorities, school, and police officials. The couple threatened the girl with bodily harm; physically assaulted her; made threats against her sister in Egypt; and told her she would be arrested if she left the house.

A seven year old boy in Pakistan was forced to weave carpets in order to pay off an alleged family debt. He was given food, little free time, and no medical care. He was never told who in his family had incurred this debt or how much was owed. He was fined and his debt increased whenever he made an error in his work. At one point when his work was considered to be too slow, his captors beat him as punishment. When he attempted to run away, he was picked up by the local police and forced to return to work.

A fourteen year old girl in India was told by her father that he could not afford to pay a dowry for her wedding. He met a woman who told him of a boy's family who was willing to pay for the wedding; her father saw this as an opportunity of a lifetime. He sent her to be married. The girl was sold to a brothel.

Four sisters, from a poor family in Kazakhstan were promised good paying jobs during a school break by a family friend. The girls were sold into slavery and forced to live and work in a massive garbage dump. The dump was surrounded by barbed wire, security guards and vicious dogs. The girls were required to rummage through the dump for plastic bottles and containers. They had a daily quota of seventy-five pounds; failure to meet this quota resulted in various forms of punishment. They were denied food during the day, forcing them to scavenge for food at night. Once they came across a case of cookies. The girls were so hungry they began to devour the cookies, unaware that the cookies were infested with maggots. This revelation came to them at daybreak. The family was concerned for the safety of their daughters and contacted other family members to help search for them. A relative found the girls and paid the recycler for the release of two of the girls. The family and a local group went to authorities to retrieve the other two children. For seven months the sisters worked at the dump, received no money, suffered physical harm, and psychological abuse.

Agriculture

Commercial farms and plantations grow coconut, banana, pineapple, tobacco and sugarcane in the Philippines, a country comprised of over seven thousand islands. Children who work on commercial plantations are at greater risk of exploitation than those who work on family farms. The agricultural sector is often falsely believed to mean working on the family farm; this sector tends to be overlooked as an area where children are often exploited. It is estimated that there are over two million children working in this sector. Agriculture is a very important source of income for the Philippines. Sugarcane is an important commercial crop in the Philippines. The workers on the sugarcane plantations are paid sixty to eighty pesos, which falls below the government established minimum wage of 153 pesos per day.

Most plantation owners offer their workers a house on the plantation. These are generally shacks built out of bamboo, cane and palm leaves. The drinking water is obtained from pump wells and there are generally no sanitation facilities near the houses. The houses are placed closely together, are small and mostly overcrowded with as many as thirteen family members living in confined quarters. Children are required to work with their families in the fields, when not in school. One man in a recent interview stated that he feared they would be evicted if his sons refused to work in the fields. The plantation owners have a lot of power over these families, as they are their employers and landlords. Families have been threatened with violence and have been subjected to physical abuse by those who work for the plantation owners. The workers are not able to question any decisions that made nor are they able to work somewhere else, due to their dependence upon the landowner. These families are living well below the poverty line due to poor wages and large families. The workers often find it difficult to feed their children. In most cases, they are not allowed to plant small vegetable gardens as a way to help feed their children. The consequences are that many of the children suffer from malnutrition. The children are susceptible to diseases and reoccurring illnesses, such as pneumonia and chronic coughs. The families lack a balanced diet because they are forced to buy food by quantity rather than by quality. The families are so poor, that in order for the children to attend school, they must work to earn the money required for their education.

Many children begin working by the age of seven, pulling weeds and planting the cane. New stalks of sugarcane must be replanted each year. Once the cane is planted, fertilizer must be added to help the canes grow. This, of course, stimulates the growth of weeds. Weeds are the number one killer of sugarcane; weeds choke out new growth. All of this work is done manually. Children are assigned to this type of work because it is simple and not as heavy as harvesting. The children manually clear the fields of weeds and grass with big cutting knives called bolos. Applying fertilizers is another chore assigned to children. Most plantations use a mixture of urea and potash, causing the cane to grow faster. The children walk the fields spreading granules of fertilizer from their buckets. The children work up to ten hours per day and earn sixty pesos per day.

Hazards faced by the children working on the plantations are many. First of all, the children are exposed to the sun all day. The children try to cover as much of their bodies as possible, however they cannot escape the heat of the sun blaring down on them throughout the day. Sudden weather changes also pose a threat to the children. They are forced to work, rain or shine. They take no time to rest and usually don't eat properly. The combination of rain and heat makes the children susceptible to colds and fever. Lack of proper nutrition lowers the immune system of the children working in the fields of the plantations. Children who weed, harvest, or prepare the soil are not supplied with the proper equipment for these tasks. They use machetes when harvesting and weeding. These are not suitable tools for children, usually too large and awkward for the children to wield properly. Children have suffered serious injury from these knives; dull blades can bounce off the canes and injure a child's leg or foot. Children as young as seven use machetes as part of their daily labor. The sugarcane, which is sharp to the touch, leaves small cuts on the children's arms and legs. Snakes and insects also pose a threat to the children. Poisonous bites have caused deadly results amongst the children living and working in the sugarcane plantations. Last but certainly not least, prolonged exposure to herbicides, pesticides, and fungicides result in respiratory damage, skin and eye irritation, reproductive problems, and overall poor health of the plantation workers.

Fisheries

Typical fishing villages in Ghana consist of square mud houses with thatched roofs. The villages lack the basic community facilities such as running water, wells, markets, and schools. Each village is organized around the family household, which is made up of the master fisherman (slave-master), his wife, and their natural children. The household also includes the trafficked children engaged in fishing for the slave-master. The boys are usually sold by their parents to the slave-masters for an average sum between $47 - $177 US dollars. In some cases the parents contract the children out for a period of one to three years. The slave-masters typically pay fifty percent of the agreed upon price when they take the children, promising to send the balance as the children earn their income. The boys work for the slave-masters in the fishing villages pulling nets out of the water. When the nets become tangled, the slave-master sends a boy under water to free the net. This is dangerous work and many children have drowned in the course of this task. The enslaved boys were never involved in the discussions between their parents and the slave-master. Some have been told by their parents that they had to go and live with their uncle, while others were told they were going off to school. It wasn't until they arrived in the fishing villages that the boys found out they were required to work as slaves. Sadly, many of the boys have spent the larger portion of their lives as slaves and are unable to recall who their parents are or where they came from.

The boys enslaved in the fishing villages begin their days at dawn and work until late afternoon. They work late into the night during the peak fishing season. The boys are fed in the morning before they begin their day and do not receive any food until they return to their huts at the end of their day. Boys who fall asleep during the day are punished and beaten. While the slave-masters know it is wrong to use these boys for such dangerous work, they justify their actions by the fact that they have to feed and take of their families.

Children working in the fishing industry in the Philippines also suffer at the hands of their traffickers. Some children are required to work up to eight hours per night, diving into the water and chasing the fish into the nets. Other children go off on fishing expeditions that last approximately six to ten months at a time. The children are forced to dive as deep as fifteen meters without protective gear. The result of this work is often ear damage, injuries from falls, shark attacks, snake bites, and drowning. Many children die as a result of this work, never having a chance to live a normal life.

Domestic Servitude

Child domestic servitude exposes children to many dangers and health hazards. The children are at risk working in an industry which is widely accepted in many countries around the world. Many families willingly give or sell their children into domestic servitude believing that their children will have a better chance at life. They are misled into believing that their children will receive a good education in return for their services. Unfortunately child domestic servants receive an education no child should ever have.

Physical, emotional, and sexual abuse are rampant among households with child domestic servants.

Quality of life and basic welfare issues are determined by the attitude of employers toward child servants. Young children suffer from injuries resulting from burns acquired while cooking and ironing. Children also cut themselves with knives while preparing meals for the family. Common tasks of child domestic servants include cooking, boiling water, using sharp utensils, working with chemicals (cleaning and gardening), lifting heavy items, caring for young children, caring for household pets, cleaning, and any other duties the family designate to the child slaves. These young domestic servants often work long hours, seven days a week, with very little time off and improper nutrition and medical care. The children are physically and mentally exhausted. They suffer from physical and verbal abuse on a daily basis. If a child should break a household object, be perceived as working too slow, or have their work judged as being inadequate, they suffer at the hands of their employers. The children are physically beaten and in some cases deprived of food as punishment. Lack of medical care prevents their cuts and burns from healing properly. Child domestic servants are not given time to heal, they must continue to work or else they will be forced to suffer from further degradation and physical abuse.
Unfortunately for these children, the combination of their injuries, sleep deprivation, and malnutrition put them at a greater risk of having additional accidents and suffering from further beatings from their employers.

Child domestic servants are forced to suffer through frequent sexual abuse by their employers and the sons of their employers. The children are too young and weak to defend themselves. Psychological abuse adds to the further victimization of the young domestic servant making them easy prey for the predators in quest of young children who can be easily used for their sexual gratification. Furthermore, the children are exposed to numerous sexually transmitted diseases. It is not uncommon for child domestic servants to contract syphilis, genital herpes, HIV/AIDS, as well as developing reproductive problems. Another problem faced by these young victims of sexual abuse is unwanted pregnancy. Employers have reacted differently to these pregnancies; some have forced these young girls to have abortions, while others have thrown them out to live in the streets. Pregnant and disgraced, these young girls are not able to return home and therefore are forced to live in the streets, begging or working as child prostitutes. They are vulnerable and often fall victim to other human traffickers. It is a vicious cycle which never ends for some of these children.

The child servant is often isolated, not just from their families, but also from peers. They are not allowed to have friends, indeed even if they were permitted to make friends, they lack the free time to do so. They are prevented from attending school and from visiting their families. The child servant is also isolated within the homes of their employers. They are considered to be subhuman and therefore not worthy of personal interaction with the members of their employer's family. This isolation leaves them extremely vulnerable to physical and sexual abuse. The degree of abuse inflicted upon the child servants varies from household to household. Sexual abuse of child servants is not limited to girls. Boys working as household servants have reported being sexually abused. The children are not related to the employer; they are hidden from view, and are unaware of the options available to them, making them defenseless against repeated sexual abuse. Sadly, it is an unspoken aspect of the child's work contract. In Peru, sixty percent of men who grew up with child domestic servants reported having their first sexual encounter with the enslaved children working in their family homes.

Debt bondage is a common reason for child domestic servitude. The children are traded or sold to pay off their parent's or guardian's debt. They are forced to work in household situations until the family's debt is paid off. They have absolutely no say in the matter and are often unaware of how much they earn or how much is owed. Rarely do child domestic servants see any remuneration at all. Some families are so poor that they send the child off to work and support themselves, while other parents send the child off to work and support the family and contribute to a sibling's education. Parents are not always aware of the conditions their children are living in. They generally believe that child domestic servitude is in the child's best interest; they have an opportunity to work and to go to school. Parents are not always aware of the horrific abuse suffered by their children. Most of these parents are very poor and live far away from where their children work.

People hire child domestic servants because they are cheaper than hiring adults to do the same work. Children are easier to control and exploit. Children are not in a position to renegotiate their work situation or a higher wage. Children are unable to demand respect for themselves and the work that they do. Child domestic servants are also easier to abuse, both physically and sexually. The children are unaware of the laws which afford them protection; they do not know that there are agencies available to help them out of their current situation; and the children do not know they are being victimized. It is a common misconception that this is the life they have been born into; too expect anything else would be seen as being ungrateful. Employers don't see the need to educate these children for a variety of reasons, including the fact that they perceive the children to be inferior and not deserving of an education. Employers feel that by providing food, shelter and in some cases a small wage is more than enough for child domestic servants. Sending these servants to school interferes with their daily tasks and reduces the number of hours child servants work. Educated child servants are unwelcome because they are not as easy to manipulate once they become aware of their rights. Education also diminishes the child servant's dependency on their employer. These are some of the reasons why the education of child domestic servants is perceived to be unacceptable by most employers of child laborers.

Long term effects on victims of slavery are complex. They suffer from an extreme fear of the outside world and remain vulnerable to further abuse throughout the course of their lives. After their release, victims of slavery continue to suffer from a number of psychological problems. They fear the outside world and become panic stricken by their sudden release and new found freedom. They have lost their bearings due to their confinement and/or frequent moving from one location to another. Victims who are used to working constantly become depressed from their sudden inactivity. These children lack self-esteem and self-confidence. They have been repeatedly beaten down, physically, spiritually, and emotionally. Their slavery has prevented them from developing healthy emotional relationships and prevented them from developing their natural personality. They have been denied their childhood and forced to live an inhumane existence. Victims suffer from post traumatic stress syndrome and have an unhealthy bond to their former employers. Family relationships do not exist for the child domestic servants; the bonds of family were severed by their confinement in domestic servitude.

The emotional abuse suffered by the children leave them with an enormous fear of rejection. Every child is a fragile creature that desperately needs love and kindness in order to grow into a healthy member of society. Child servants are denied this basic need; they are forced to grow up without love in a hostile and vicious world. Their lack of childhood friendships prevents them from learning basic social skills. Many become incapable of being able to develop normal loving relationships, in fact most of these children lose their faith in basic human kindness. They live a life suspicion, unable to accept compassion or hospitality. A sad reality is that these children who have lived their lives in servitude with little or no education grow up to become the next generation of human traffickers and slave owners.

Tanzanite Mines

Tanzanite gems have gained much popularity in recent years, especially in Western countries. Exporters say that tanzanite, which is a $300 million a year business, is as sort after and popular as diamonds. Tanzanite is a blue-violet colored precious stone and it can only be found in Tanzania Africa. Children are used to mine these precious stones and are often referred to as the "snake boys" of Tanzania. They got this name because they crawl through underground tunnels like snakes. The mines are made up of pits and tunnels; reports state that the pits can be up to fifty meters deep and the tunnels are up to 300m long. These boys breathe in harmful graphitic dust and work up to eighteen hours at a time, while receiving only one meal of bread and boiled cassava. Those who receive wages earn less than one dollar (US) per day; others receive a meal in exchange for their labor.

The "snake boys" compromise their physical and mental well being by toiling in deep and weakly constructed mines. Respiratory problems are just one of the results due to dust and harmful gases they breathe in each day in these poorly ventilated pits. The children endure excessive heat and loud noises which result in further consequences, health-wise. The children work in their bare feet, while wielding the crudely made hammers they use to break the rocks in their desperate search for tanzanite stones. To make matters worse, the children are placed at further risk by remaining in the mines while explosives are detonated. They stay in the mines hoping to be the first to retrieve the newly exposed precious stones; desperate to earn the meager wages offered by the mine owners. An additional risk to their safety occurs during cave-ins; the children work without safety equipment, in mines that are poorly constructed. Many children have drowned in these make shift tunnels when the floods come. It is so sad to think of these children living in impoverished slavery so that foreigners can wear the beautiful blue-violet tanzanite stones. The only thing sadder is knowing that so many of the "snake boys" die while trying to uncover these gems.

IRIN Films recently released a documentary entitled *Gem Slaves: Tanzanite's Child Labour*. This film tells the story of the child miners in Merenani in Northern Tanzania; it poignantly shows the horrid conditions that these children live and work in. This controversial documentary has the Tanzanian government scrambling to launch a counter-campaign denouncing the IRIN film in an effort to stave off the fallout they fear will crush this $300 million a year industry.

Child Labor in Mines and Quarries

There is an estimated one million children who work in small scale mines and quarries around the world. In Africa, children have been found working in mines in West African Countries, Tanzania, and Zimbabwe. They mine for gold, diamonds, tanzanite, chrome, tin, and other precious and semi-precious stones. In India, child bonded labor is widespread and can be found in quarries of granites and marble. Guatemalan children work to mine and refine lime, a mineral compound. These children are forced to lift and crush heavy rocks; they are in constant danger from landslides, and suffer from broken bones, burns and respiratory problems. Other health risks include a variety of lung diseases, damaged eyesight, physical deformities, loss of limbs, exposure to hazardous working conditions, physical and sexual abuse, and in some cases death. Children working in mines are at risk from cave-ins as well as injuries resulting from using hazardous equipment. In Côte d'Ivoire, while the average child worker is seven years old, children as young as three have been found working in the mines. They lack proper nutrition, hygiene, drink from contaminated water sources and are forced to work in uncomfortable positions for hours on end. Child miners suffer from malnutrition, dehydration, kidney diseases, gashes, severe accidents, deformities and death while working in hot, dusty, gas-filled tunnels for a few cents a day, sometimes just for a meal.

Forced Labor

Forced labor victims can be found in the agricultural fields, sweatshops, restaurants, hotels, private homes, and in the sex trade. There are approximately twenty-seven million victims who are forced to work as slaves in nations around the world each year. These victims can be found in wealthy nations, such as the United States of America, as well as in underdeveloped nations. It is a common misconception that the United States has not been involved in the slave trade since Abraham Lincoln signed the Emancipation Proclamation in 1863; however human trafficking has proven to be a very lucrative enterprise. Forced labor victims come from nearly every nation in the world and from a wide variety of ethnic, racial, and socio-economical backgrounds. They fall prey to traffickers through force, fraud or coercion. Many have entered into transportation or smuggling agreements only to find themselves deeply indebted to these unscrupulous profiteers at the end of their journey. Once the victims have reached their final destination, they are held captive, forced to work inhumane hours, in harsh conditions in an attempt to work off a debt that continues to grow each day. Victims of forced labor are reluctant to contact law enforcement and report these crimes against them because they have an inherent fear instilled in them by their traffickers. We must remember that victims of human trafficking do not identify themselves as victims; they often feel ashamed for having "gotten" themselves into this situation, and feel shame for the acts they have been forced to commit. Another reason they are not compelled to report the crimes against them is because many of them come from places where officials are often corrupt and vicious.

Forced labor victims are difficult to detect because they are hidden from society. They are rarely seen in public places; locked away in sweatshops, factories, labor camps, farms, brothels, restaurant kitchens, and private homes. Their captors have complete control of every aspect of their daily lives, and in some cases, the victims are forced to ask for permission to use the bathroom, eat or sleep. These are normal functions we all take for granted as a basic human right. Many have been tortured, maimed, raped, and killed. Victims have been killed as punishment for trying to escape, to set an example to the other slaves, and for failure to meet production requirements. Many have died as a result of repetitive and extreme physical abuse, substantial neglect of proper nutrition and lack of medical attention. Forced labor covers the gamut of modern day slavery; as a result of following news and press reports it is apparent that forced labor is broken down into the following categories, listed in order of the most lucrative to the least populated. Sexual exploitation, domestic servitude, forced agricultural work, sweatshop factories, restaurant and hotel work, entertainment, and mail order bride services all provide opportunities for the profiteers of human trafficking.

Forced Sexual Exploitation

Out of all of the industries included in forced labor, forced sexual exploitation is the largest sector. The trafficking of women for forced prostitution, exotic dancing, and forced participation in pornography combined with child sexual exploitation makes this a highly profitable industry. These activities are generally associated with organized crime. The commercial sex industry is driven by the demand for cheap sex services and the ever-increasing desire for child sexual exploitation.

Sex traffickers generally recruit women and children from their own geographic regions or ethnic backgrounds. Victims are more trusting of those who have similarities to themselves; it is easier to trust someone who speaks your language and who approaches you using culturally sensitive tactics. Sex trafficking in the United States is closely linked to migrant smuggling controlled by Asian, Mexican, and Eastern European organized criminal networks. Sex trafficking enterprises around the world are also tied to organized criminal networks. Many victims are deceived into believing that they will be employed as waitresses, nannies, household staff, while others are misled into thinking they will become models. Those who have been promised acting careers, generally end up in pornographic videos. Some women have entered into agreements to work as prostitutes, having been promised great sums of money, only to discover they are completely enslaved without any financial remuneration.

There have been several sex trafficking rings busted in Florida in recent years. Information revealed from these arrests has been very disturbing in relation to the living situations of these victims. They were forced to live in filthy unsanitary conditions, locked in trailers, duplexes and houses, located in isolated areas in citrus fields, which were accessible by dirt roads leading into the groves. The living quarters had garbage and condoms scattered all over the place. The limited bathroom facilities were deplorable. In some situations, the women were forced to sleep on the very mattresses where they forced to service clients. The mattresses were separated from each other by hanging sheets.

The isolation and location were contributing factors to law enforcement's lack of awareness about these situations. The traffickers normally had look-outs posted who can radio ahead whenever law enforcement officers were approaching the area. In one case, a "john" notified the police about the situation, because he had become attached to one of the girls who was being prostituted. A marked police car arrived on the scene to investigate. Neither officer spoke Spanish and needed to rely on the trafficker to translate for the victim being interviewed. What ensued was the trafficker informed the police that the woman in question was his wife and that she was both safe and happy. The woman was told that the police were here to arrest her, but her trafficker told her if she smiled and nodded, he could protect her from the police. As a result, the police left. Later that week, another police car arrived at the location with a Spanish speaking officer. Once again the woman smiled, and told him she was fine. Fortunately for her and the others who were locked inside with assault rifles aimed at them, the officer felt something was "off" with the situation. Further investigation, led the authorities to uncover the truth. The raid took place in the early hours of the morning before daybreak; the authorities were able to round up many of the traffickers, and rescue the women.

Two Men Arrested in Michigan for Human Trafficking Scam

Michail Aronov and Aleksander Maksimenko were arrested by Immigration and Customs Enforcement (ICE) special agents for forcing at least four women from the Ukraine to work as exotic dancers at a strip club. The women were recruited under the guise of working as waitresses in the United States; however once they arrived they were forced to work at a strip club in Detroit. They were forced to work twelve hours per day, six days a week to pay off $12,000 in travel expenses and another $10,000 for identification documentation.

The two men took all of the money the women were paid by customers in the strip club, under the guise of payment for their "expenses." Two of the women arrived in the United States with their husbands but they have not seen or spoken to their spouses since their arrival. The victims were driven back and forth from work to their apartment each day. They did not have access to a telephone and the women were kept under control through intimidation, physical abuse, and death threats.

Three Plead Guilty in Sex Trafficking Case

New York City - Josue Flores Carreto, Gerardo Flores Carreto and Daniel Perez Alonso, plead guilty in a sex trafficking case which stemmed from as far back as 1991. The men admitted that they physically assaulted the women and girls on numerous occasions, causing serious bodily injury, forced the victims into prostitution, and used threats of serious harm in order to get their victims to comply with their demands. Acts of violence were also used whenever the women tried to hide money from the men, failed to make enough money, and disobeyed orders.

On April 27, 2006, Josue Flores Carreto and Geraldo Flores Carreto were each sentenced to fifty years in prison; the longest sentences ever to be imposed in a sex trafficking case. Daniel Perez Alfonso was sentenced to twenty-five years in prison on the same day. On February 2, 2006, Edith Mosquera de Flores was sentenced to twenty-seven months incarceration for conspiring to force young Mexican women into prostitution. Eliu Carreto Fernandez was sentenced to serve eighty months in prison on June 1, 2006. Consuelo Carreto Valencia and Maria De Los Angeles Velasquez Reyes were indicted in the United States on charges of conspiracy, sex trafficking, forced labor or services, Mann Act, and immigration offenses. They are incarcerated in Mexico on Mexican federal charges related to the human trafficking conspiracy. Elroy Carreto Reyes pled guilty to sex trafficking, his sentencing is pending.

Texas Sex Slaves

Six Texas men were sentenced for sex trafficking receiving a combined fifty-one years. Four women from Central America agreed to pay the men $5000 in smuggling fees. They paid half up front and were to pay the balance upon arrival into the United States. Once they arrived in Texas, the smugglers demanded more money. When they failed to pay the additional money, they were forced to work as unpaid servants during the day. At night, they were the gang's sex slaves, often beaten and brutalized. Two of the women turned to neighbors for help, however when the ring leader found out about it, he ordered them killed. His men beat and raped the women, but did not kill them. Once they were let go, they turned to the police for help, who were able to locate the other two women and rescue them. The men involved in this case eventually pled guilty to the charges. It was discovered in the course of the investigation that the smuggling and human trafficking ring had been in operation since the early 1980's.

Domestic Servitude

Domestic servitude is ranked as being the second highest incidence of forced labor in the United States. This is due to the high demand for cheap household service, and it is easily exploitable. The lack of a monitoring system combined with a lack of legal protection in the domestic service industry facilitates this form of exploitation. Thousands of domestic workers are brought into the United States each year to work in private households; many suffer from various forms of abuse, including sexual assault. Unscrupulous employers have confiscated travel documents and work visas, charged the employees for room and board at exorbitant rates, and forced the victims to work inhumanely long hours without benefit. Foreign domestic household workers have been denied the freedom to come and go as they want; they have been deprived of any contact with their families, and do not have the right to change jobs.

Woman Sentenced in Human Trafficking Case

Mariska Trisanti was sentenced to forty-six months in prison for holding a young Indonesian woman in involuntary servitude. Trisanti had arranged for the young woman to travel from Indonesia on a tourist visa back in 1997. The arrangement was for the victim to work as a domestic and a nanny for two years, however when she arrived in Los Angeles, her passport was confiscated and she was forced to work seventeen hours a day, seven days a week. The victim received very little compensation for her work; she was kept under control through constant threats, acts of violence, and fear that she would be arrested and sent to prison. The victim escaped in the spring of 2000, when Trisanti took a trip to Indonesia, leaving the victim and another young Indonesian girl in her husband's care.

Wisconsin Couple Indicted On Human Trafficking Charges

Jefferson and Elnora Calimlim, of Brookfield Wisconsin are charged with holding a woman in domestic servitude for nineteen years. The couple used threats, physical abuse and coercion to keep the Filipino woman captive in their home. Jefferson and Elnora Calimlim, both physicians, forced the victim to work long hours, seven days a week. She was not allowed to play outside in the yard with the children she cared for; instead she was forced to play with them in the garage with the door closed. Her captors refused to allow her to go out for walks, keeping her hidden from friends and neighbors during the nineteen years she was in their household.

During the trial of Drs. Calimlim, the victim testified she had been refused medical attention and freedom. She was constantly told that she would go to prison if she did not obey them. The victim was not allowed to answer the door, the telephone or to be seen by guests. Neighbors testified that they did not know the Drs. Calimlim even had a maid. In the nineteen years of domestic servitude, the victim was allowed to answer the door once, on Halloween; however she was forced to wear a mask to cover her face. The victim was paid one hundred dollars a month for the first ten years and about four hundred dollars a month thereafter. She was forced to serve as a maid, a nanny, and made to clean the Calimlims' investment rental apartments, medical offices, and medical instruments. She also washed, waxed and changed the oil in the family's cars; however she had to do this inside the garage to avoid being seen.

During the trial, the victims testified against her captors. She stated that whenever the family had guests over, she was told to hide in her basement bedroom and lock the door from inside. These parties would last five to eight hours, and they would be held in the basement right outside her bedroom. She was not allowed to leave the bedroom to go to the bathroom until after all of the guests had left. She would then be made to clean up the party mess. In May 2006, the Calimlim's were convicted of human trafficking.

Couple Arrested on Slavery Charges

Abdel Nasser Eid Youssef Ibrahim, and Amal Ahmed Ewis-abd Motelib, were named in a four count indictment for conspiring to hold the victim in involuntary servitude and obtaining her services by force and coercion. The twelve year old girl was kept locked in their garage for two years and forced to work as a domestic servant for their family of seven. The victim was forced to comply through threats of violence against her sister living in Egypt. The couple obtained a visa for the girl through a third party on fraudulent grounds in order for her to travel to the United States. Her presence was concealed from immigration authorities, local law enforcement, and school officials. She was forced to live in squalid conditions, she received little or no pay during the two years, endured physical abuse, constant threats, and lived in a constant state of fear. The twelve year old child was kept in captivity and unable to go outside during her during her years of enslavement.

Forced Agricultural Labor

Farm workers are especially vulnerable to human traffickers. This is due to the fact that monitoring systems in the fields are inadequate, the wages are insufficient, the working conditions are poor, the legal protections are weak and lacking, and generally the agricultural workers are poor, uneducated, and usually have language barriers. The majority of agricultural workers are migrants who tend to travel across the United States for seasonal employment. There are approximately one and half million seasonal farm workers each year. Without the proper farm inspections, many laborers fall victim to trafficking schemes. The same goes for the horse industry; unscrupulous farm owners and farm managers take advantage of the migrant workers, many of whom may be undocumented. Unfortunately, even workers who are in the United States legally also fall prey to traffickers and unfair labor practices. The threat or use of violence is commonly used to maintain order amongst the farm workers. Those who come from countries with corrupted officials and law enforcement are afraid to contact authorities out of fear of retribution.

Many migrant workers are required to sign a contract to work for their traffickers; these contract stipulate fees listed as "employment fees" or "job placement fees" and range from $4,000

- $11,000. Exorbitant employment fees are illegal in many countries and are banned by international covenants. Traffickers will usually charge high interest rates on these fees, as most migrant workers do not have that amount of cash available to them. Agricultural slaves receive very little payment, due to the weekly deductions taken by their employers for fees, interest, and living expenses. Migrant workers generally spend their money at the company store, whether it is for cigarettes, alcohol, or prostitutes that are brought in for the workers. The workers who are enslaved are confined to the farms to prevent them from running off or seeking help.

Group Forced Illegal Aliens to Work for Little or No Pay

Maria Garcia, a labor contractor from Texas, recruited illegal Mexicans and smuggled them into western New York. Garcia, her husband, and their two sons approached the illegal aliens once they were smuggled into Arizona from Mexico. They charged the illegal aliens exorbitant fees for transporting them to farm jobs in western New York. When the farm workers were paid, Garcia would take their checks, cash them and keep the money. The men were told that they were not free to leave until all of their debts had been paid off. Two groups of victims were able to escape and seek help from the authorities. The victims, some of them as young as fifteen years old were forced to work long hours for little or no wages. The family pled guilty to charges of forced labor, conspiracy to commit forced labor, and harboring illegal aliens.

Ramos Case

Juan and Ramiro Ramos were convicted of conspiring to commit involuntary servitude, violating the Hobbs Act, and illegally transporting Mexican workers to work in their fields. The Hobbs Act criminalizes extortion by the wrongful use of actual or threatened force, violence, or fear. The Ramos brothers were convicted on June 27, 2002. Jose Ramos, another brother was also convicted of a Hobbs Act offense for his part in the criminal enterprise.

Upon arrival at the camps, the workers were informed that they were not free to leave their employment until they had paid off their transportation fees. Juan and Ramiro Ramos created an environment of fear by keeping the workers under constant surveillance and constant threat of violence if they attempted to leave. The Ramos brothers violently beat a van driver and several employees in order to prevent them from freeing the workers.

Jose Ramos was sentenced to more than ten years of imprisonment and ordered to pay a $10,000 fine, while his brothers Ramiro and Juan were sentenced to more than twelve years of imprisonment and ordered to pay over $3 million in proceeds, they were forced to forfeit vehicles and real property. Shortly after their conviction, the Supreme Court of the United States rendered a decision in another case which held that action which did not amount to obtaining property could not be a basis of a Hobbs Act violation. The Ramos brothers had been convicted of a Hobbs Act however the evidence did not show the obtainment of property in the commission of their crimes. At the government's request the United States Court of Appeals for the Eleventh Circuit reversed Juan and Ramiro Ramos' Hobbs Act conviction and remanded the case for resentencing. They were each resentenced to fifteen years of imprisonment and ordered to pay $20,000 in fines and ordered to pay restitution to the victims.

Sweatshops

One of the largest cases of forced labor took place in America Samoa, a United States territory. The garment factory held over two hundred enslaved workers, who were malnourished, mistreated, and brutally beaten when they did not comply with the demands placed upon them. The garment factory produced merchandise carrying the label "Made in the U.S.A." however they workers did not receive American wages or benefits. The abuse went on for several years due to the lack of inspections, labor law enforcement, and regulatory conditions. The Samoan immigration board has the authority to cancel work visas and deport immigrant workers, and always complied with the employers' wishes. Most of the employees went into debt for the opportunity to work in this garment factory and could not afford to pay off their debts or to return to their countries without money for loan repayments. The minimum wages in American Samoa are much lower than they are in the mainland United States.

United States Response to Human Trafficking

The United States has been active against the slave trade ever since Abraham Lincoln was president. He signed the Emancipation Proclamation which led to the Thirteenth Amendment being added to the Constitution. Further legislative actions include the Mann Act, The Hobbs Act, The TVPA, the PROTECT Act, and the Palermo Protocol. Currently twenty-seven states have passed anti-trafficking legislation, and other states are currently working to develop human trafficking laws. The trafficking of persons is a federal offense, which is tried by federal prosecutors in federal court. States with anti-trafficking legislation have the opportunity to try human traffickers in their courts, once the federal government has completed their prosecution.

Prior to the Trafficking Victims Protection Act, the United States government had enacted a law called the Mann Act back in 1910, for the purpose of criminalizing "white slavery", otherwise known as sex trafficking. Illinois congressman James Robert Mann authored the "White Slavery Act" which is better known as the Mann Act in reaction to the "white slavery" hysteria of the early twentieth century. The Mann Act made it a crime to transport women across state lines "for the purpose of prostitution, debauchery, or for any other immoral purpose." The industrial revolution brought an onslaught of change and immigration to American society; one of the most frightening changes of the time period was that young single women were moving into the cities and entering the work force without the protection of traditional family centered courtships. The puritanical society of the era was anxious to prevent the decay of moral values; they feared for the safety of the young women, and wanted to protect them from forced prostitution and the increase of the "white slavery" movement.

Boxer John Arthur Jonson, better known as Jack Johnson, was the first black heavyweight champion of the world and he was convicted under the Mann Act for transporting a white prostitute from Pittsburg to Chicago. In 1920 Johnson was sentenced and spent one year in Leavenworth prison. In 1949, actor Rex Ingram was arrested for violating the Mann Act. He pled guilty to the charge of transporting a teenage girl to New York and sentenced to eighteen months in prison. Chuck Berry was convicted in 1959 for transporting an underage Apache girl across state lines. The girl was arrested on prostitution charges a few weeks later. Chuck Berry served twenty months in prison. The Mann Act is still enacted today and being used to convict sex traffickers. The full text of the Mann Act can be found in the Appendix.

Trafficking Victims Protection Act

In October 2000, the Trafficking Victims Protection Act (TVPA) was signed and enacted. The TVPA is the first comprehensive federal law which specifically protects victims of human trafficking and also provides the necessary statutes for prosecuting the criminals engaged in human trafficking. Organized criminal enterprises profit from the trafficking industry world-wide. The United States government is taking a proactive approach to combating this fast growing industry. Three main goals have been set forth in the TVPA, they are to prevent human trafficking oversees, to protect victims and help them rebuild their lives in the United States, with federal and state support, should they choose to stay in the U.S., and the last goal is to prosecute traffickers under stiff federal penalties. The TVPA is comprehensive in addressing the numerous ways to combat human trafficking. Prevention measures include educational and public awareness programs designed to bring this topic into the public domain, as well as increasing training to those in the fields of law enforcement and social services.

The TVPA defines "severe form of trafficking in persons" as:

a. *Sex trafficking in which a commercial sex act is induced by force, fraud, or coercion, or in which the person induced to perform such an act has not attained eighteen years of age;*
b. *The recruitment, harboring, transportation, provision, or obtaining of a person for labor or services, through the use of force, fraud or coercion for the purpose of subjection to involuntary servitude, peonage, debt bondage, or slavery.*

Protection measures for victims of human trafficking include housing, health care, and federally funded social service programs geared towards rebuilding their shattered lives. The TVPA established the *T Visas* as an additional protective measure for these victims. *T Visas* provide a temporary legal status, which allows victims of human trafficking to stay in the United States for up to three years, once they have been certified as trafficking victims. The TVPA authorizes up to 5,000 *T Visas* annually. Additionally, the TVPA makes provisions for the *U Visa* and authorizes up to 10,000 *U Visas* annually. The law provides victims of trafficking with these protective measures as a way to shift immigration law, which previously resulted in trafficking victims being deported as illegal aliens. Deportation could result in victims being returned to the very people who were responsible for their exploitation, thus perpetrating a vicious cycle where the victims end up being trafficked to another location. The TVPA also makes victims eligible for the Witness Protection Program. Before a trafficking victim becomes eligible for these services they must be certified by the U.S. Department of Health and Human Services. Further requirements of the TVPA state that the victim must be helpful and cooperative in the investigation and / or prosecution of their traffickers. Child victims under the age of fifteen are exempt from this requirement. Once certified under the guidelines set forth by the TVPA, human trafficking victims are eligible to apply and receive benefits, social services, and work visas.

T Visas

T Visas are for victims of severe forms of human trafficking, who have cooperated and complied with any reasonable requests for the purpose of investigating and prosecuting the traffickers who forced them into modern day slavery. A victim of trafficking is only eligible for a *T Visa* if he or she is present in the United States, American Samoa, or the Commonwealth of the Northern Mariana Islands. Additionally, it must be shown that he or she would suffer extreme hardship or harm to be removed from the United States, American Samoa, or the Commonwealth of the Northern Mariana Islands. I have included an excerpt in italics below from the *T visa* application.

Excerpt from T visa application:

To qualify for T-1 nonimmigrant status, an applicant must demonstrate that he or she:

- *Is physically present in the United States, American Samoa or the Commonwealth of the Northern Mariana Islands as a result of trafficking;*

- *Is a victim of a severe form of trafficking in persons;*

- *Would suffer extreme hardship involving unusual and severe harm upon removal; and*

- *Has complied with any reasonable request for assistance in the investigation and prosecution of acts of trafficking in persons, unless the applicant is less than 15 years old.*

To establish that he or she is a victim of a severe form of trafficking in persons, the applicant must demonstrate that he or she was brought to the United States either:

(1) For the purpose of a commercial sex act, which act was either induced by force, fraud or coercion, or occurred when the applicant had not reached 18 years of age, or

(2) For the purpose of labor or services induced by force, fraud, or coercion for the purpose of subjecting the applicant to involuntary servitude, peonage, debt bondage, or slavery.

An applicant is encouraged to raise all arguments and to document all elements of his or her claim, including allegations of extreme hardship, in his or her initial application.

You must also provide a personal declarative statement. That statement should describe the trafficking crime of which you were a victim, including:

- *How you were induced to enter the United States;*

- *The purpose for which you were brought to the United States;*

- *When these events took place;*

- *Who was responsible;*

- *How long were you detained by the traffickers;*

- *How and when you escaped, were rescued, or otherwise became separated from the traffickers;*

- *What you have been doing since you were separated from the traffickers;*

- *Why you were unable to leave the United States after you were separated from the traffickers;*

- *What harm or mistreatment you fear if you are removed from the United States; and*

- *Why you fear you would be harmed or mistreated.*

U Visas

U Visas are for victims of human trafficking who have suffered substantial physical or mental abuse during the course of their enslavement. The applicant must possess information concerning the crime and be willing to cooperate with federal law enforcement authorities for the purpose of the investigation and or prosecution of the perpetrators of this criminal activity. The application must also include a certification from federal, state or local law enforcement stating that the victim has helped, is helping, or will likely be of helpful in the course of the investigation and or prosecution of the crime.

As mentioned previously, there are only 5,000 *T Visas* and 10,000 *U Visas* issued annually to victims of human trafficking. Family members of the victim are also eligible to apply for immigration status, once the victim has been certified. Their immigration status is not deducted from the 5,000 *T Visas* or the 10,000 *U Visas*.

Trafficking Victims Protection Reauthorization Act 2003

Under the Trafficking Victims Protection Reauthorization Act of 2003 (TVPRA), the Bush administration authorized over $200 million to combat human trafficking. Additional benefits of the TVPRA 2003 include the empowerment of trafficking victims enabling them to bring federal civil suits against their traffickers for actual and punitive damages, it also provides for the inclusion of sex trafficking and forced labor under the Racketeering Influenced and Corrupt Organization (RICO) statute.

Trafficking Victims Protection Reauthorization Act 2005

On January 10, 2006, President George W. Bush signed the Trafficking Victims Protection Reauthorization Act 2005 (TVPRA 2005). The TVPRA 2005, also known as H.R. 972 was introduced by Representative Smith (R) of New Jersey and cosponsored by 103 supporters on the hill. The TVPRA 2005 authorized $361 million over a two year period to combat human trafficking. President Bush signed the TVPRA 2005 on January 10, 2006. Since 2001, the Department of Justice has prosecuted 277 traffickers.

The TVPRA 2005 provides improvements for the TVPA. The improvements include strengthening anti-trafficking and protection measures, supporting domestic efforts to combat trafficking, and bringing attention to reducing the demand for commercial sex acts. The TVPRA 2005 requires local and state law enforcement to use the best practices and methods in training their officers. Human trafficking is a federal offense and therefore must be prosecuted in federal court. That means that individual states are unable to prosecute a human trafficking offense. However, that does not mean that states are helpless or have their hands tied. States are allowed to prosecute for the individual crimes committed in the course of human trafficking. Currently, twenty-seven states have human trafficking criminalization statutes and many others are in the process of enacting human trafficking statutes into their state constitutions.

HR 270

HR 270 was brought to the floor in the United States House of Representatives on January 5, 2007. The purpose of this proposed legislation is to authorize appropriations for fiscal years 2008 through 2010 for the Trafficking Victims Protection Act of 2000. The Act is also cited as the Trafficking Victims Protection Reauthorization Act of 2007. The minimum standards can be found in the Appendix.

TIP Report

Each year the United States Department of State puts out the Trafficking in Persons (TIP) report containing information regarding the progress or lack of progress made by other nations. The Department of State is required by law to submit a report to Congress on what foreign governments are doing to eliminate human trafficking, as mandated by the TVPA. The nations are listed in a tier system based on their level of achievement.

The TIP report classifies countries on a tier system according to their efforts in the fight against human trafficking. A Tier 3 country is classified as failing to make significant efforts to come into compliance with the minimum standards to eliminate trafficking as specified under U.S. law. A Tier 3 status could cause the US to withhold any non-humanitarian, non-trade assistance from that country. The 2006 tier list is located at the end of this chapter.

The Tiers

Tier 1 countries are nations whose governments fully comply with the TVPA's minimum standards.

Tier 2 countries are nations whose governments do not fully comply with the TVPA's minimum standards but are making significant efforts to bring themselves into compliance with those standards.

Tier 2 Special Watch List countries are nations whose governments do not fully comply with the TVPA's minimum standards but are making significant efforts to bring themselves into compliance with those standards. Plus, the country must meet at least one of the following provisions:
a) the absolute number of victims of severe forms of trafficking is very significant or is increasing significantly
b) there is a failure to provide evidence of increasing efforts to combat severe forms of trafficking in persons from the previous year
c) the determination that a country is making significant efforts to bring themselves into compliance with minimum standards was

based on commitments by the country to take additional future steps over the next year.

Tier 3 countries are nations whose governments do not fully comply with the minimum standards and are not making significant efforts to do so.

U.S. Department of Justice Civil Rights Division Report on Activities to Combat Human Trafficking Fiscal Years 2001 – 2005

The U. S. Department of Justice, Civil Rights Division issued the above named report which includes activities the Department is doing to combat human trafficking. Included in this report is the Model State Anti-Trafficking Criminal Statute. This model statute can be found in Appendix I of the U.S. Department of Justice Civil Rights Division Report on Activities to Combat Human Trafficking Fiscal Years 2001 - 2005. This is an important tool for states seeking to implement anti-trafficking laws. I have included the model statute in this book for your convenience. Model statutes can be found in the Appendix.

TIER 1			
AUSTRALIA	FRANCE	MALAWI	SOUTH KOREA
AUSTRIA	GERMANY	MOROCCO	SPAIN
BELGIUM	HONG KONG	THE NETHERLANDS	SWEDEN
CANADA	IRELAND	NEW ZEALAND	SWITZERLAND
COLOMBIA	ITALY	NORWAY	UNITED KINGDOM
DENMARK	LITHUANIA	POLAND	
FINLAND	LUXEMBOURG	SINGAPORE	

TIER 2			
AFGHANISTAN	EAST TIMOR	LATVIA	RWANDA
ALBANIA	ECUADOR	LEBANON	SENEGAL
ANGOLA	EL SALVADOR	MACEDONIA	SERBIA-MONTENEGRO
AZERBAIJAN	ESTONIA	MADAGASCAR	SIERRA LEONE
BANGLADESH	ETHIOPIA	MALI	SLOVAK REPUBLIC
BELARUS	GABON	MALTA	SLOVENIA
BENIN	THE GAMBIA	MAURITIUS	SRI LANKA
BOSNIA/HERZ.	GEORGIA	MOLDOVA	SURINAME
BULGARIA	GHANA	MONGOLIA	TAJIKISTAN
BURKINA FASO	GREECE	MOZAMBIQUE	TANZANIA
BURUNDI	GUATEMALA	NEPAL	THAILAND
CAMEROON	GUINEA	NICARAGUA	TUNISIA
CHAD	GUINEA-BISSAU	NIGER	TURKEY
CHILE	GUYANA	NIGERIA	UGANDA
CONGO (DRC)	HONDURAS	PAKISTAN	UKRAINE
COSTA RICA	HUNGARY	PANAMA	URUGUAY
COTE D'IVOIRE	JAPAN	PARAGUAY	VIETNAM
CROATIA	JORDAN	PHILIPPINES	YEMEN
CZECH REPUBLIC	KAZAKHSTAN	PORTUGAL	ZAMBIA
DOMINICAN REP.	KYRGYZ REPUBLIC	ROMANIA	

TIER 2 WATCH LIST			
ALGERIA	CHINA (PRC)	JAMAICA	OMAN
ARGENTINA	CYPRUS	KENYA	PERU
ARMENIA	DJIBOUTI	KUWAIT	QATAR
BAHRAIN	EGYPT	LIBYA	RUSSIA
BOLIVIA	EQUATORIAL GUINEA	MACAU	SOUTH AFRICA
BRAZIL	INDIA	MALAYSIA	TAIWAN
CAMBODIA	INDONESIA	MAURITANIA	TOGO
CENTRAL AFRICAN REP.	ISRAEL	MEXICO	UNITED ARAB EMIRATES

TIER 3			
BELIZE	IRAN	SAUDI ARABIA	UZBEKISTAN
BURMA	LAOS	SUDAN	VENEZUELA
CUBA	NORTH KOREA	SYRIA	ZIMBABWE

Courtesy of the Trafficking In Persons Report June 2006

States with Human Trafficking Laws

While human trafficking is a federal offense and can only be tried in federal court, individual states are encouraged to adopt state anti-trafficking criminal statutes. As of this publication there are twenty-seven states with anti-trafficking criminal statutes. Many other states are in the process of passing laws against human trafficking which should be enacted before the end of 2008.

Alaska – SB 12

July 1, 2006, Alaska enacted SB 12. Under SB 12, human trafficking in the first degree is a class A felony and human trafficking in the second degree is a class B felony. SB 12 also includes sex tourism as a criminal act in the second degree. This statute requires the legislative council, the court system, and the commissioner to adopt provisions prohibiting procurement from a person that has headquarters in or conducts business in a country in Tier 3 of the most recent US State Department TIP report.

The included provision regarding prohibiting procurement from a person associated with a Tier 3 country is in my opinion a stroke of brilliance. The purpose of being listed as a Tier 3 country is to withhold economic opportunities to these nations until they comply with the minimum standards set forth by the State Department.

Arizona – SB 1372

August 12, 2005, Arizona enacted SB 1372. Under SB 1372, it is a first degree felony to engage minors under the age of fifteen in sex trafficking and a second degree felony to attempt to engage minors in sex trafficking. SB 1372 also establishes two class 2 felonies: sex trafficking, and trafficking of persons for forced labor or services. The bill also establishes a class 4 felony, unlawfully obtaining labor or services. The bill makes a provision requiring the courts to order restitution to the victim.

Arkansas – HB 2979

August 11, 2005, Arkansas enacted HB 2979. Under HB 2979, it is a class A felony to engage in trafficking of persons for the purposes of involuntary servitude, peonage, debt bondage, slavery, marriage, adoption or sexual conduct. It is also a class A felony to benefit financially from human trafficking.

California – AB 22

On September 21, 2005, California enacted AB 22. Under AB 22, human trafficking for the purpose of forced labor or services is a felony crime and is punishable with a sentence of 3, 4, or 5 years in a state prison. The trafficking of a minor is a felony that is punishable with a sentence of 4, 6, or 8 years in a state prison. AB 22 also provides for mandatory restitution and allows trafficking victims to bring a civil action against his or her traffickers. AB 22 has strict guidelines and timetable for the issuance of law enforcement agency endorsements for trafficking victims. Law enforcement agency endorsement is necessary for those victims seeking either a *T Visa* or a *U Visa*. Additionally, AB 22 also an interagency statewide task force on human trafficking.

SB 1569

September 29, 2006 California enacted SB 1569. This bill amends California's Welfare and Institutions Code allowing non-citizen victims of trafficking, domestic violence, and other serious crimes to be eligible to receive state funded social services. This includes cash assistance, social services, health care, and employment under the Cuban-Haitian Entrant Program and the Refugee Resettlement Program. Guidelines for determining whether a person is a victim of severe forms of trafficking are provided in this bill.

SB 180

September 21, 2005, California enacted SB 180 which created the California Alliance to Combat Trafficking and Slavery (California ACTS) Task Force. The California ACTS Task Force consists of government and nongovernment agencies and organizations to work together for the purpose of gathering and examining data, evaluate programs, and evaluate criminal statues which address human trafficking victims. The task force must submit a report on their findings to the Legislature, Governor, and Attorney General by July 1, 2007.

Colorado – SB 207

July 1, 2006, Colorado enacted SB 207. This bill establishes the crime of trafficking in adults as a class 2 felony and the trafficking in minors as a class 3 felony. SB 207 classifies adults as being a person who is 16 years of age or older and a child is a person under the age of 16.Trafficking is defined as the sale, exchange, barter, or lease of an adult or child in return for money or other consideration or item of value for the adult or child victim of trafficking.

HB 1143

April 5, 2005, Colorado enacted HB 1143 creating an interagency task force on human trafficking. The task force was charged with the collection and analyzing of all data pertaining to the crime of trafficking in persons within the state.

Connecticut – SB 153

July 1, 2006, Connecticut enacted SB 153 which established the trafficking of persons as a class B felony. SB 153 also provides a victim of trafficking with the right to a civil case to recover penalties, actual damages, and statutory damages. This bill also provides for the training of state police, the office of the Chief State's Attorney, local police departments, and community organizations.

HB 5358

October 1, 2004 Connecticut established HB 5358 creating an interagency task force on human trafficking. The task force was charged with the collection and analyzing of all data pertaining to the crime of trafficking in persons within the state, including evaluating public awareness programs. The task force was charged with these duties and required to present their findings to the General Assembly by January 1, 2006.

Florida

Florida has been proactive in its battle against human trafficking. For further information, please see the chapter on Florida's response to human trafficking.

Georgia – SB 529

July 1, 2006 Georgia enacted SB 529 establishing the felonies of trafficking in persons for labor servitude and sexual servitude. Conviction for the trafficking of an adult (eighteen years and older) brings the minimum sentence of one year to the maximum sentence of twenty years. The trafficking of a minor results in the minimum sentencing of ten years and the maximum sentence of twenty years. SB 529 allows a corporation to be prosecuted if an agent of the corporation acts within his/her capacity on behalf of the corporation.

Hawaii – HB 135

July 1, 2004 Hawaii enacted HB 135 allowing persons living abroad who use International Marriage Brokers (IMB) or International Marriage Organizations (IMO) to obtain information regarding criminal convictions and marital histories of prospective spouses. Each IMB/IMO must notify each recruit in their native language that criminal records and marital histories of Hawaii residents are available upon request. Failure to do so can result in a fine up to $500 and imprisonment up to thirty days.

HB 2050

January 1, 2007 Hawaii expanded their current law to include the history of abuse orders in the disclosure given to recruits utilizing the services of International Marriage Brokers (IMB) or International Marriage Organizations (IMO).

HB 2051

July 1, 2006 Hawaii enacted HB 2051 establishing a human trafficking task force to review laws and information from other states. The task force is required to develop protocol and training related to providing services for victims of human trafficking. Additionally, the task force is to conduct needs assessment and victim protection. The task force is required to work with government agencies and nongovernment organizations, seek federal grants, and report their findings to the state legislature at least twenty days before the 2007 session begins.

HB 2020

On May 19, 2004, Hawaii enacted HB 2020. Under HB 2020, it is a class C felony to knowingly sell or offer to sell services that include or facilitate travel for the purpose of engaging in prostitution. HB 2020 emphasizes that sex tourism and prostitution contribute to human trafficking. HB 2020 also authorizes the suspension or revocation of a travel agency's registration for engaging in these acts.

Idaho – HB 536

July 1, 2006 Idaho enacted HB 536 establishing human trafficking as a felony punishable by imprisonment in the state prison for up to twenty-five years. This bill authorizes the court to order restitution to trafficking victims and to order payment for mental and physical rehabilitation of the victim.

HCR 18

April 1, 2005 Idaho established HCR 18 creating an interagency task force on human trafficking. The task force was mandated with the collection and analyzing of all data pertaining to the crime of trafficking in persons within the state, including evaluating public awareness programs. The task force was charged with these duties and required to present their findings and recommendations to the Legislature, the Governor, and the Idaho Supreme Court by January 1, 2006.

Illinois – HB 1469

On January 1, 2006, Illinois enacted HB 1469. Under HB 1469, the following felony offenses were established: involuntary servitude, involuntary servitude of a minor, and trafficking of persons for forced labor or services. Causing or threatening physical harm; destroying, confiscating, concealing, removing, or possessing any actual or alleged immigration documentation; and the use of intimidation can be used to determine the severity of the charge against the alleged trafficker. HB 1469 also makes a provision to include the trafficker's behavior as a consideration during sentencing. This includes extreme violence, bodily injury, the number of trafficking victims, and sexual assault. HB 1469 also requires the court to order restitution to the victim of human trafficking and the forfeiture of any and all assets obtained as a result of the human trafficking criminal activities.

HB 1299

July 3, 2006, Illinois enacted HB 1299, the Predator Accountability Act. This Act provides victims of the sex trade and victims of trafficking, with the right to bring a civil action against those responsible for recruiting, harming, profiting from or maintaining them in the sex trade. HB 1299 establishes a ten year statute of limitations for those seeking damages under this Act. Victims of sex trafficking under the age of eighteen or whose disability precludes them from bringing a civil suit are provided with an exception under this bill. The statute of limitations does not begin to run until the victim reaches the age of eighteen or the victim is declared to be free of their disability.

Indiana – HB 1155

July 1, 2006 Indiana enacts HB 1155, establishing that the sex trafficking of a minor as a class A felony; the promotion of human trafficking as a class B felony; and human trafficking as a class C felony. HB 1155 requires court ordered restitution and provides for the protection of victims.

Iowa – SF 2219

July 1, 2006 Iowa enacted SF 2219 establishing human trafficking as class B, C, or D felonies. This bill requires the development of training curricula; provides for an affirmative defense for trafficking victim facing criminal charges; provides trafficking victims the same rights as other crime victims; and allows them access to the victim compensation fund. SF 2219 also requests a legislative study on human trafficking which must be presented during the 2007 legislative session and should include the study's findings regarding the needs of trafficking victims and the services provided to victims.

Kansas – SB 72

On July 1, 2005, Kansas enacted SB 72. Under SB 72, human trafficking is a level 2 felony offense and aggravated trafficking is a level 1 felony offense. Aggravated trafficking is defined as kidnapping or attempted kidnapping; sexual gratification of the defendant or another person; death of the victim; or the trafficking of a person under the age of eighteen.

Louisiana – HB 56

On August 15, 2005, Louisiana enacted HB 56. Under HB 56, human trafficking is punishable by a maximum sentence of ten years in prison and a maximum fine of $10,000. However, if the trafficking is committed for the purpose of commercial sexual activity, then the maximum sentence is twenty years in prison and a maximum fine of $15,000. Under HB 56, the trafficking of a minor carries a maximum prison sentence of twenty-five years and a maximum fine of $25,000.

Maine – HP 893

April 28, 2006 Maine enacted HP 893 establishing a human trafficking task force to review laws and legislation from other states for the purpose of making recommendations for statutory language to criminalize human trafficking. The task force is responsible for researching and evaluating public awareness programs, federal, state, and local programs in order to make their recommendations. A report must be submitted to the legislature along with their recommendations by November 30, 2006.

Michigan – HB 5747

August 24, 2006 Michigan enacted HB 5747 establishing human trafficking for forced labor or services as a felony punishable by imprisonment up to ten years. Financial gain through human trafficking also brings a punishment of up to ten years in prison. HB 5747 provides enhanced penalties for injury or death of the victim, attempted murder, kidnapping, attempted kidnapping, criminal sexual conduct, or attempted criminal sexual conduct.

Minnesota – HF 1

On April 26, 2005, Minnesota enacted HF 1. Under HF 1, the following criminal activities are felonies: labor trafficking, sex trafficking, and unlawful conduct with respect to documents in furtherance of labor or sex trafficking. Labor trafficking is punishable by up to fifteen years in prison and / or a $30,000 fine. Sex trafficking is punishable by a maximum prison sentence of either fifteen years or twenty years, depending upon the age of the victim. The document offense carries a maximum punishment of five years in prison, a $10,000 fine, or both. HF 1 includes appropriations funding for a task force charged with providing an annual study to be presented to the legislature. The study should include the number of arrests, prosecutions, and convictions of traffickers.

Mississippi – HB 381

July 1, 2006 Mississippi enacted HB381 human trafficking for forced labor or services as a felony punishable by not more than twenty years in prison. The trafficking of a minor for the purpose of commercial sexual activity is punishable by not more than thirty years in prison. A minor is described as a person under the age of eighteen years old.

Missouri – HB 1487

On August 28, 2004, Missouri enacted HB 1487. Under HB 1487, makes the sexual trafficking of a child a class A felony. HB 1487 establishes the following class B felonies: abusing an individual through forced labor and trafficking for either forced labor or sexual exploitation. Under HB 1487, contributing to human trafficking through the misuse of documentation is a class

D felony. Sentencing guidelines under HB 1487 require the perpetrator to pay restitution to the victim.

HB 1698

July 1, 2006, Missouri enacted HB 1698 making sex tourism a class C felony. HB 1698 authorizes the revocation of the articles of incorporation of any company facilitating sex tourism, and it allows the freezing of bank and deposit accounts. Sex tourism is defined as selling or offering to sell travel services for the purpose of engaging in prostitution.

HB 353

July 13, 2005 Missouri enacted HB 353 which requires International Marriage Brokers (IMB) or International Marriage Organizations (IMO) to provide their recruits with the criminal history record and the marital history record of their clients. IMB / IMO are required to provide their recruits with basic rights information in the recruits' native language, at the expense of the IMB/IMO. Failure to provide this information as set forth in the guidelines is a class D felony. Recruits are defined as non-citizen or non-resident and clients are defined as citizens seeking mates.

Nebraska – LB 1086

July 14, 2006 Nebraska enacted LB 1086 establishing the trafficking of persons for the purpose of forced labor or services as a Class IV felony. This includes anyone who benefits from the trafficking of persons. Enhanced sentencing is included in LB 1086 for the trafficking of minors under the age of eighteen for the purpose of forcing them to participate in the commercial sex industry. Enhanced penalties are included for inflicting or threatening to inflict serious personal injury, and/or physically restraining or threatening to physically restrain a person. LB 1086 establishes that knowingly destroying, concealing, removing, confiscating or possessing any actual or purported immigration document as a Class IV felony offense.

New Jersey – AB 2730

On April 26, 2005, New Jersey enacted AB 2730. Under AB 2730, committing the offense of human trafficking for the purpose of engaging in sexual activity or providing labor or services is a first degree felony. This brings a maximum punishment of twenty years in prison without the possibility of parole, or a sentence up to life in prison with the possibility of parole after the offender has served twenty years of his or hers sentence. AB 2730 requires the court to sentence the perpetrator to make restitution to the victim. The court is able to order forfeiture of any assets related to the trafficking violation. AB 2730 mandates that the county prosecutor's office or the victim-witness advocacy office ensures that trafficking victims receive available benefits and services.

North Carolina – HB 1896

December 1, 2006 North Carolina enacted HB 1896 establishing the trafficking of a minor for sexual servitude or involuntary servitude as a Class C felony and the trafficking of an adult for sexual servitude or involuntary servitude as a Class F felony. Human trafficking is defined as the recruiting, enticing, harboring, transporting, providing or obtaining a person with the intent to hold that person in involuntary servitude or sexual servitude.

Pennsylvania – HB 1112

January 9, 2007 Pennsylvania enacted HB 1112 establishing the trafficking of persons as a second degree felony, the trafficking of persons under the age of eighteen as a first degree felony, and the bodily injury of a trafficking victim as a first degree felony. Factors including the kidnapping, rape or involuntary deviate sexual intercourse of trafficking victims are considered in determining the severity of the charge. Mandatory victim restitution along with property and asset forfeiture are included in HB 1112.

South Carolina – HB 3060

May 2, 2006 South Carolina enacted HB 3060 establishing human trafficking for the purpose of forced labor or services as a felony. Human trafficking is defined as the recruiting, enticing, harboring, transporting, providing or obtaining another person knowing that person will be subjected to forced labor or services. The felony charge brings a sentence of imprisonment up to fifteen years.

Texas – HB 2096

On September 1, 2003, Texas enacted HB 2096. Under HB 2096, the trafficking or transporting of persons under the age of fourteen is a first degree felony. It is a first degree felony if the commission of the offense results in the death of the person who is trafficked. It is a second degree felony if the trafficked person is over the age of fourteen. The punishment range for a first degree felony is from five to ninety-nine years imprisonment in a penitentiary. The range of punishment for a second degree felony is from two to twenty years imprisonment in a penitentiary.

HB 177

September 1, 2003 Texas enacted HB 177 which requires International Marriage Brokers (IMB) or International Marriage Organizations (IMO) to provide their recruits with the criminal history record and the marital history record of their clients. IMB / IMO are required to provide their recruits with basic rights information in the recruits' native language, at the expense of the IMB/IMO. An IMB/IMO which violates the law is subject to a civil penalty up to $20,000 per offence.

Washington – HB 1175

On July 27, 2003, Washington enacted HB 1175. Under HB 1175, sex trafficking and labor trafficking is a class A felony in the first and second degree. Victims of human trafficking have the right to sue for damages, as well as the cost of bringing the suit. The court may impose a civil fine of up to $250,000. The standard sentencing guideline for a first degree felony carries a maximum prison term of fourteen years. A second degree class A felony carries a maximum sentence of nine years. HB 1175 allows factors such as the age of the victim; whether the victim was kidnapped; and whether the victim was killed to be considered in the determination of the severity of the charge.

HB 1826

July 27, 2003 Washington enacted HB 1826 requiring International Marriage Brokers (IMB) or International Marriage Organizations (IMO) to provide their recruits with the state background checks and personal histories of Washington residents, upon request. The IMB's/IMO's are required to notify all recruits that state background checks and personal histories are available to them upon request.

SB 6731

June 7, 2006 Washington enacted SB 6731 establishing sex tourism as a class C felony. Travel agents are prohibited from knowingly selling or offering to sell services that include or facilitate travel for the purpose of engaging in commercial sex acts. Sellers are prohibited from promoting and/or advertising travel services for the purpose of participating in sex tourism.

HB 2381

June 13, 2002 Washington enacted HB 2381 creating the Washington State Task Force Against the Trafficking of Persons for the purpose to measure and evaluate trafficking prevention activities; identify federal, state, and local trafficking programs; and to make recommendations for improvement in support services.

This task force was reauthorized yearly through various legislative acts: HB 1090 (May 14, 2003), HR 4707 (March 4, 2004), and SB 5127 (April 13, 2005).

States with Pending Statutes

Many states have entered the battle against human trafficking. They have drafted laws to combat trafficking and are waiting for the legislature to pass. These states include Delaware, Kentucky, Maine, Maryland, Massachusetts, Montana, New Hampshire, New Mexico, New York, Oklahoma, Oregon, Rhode Island, South Dakota, Utah, Virginia, Wisconsin, and West Virginia. Continued education and public awareness on human trafficking is an important component in the war on trafficking. Continued diligence is an essential aspect for both the public and the legislators, particularly in states which are currently without anti-trafficking laws. The Department of Justice has drafted a model state anti-trafficking criminal statute; I have included this in the appendix.

Florida Responds to Trafficking

The state of Florida has taken a proactive stance against human trafficking. Florida is currently the second busiest destination port for criminal activity involving the trafficking of persons. The top three industries are sex trafficking, forced labor, and domestic servitude. Florida is a popular destination state due to the many opportunities presented to criminals trafficking human beings for commercial exploitation. A tourist destination, an agricultural state, and temperate climate are contributing factors to the popularity of Florida. Victims of forced labor are moved from one citrus grove to another; from one produce farm to another; and from one construction site to another. Enslaved laborers are forced to work long hours in the fields or on construction sites, receive little or no remuneration, and are subjected to physical violence, psychological abuse, and threats on a daily basis. Many of them have been trafficked from other countries, speak little or no English and live in constant fear of law enforcement authorities, whom they believe are actively looking for them. They are told that they are criminals who will suffer from severe abuse by the police once they are caught and imprisoned. Subjugated workers, who do receive payment for their services, are charged over inflated rates for room and board. These accommodations are typically a single wide trailer, packed with twenty to thirty men living together, with poor sanitation conditions.

Victims of sexual exploitation can be found in many of the same work camps as the enslaved laborers. The traffickers provide the women (and sometimes children) to the laborers, who will spend the little money they receive in order to have their fifteen minutes with the sex slaves. Neither the women nor the laborers will ever be able to pay off their debts to the traffickers. Constantly surrounded by armed guards, the victims of human trafficking are unable to escape. Those who try to escape are typically killed or tortured; this is one method the traffickers use to set an example to the others. Once in a while, someone does get away; in a few instances this has led to raids and arrests. There are several organizations in Florida that provide services to the rescued victims. These services include interpreters, shelter, food, medical, immigration attorneys, financial support, and psychological services. Many of the organizations involved in the campaign to end human trafficking have partnered with Rescue and Restore, a human trafficking program from the Department of Health and Human Services.

Women In Need Network began working on behalf of human trafficking victims several years ago. They have launched a website dedicated to combating human trafficking. The site www.ModernDaySlavery.org provides information, resources, and an RSS news feed which supplies the latest breaking news on human trafficking and human trafficking cases. Women In Need Network has a training institute which offers up to date and informative seminars, conferences, and professional training. All of their programs include the latest information and regionally pertinent case studies. Women In Need Network also provides certification to those who participate in their training program. They offer a human trafficking program kit designed to assist organizations and agencies interested in helping human trafficking victims. The organization, which is an NGO, offers several opportunities for interested parties to participate in the war on human trafficking. You can sign up to receive their monthly newsletter on the Modern Day Slavery website. Women In Need Network has a college program designed to coordinate students interested in raising awareness on college campuses on the subject of human trafficking. These programs are being integrated at a number of campuses and the campaign continues to grow. Another innovative program they have created is called the FIGHT Task Force. FIGHT stands for "First Internet Global Human Trafficking." This task force meets monthly for the purpose of uniting government officials, NGO's, missionaries, and persons interested in combating the trafficking of persons. The task force is comprised of dedicated professionals and advocates who are committed to ending the practice of slavery world-wide. FIGHT Task Force currently has three projects underway, they are:

>1. Lobby – involvement in the political process, to work on improving international and national policy pertaining to the trafficking of persons.

>2. Research & Policy Reform - gathering and sharing of information on human trafficking offenses; issues; advocacy; and events will facilitate the lobbying efforts

and assist the efforts to improve policies on human trafficking.

3. Public Awareness and Education - education is an important step in fighting human trafficking. The FIGHT Task Force will participate in the implementation of programs promoting awareness while providing educational opportunities throughout the world.

In response to the need for action against the trafficking of persons, Florida has enacted several statutes to combat and prosecute human traffickers under state law.

HB 1977 was introduced by the House of Representatives in 2004, sponsored by Representatives Barreiro, Bucher, Fiorentino, Gannon, Joyner, Kallinger, Kottkamp, Rich, Roberson, Sobel. The original bill stated:

> *"An act relating to human trafficking; creating s. 787.05, F.S.; specifying elements of the offense of unlawfully obtaining labor or services; providing criminal penalties; creating s. 787.06, F.S.; providing definitions; specifying elements of the offense of human trafficking; providing criminal penalties; providing applicability; providing an effective date."*

Once the bill was passed in the House it was taken up in the Senate under **SB 1962**.

SB 1962 establishes the first degree felony of sex trafficking for parents, legal guardians, or other persons having custody of a minor who sell, transfer custody, or offer to sell or transfer custody of the minor for the purpose of sex trafficking or prostitution. The bill further establishes two second degree felonies: obtaining forced labor; and, sex trafficking and human trafficking for anyone who knowingly participates in trafficking for purposes of forced labor or prostitution. Any sex trafficking activity which results in death or is committed against a person who is under the age of 14 is considered a first degree felony. SB 1962 became enacted on October 1, 2004. The bill was sponsored by Senators Wasserman Schultz, Smith, Aronberg, Haridopolos.

HB 865 was introduced in to the House of Representatives in 2004, sponsored by Representatives Gannon, Brandenburg, Bullard, Fiorentino, A. Gibson, Harrell, Hasner, Holloway, Joyner, Kravitz, Stargel, Zapata. The original language of the bill stated:

> "*Sex Trafficking: Provides that it is a felony of the first degree for a parent, legal guardian, or other person having custody or control of a minor to offer to, or to actually, sell or otherwise transfer custody or control of such minor, with knowledge that such sale or transfer, will result in force, fraud, or coercion being used to cause that minor to engage in prostitution or otherwise participate in the trade of sex trafficking; provides for the offense of sex trafficking; provides that it is a felony of the second degree to knowingly recruit, entice, harbor, transport, provide, or obtain a person, knowing that force, fraud, or coercion will be used to cause that person to engage in prostitution; provides that it is a felony of the first degree if sex trafficking involves a person under the age of 14 or results in death; provides criminal penalties; expands the definition of racketeering activity to include the offenses created by the act.*"

These bills were the basis of the four new statutes created in 2004, to specifically deal with human trafficking. The new laws came into effect in October 2004 and are listed below.

Florida Statute 787.05 deals with labor and service issues in regard to human trafficking victims. 787.05 Unlawfully obtaining labor or services. Any person who knowingly obtains the labor or services of a person by:

(1) Causing or threatening to cause bodily injury to that person or another person;
(2) Restraining or threatening to restrain that person or another person without lawful authority and against her or his will; or
(3) Withholding that person's governmental records, identifying information, or other personal property.

Florida Statute 787.06 specifically addresses human trafficking.

787.06 – Human trafficking
(1) As used in this section, the term:
(a) "Forced labor or services" means labor or services obtained from a person by:
1. Using or threatening to use physical force against that person or another person; or
2. Restraining or confining or threatening to restrain or confine that person or another person against her or his will.
(b) "Human trafficking" means transporting, soliciting, recruiting, harboring, providing, or obtaining another person for transport.

(2) Any person who knowingly engages in human trafficking with the intent that the trafficked person engage in forced labor or services commits a felony of the second degree, punishable as provided in s. 775.082, s. 775.083, or s. 775.084.

Florida Statute 796.035 concerns child sex trafficking. 796.035 – Selling or buying of minors into sex trafficking or prostitution; penalties. Any parent, legal guardian, or person having custody or control of a minor who sells or otherwise transfers custody or control of such minor, or offers to sell or otherwise transfer custody of such minor, with knowledge that, as a consequence of the sale or transfer, force, fraud, or coercion will be used to cause the minor to engage in prostitution or otherwise participate in the trade of sex trafficking, commits a felony of the first degree, punishable as provided in s. 775.082, s. 775.083, or s. 775.084.

Florida Statute 796.045 defines penalties in regard to sex trafficking offenses.

796.045 – Sex trafficking; penalties.
Any person who knowingly recruits, entices, harbors, transports, provides, or obtains by any means a person, knowing that force, fraud, or coercion will be used to cause that person to engage in prostitution, commits the offense of sex trafficking, a felony of the second degree, punishable as provided in s. 775.082, s. 775.083, or s. 775.084, if the offense of sex trafficking is committed against a person who is under the age of fourteen or if such offense results in death.

In the 2006 session, Senator Gwen Margolis introduced bill SB 250. Senator Margolis has been extremely active in her fight against human trafficking. This bill is designed towards prosecution of traffickers as RICO (Racketeering Influenced and Corrupt Organization) crimes. Under SB 250, victims of trafficking will be able to seek restitution from their traffickers including punitive damages that may be awarded up to three times the actual damages. The bill passed and was signed into law by Governor Jeb Bush becoming effective October 1, 2006.

Senator Burt Saunders has taken a hard stance against human trafficking. He co-sponsored Senator Margolis' bill and added money into the appropriations budget for a state-wide education program to fight human trafficking. I have worked with Senator Saunders through my organization, Women In Need Network, to educate the public, service providers, law enforcement, legislators, and the faith community on the evils of human trafficking. We have discussed this problem at great length on many occasions. This is what Senator Saunders had to say about human trafficking in Florida:

"I first learned about this terrible problem from news accounts of human trafficking in southwest Florida. I was shocked to learn the extent of this problem in Florida. My assumption has always been that this was a problem in Mexico, South and Central America, but not in the United States.

As I was becoming aware of this issue, I began to work with law enforcement on gang issues. I did research on the ultra-violent gangs that are proliferating throughout the United States. The most notable of those gangs is Mara Salvatrucha 13 or MS 13. These gangs are beginning to take root in Florida and they are adept at smuggling illegal aliens into the United States. They are involved in drug dealing and prostitution, along with home invasion robberies and internet crimes. There is likely a connection between gang activity and human trafficking.

When I tell people that slavery exists in Florida, the reaction is usually one of disbelief. Fortunately, the media has done an excellent job of informing the public and many organizations such as yours(Women In Need Network) have been effective in dealing with the aftermath. The women and children who are victims need a tremendous amount of resources once they are freed from their bondage.

I am hopeful that the Florida Legislature will continue to provide the resources necessary to make sure law enforcement has the resources and legal tools to deal with the criminal aspects. But, also it is necessary that social services agencies have the resources necessary to deal with the victims once they are freed."

Senator Gwen Margolis is another strong advocate for the victims of human trafficking in the state of Florida. She has successfully sponsored and helped pass SB 250 making human trafficking a RICO Act violation in Florida. I have spent much time discussing this problem with Senator Margolis and her staff. I had a few questions for the Senator, which she graciously answered. I have included both the questions and the Senators answers below.

What sparked your interest in human trafficking?

"In a span of several months there were numerous articles that appeared in the local and national papers regarding Human Trafficking and Sex Trafficking. Representing South Florida in the Florida Senate poses difficult immigration challenges. With this in mind it is in the interest of all to ensure the humanity and safety of all those who reside legally and illegally in Florida."

Have you had any encounters with human trafficking victims?

"I have never had any personal experience and or contact with this growing issue however; I felt that something had to be done."

Please discuss what you hope to see accomplished by your involvement in the human trafficking movement within the next two years.

"Raising awareness and educating our citizens that this issue is very present here and thus a relevant issue. I hope that what we have done this Legislative Session of 2006 in terms of adapting the RICO Statutes to changing times is used properly and prudently by the proper entities."

Please discuss any changes you feel needs to be made by the legislature?

"We have made the central changes necessary for the time being. After these changes have been implemented and results have been documented we can move on and re-evaluate."

Senator Saunders and Senator Margolis are just two of the Florida legislators involved in the battle against human trafficking. State Representatives Dennis Baxley and Larry Cretul have taken a very strong stance against human trafficking. They have participated in public forums on this topic and were implemental in helping the latest legislature get the necessary exposure in order to pass in the House.

Representative Baxley and I have met on many occassions to discuss the issues related to human trafficking in our state and in our nation. Dennis Baxley is a man of faith and conviction; he has always stood firm in his fight for justice. *"Human trafficking is a very important issue to me. We need to stop trafficking and we need to help the victims of human trafficking. Education is key to putting an end to trafficking."* stated Representative Dennis Baxley. I have had the priviledge to work with Dennis on this issue, I have gotten to know him, and I can testify to his commitment to end this blight on our society.

Representative Cretul is another legislator that I have had the priviledge of working with in my ongoing battle against the trafficking of persons. We have met on many occassions to discuss human trafficking; we have discussed legislation and Representative Cretul made a commitment to help us eradicate trafficking in our state. *"When you think of human trafficking, you realize what a terrible situationthis is for people who are subjected to the true horrors of slavery. I will do whatever I can to help rid our society of the filth who preys on these unfortunate victims. Education is essential in the fight against human trafficking."* stated Representative Cretul.

Both Representative Dennis Baxley and Representative Larry Cretul have participated in events with Women In Need Network's fight against trafficking. They have attended several press conferences with me as part of our public awareness campaigns. Representatives Baxley and Cretul have sent their staff members to our seminars and training programs as part of their effort to educate their team on the horrors of trafficking. It is very gratifying to see these two men live up to their commitment in the ongoing battle against trafficking. The citizens of Florida are very fortunate to have so many people working towards a solution that I am unable to list them all separately.

Global Response to Human Trafficking

Human trafficking is a global issue of astronomical proportions. Intelligence and law enforcement agencies around the world have calculated that there are over twenty-seven million victims of human trafficking. It is estimated that 600,000 to 900,000 additional people are trafficked worldwide each year. Human trafficking has a tremendous impact on the world and is a multi-dimensional threat. Victims are deprived of their basic human rights, dignity, and freedom. Trafficking in persons fuels the growth of organized crime and presents a global health risk. The devastating impact human trafficking has on individual victims varies depending on the type and degree of abuse sustained by each individual case. The victims often suffer physical and emotional abuse, sexual assault, threats against themselves or their families, theft of identification documents, and in many cases, death. Unfortunately for the rest of the world, we are not immune from the affects of human trafficking; this crime undermines the safety, health and security of nations around the world. Human trafficking affects all of us, whether we realize it or not. Economic development and the advancement of human rights worldwide are affected by this scourge upon humanity.

Victims of human trafficking suffer from both psychological and physical harm. Psychologically speaking, these victims suffer from a wide range of mental disabilities brought on by the degradation, torture, abuse, and humiliation they endure at the hands of their captors. Victims suffer from post-traumatic stress syndrome, commonly referred to as PTSD. Substance abuse problems or addictions are not uncommon among victims of trafficking. Often times, traffickers use drugs to control their victims, while some victims seek out drugs and alcohol as a way to deal with the horrendous factors of their daily lives. Other psychological trauma resulting from daily mental abuse and torture, include depression, stress-related disorders, disorientation, confusion, phobias and panic attacks. Feelings of helplessness, shame, humiliation, shock, denial, and / or disbelief are also a part of the psychological damage trafficking victims suffer from. Cultural shock from finding themselves in a strange country is yet another way these victims suffer from psychological manifestations.

Physical harm includes exposure to disease, stunted growth, malnutrition, and physical deformities brought on by torture and hazardous work conditions. Health problems are typically not treated in the early stages, they tend to fester until they become critical and/or life-endangering situations. Health care is frequently administered by an unqualified "doctor". The doctor more than likely is someone who has lost their license to practice due to unscrupulous acts or may even be a veterinarian. Preventative health care is virtually non-existent. Victims of human trafficking are seen as a commodity and therefore are unworthy of proper health care. When a person can be bought for as little as twenty dollars, it is not cost effective for traffickers to spend money on health care and proper nutrition. Human traffickers have absolutely no regard for human life. Their priority is to make as much money as possible while keeping their overhead low. They dispose of the slaves who are no longer useful to them; replacing them with newer healthier stock, and have absolutely no regard for their welfare. Sexually transmitted diseases, HIV/AIDS, pelvic pain, and urinary difficulties are just a few of the physical effects suffered by those who are sexually abused. Forced prostitution and rape also results in unwanted pregnancy. In most cases, pregnancies are terminated and the abortions are generally performed in unsanitary conditions by unqualified persons. It is not uncommon for some of the girls and women to die as a result of these procedures. Infertility from chronic untreated sexually transmitted infections or botched abortions are yet another aspect of the physical harm incurred by victims of sex trafficking.

Health issues associated with victims of human trafficking include infections or mutilations caused by unsanitary and dangerous medical procedures performed by unqualified individuals. Chronic back problems, hearing loss, cardiovascular ailments, or respiratory problems result from endless days toiling in dangerous agricultural fields, poorly ventilated sweatshops, or dangerous construction conditions. Weak eyes and other eye problems occur from working in dimly lit sweatshops. Additional health related problems include malnourishment which is especially acute with child trafficking victims who often suffer from retarded growth. Infectious diseases like tuberculosis are on the rise again due to poor health care and unsanitary living conditions. Bruises, scars and other signs of physical abuse and torture are commonly found on victims of trafficking. Undetected or untreated diseases, such as diabetes or cancer are also a serious problem for these victims.

United Kingdom

The United Kingdom (UK) addressed the crime of sex trafficking back in 2002. Trafficking for the purposes of sexual exploitation was first criminalized by the Nationality, Immigration and Asylum Act 2002. This Act has been superseded by the Sexual Offenses Act 2003, which allows a maximum sentence of fourteen years when tried in the Crown Court. If the offense is tried in the Magistrates Court, then there is a maximum sentence of six months. Currently, other forms of trafficking is not an offense in the UK at this time, however, that situation is due to change in the very near future. Parliament is considering the Asylum and Immigration Bill, which will establish the offense of trafficking for exploitation around forced labor, slavery, and the trafficking of organs. Up until now, all trafficking cases in the United Kingdom have been prosecuted under different legislation. Traffickers were prosecuted under the following legislation: false imprisonment; controlling prostitution; procuring women for prostitution; living on the earnings of prostitution; rape; assault; incitement to rape; and immigration offenses.

Italy

In Italy, the major sector for trafficked women is forced prostitution. There are a variety of levels of forced prostitution taking place in Italy today, for instance there is the common practice of street prostitution followed by brothels, private escort services and clubs which specialize in exotic dancing and prostitution. Most victims of sex trafficking in Italy come from the Balkans, specifically from Albania and the countries of former Yugoslavia. These victims also come from the continent of Africa. They come from Ghana, Liberia, Sierra Leone, Morocco, Nigeria, and Tunisia. Victims from Eastern Europe mainly come from Russia, Moldova, Ukraine, Romania, Hungary, and Bulgaria. There are a small percentage of sex trafficking victims from Latin America and China.

On August 11, 2003 Italy enacted its first law specially designed to punish those who traffic persons. This was created in compliance of the United Nations protocol: law number 228/2003 "Measures against trafficking in persons". This law inserts the specific crime of human trafficking in the Penal Code; it covers all forms of human trafficking and it contains the elements of the crime. Another tool Italy has in its fight against human trafficking is the Legislative Decree number 286/98, article 18. The article 18 permit applies to foreign victims of human trafficking who are situations of severe exploitation, abuse, and situations where the safety of the victim may be jeopardized due to their attempt to escape from their traffickers. Anyone who is granted an article 18 permit must participate in social assistance and integration programs offered by local public authorities and NGO's. There are two avenues for obtaining this permit, one is through a judicial procedure and the other way is through a social procedure. The judicial procedure is available when the public prosecutor has determined that the victim is an important aspect of the case. Much like the T Visa issued in the United States, the victim is obligated to cooperate with law enforcement and the prosecutor. The permit issued through a social procedure requires the victim to make a statement containing provable information (evidence); however the permit is issued through the social procedure because the victim does not have relevant information about the criminal organization involved in their trafficking. A victim can also be issued a permit through social procedure in cases where their trafficker has already been prosecuted. A victim issued an article 18 permit is allowed to stay in Italy, even after the case is resolved. They are eligible to obtain a residence permit for education or for work. If a victim is gainfully employed at the end of the program, they can remain in Italy and eventually apply for permanent residence. This is especially beneficial in situations where it would be unsafe for the victim to return to their home or village.

Italy has implemented a social assistance and integration program to promote awareness on human trafficking. This campaign uses a variety of avenues to reach the public. They print and distribute stickers with the toll-free telephone number in the main languages spoken by their target audience, including several dialects of Nigerian. Public awareness campaigns are played over the radio and television, publicizing the toll-free number. National seminars aimed at the social organizations which assist victims of human trafficking are conducted throughout the country. On-going research into the areas of trafficking and smuggling continues in an effort to remain well informed and effectual. Italy continues to find new ways to combat human trafficking, but like most nations they are still learning and trying to find the most effectual way to help these unfortunate victims while trying to bring the criminal elements to justice.

The Netherlands

The Netherlands have signed or ratified several international treaties regarding migration and the safe return and inclusion for victims of human trafficking.

- ILO Convention Number 29 on Forced Labor, 1930 (ratified 1933)
- ILO Convention Number 97 on Migration for Employment, 1949 (ratified 1952)
- UN Convention Relating to the Status of Refugees, 1951 (ratified 1953)
- ILO Abolition of Force Labor Convention, 1957
- UN Convention on the Elimination of All Forms of Discrimination Against Women, (CEDAW ratified 1991)
- UN Convention Against Transnational Crime, 2000 (ratified 2004)
- UN Protocol to Prevent, Suppress and Punish Trafficking in Human Beings, Especially Women and Children, supplementing the UN Convention Against Transnational Crime, 2000 (ratified 2004)

What happens when a person is identified as a trafficking victim in the Netherlands? First they are identified, either by the police, social worker or a private citizen. Next they are registered as a victim of trafficking. This is followed by case management and when necessary, they are placed in a shelter. If the victim does not want to accept this help, then they must leave the country; their only other choice would be to stay in the country illegally. A victim who chooses to accept this help is normally faced with a waiting period of approximately three months. This is the point when the victim must decide whether or not to press charges against their trafficker. A victim who chooses to press charges is then granted a temporary residence permit. Case management begins at this juncture; the case manager will help the victim find accommodations, assist with daily activities, and look into work options. Once again the victim must choose whether or not they will press charges; a victim who chooses not to press charges must then leave the country. Victims who do not leave the country are now considered to be illegal aliens. Unfortunately a victim who does leave the country is faced with the possibility of being re-trafficked once they arrive back to their place of origin. Once the case is closed, the temporary permit expires and the victim must leave the country. In some situations, the case manager may be able to contact a social service organization in the victim's home country to provide further assistance. The victim also has the right to request a residence permit based on humanitarian grounds or in cases where the victim has formed a relationship with a Dutch citizen. It is important to remember that filing a request does not guarantee approval.

Australia

Australia is a destination country for a relatively small number of women who are trafficked in for the commercial sex trade. The women originate from countries in South Korea, Southeast Asia, and the Peoples Republic of China. Government authorities are fairly confident that the sex trafficking networks are mainly comprised of small criminal organizations as well as individual criminals. Australia has coordinated with neighboring countries in a campaign against human trafficking; this includes investigating the problem and funding awareness campaigns in the very countries that are a source of trafficking victims.

Australia has funded specialized anti-trafficking law enforcement units as part of its campaign against human trafficking. In 2003, Australia signed anti-trafficking agreements with Thailand, Cambodia, Burma, and Laos as part of their endeavor to improve international cooperation.

Cambodia

A significant number of women and children are trafficked from Cambodia for the purposes of labor and commercial sexual exploitation. Men are also victimized by the traffickers and propagators slavery. Cambodian men are mainly trafficked into Thailand for forced labor in the agriculture, construction, and fishing industries. Women and children are trafficked into Cambodia from Vietnam for the purpose of forced prostitution and child sex tourism.

Police raided a notorious brothel at the Phnom Penh hotel where they successfully captured eight traffickers and rescued eighty-three women and young girls who were held hostage and forced to work as prostitutes. The victims were placed into the care of an NGO who worked to help victims of human trafficking. The following day, the authorities released the eight suspects rounded up in the raid. Subsequently, a mob of family members and other unidentified persons removed ninety-one women and girls from the NGO shelter, including the eighty-three freed from the Phnom Penh hotel. The Cambodian government and local authorities failed to protect these victims.

In the 2005 Trafficking in Persons report, the United States Department of State placed Cambodia on Tier 3 for its lack of progress in the campaign against human trafficking. In an attempt to remove itself from the Tier 3 category, Cambodia increased its efforts to raise awareness of human trafficking by collaborating with NGOs as well as international organizations. The Ministry of Tourism created pamphlets and advertising campaigns to warn tourists of the penalties for child sex tourism. Cambodia established protocol for monitoring and reporting crimes of human trafficking, created anti-trafficking units, created public education programs, and provided support for NGOs offering long-term shelter to victims of trafficking as part of their determination to be removed from Tier 3. In June 2006, the United States released their 2006 Trafficking in Persons report; this time Cambodia was not on the Tier 3 list. Cambodia had been placed on the Tier 2 Watch List for beginning work on the battle against human trafficking.

The Trafficking in Persons Interim Assessment was released on January 19, 2007 by the Office to Monitor and Combat Trafficking in Persons. According to this report, Cambodia has made significant progress in combating human trafficking since the release of the 2006 Trafficking in Persons report. The National Police reports that as of September 2006, fifty-eight pimps and traffickers were turned over to the judiciary for prosecution. There have been thirty-four convictions, with sentences ranging from three years to twenty-four years of imprisonment. Thirty-two establishments selling trafficking victims have been shut down according to police statistics released in October 2006.

New Zealand

New Zealand is a destination country for sex trafficking with the majority of the women trafficked from Thailand and other countries in Asia. Prostitution has been decriminalized in New Zealand; however it is illegal for nonresidents to work in the commercial sex industry. The government supports NGO's working on behalf of trafficking victims, including organizations that provide services to women in the commercial sex industry. New Zealand provides physical protection, medical services, travel documents, and repatriation for human trafficking victims. The government has programs designed to help protect children from becoming victims of trafficking; additionally, New Zealand has been working with NGO's to address the issue of child trafficking. This campaign includes funding organizations that work on behalf of child victims. The result of this county's commitment to combating human trafficking is their placement on Tier 1 by the United States.

Indonesia

Indonesia is a source and transit country for men, women, and children who are trafficked across international borders for the purpose of sexual exploitation and forced labor. Indonesia also suffers from an internal trafficking problem. Victims are trafficked to Malaysia, Saudi Arabia, Kuwait, United Arab Emirates, Hong Kong, Taiwan, Uzbekistan, Japan, South Korea, Singapore, and Australia. Within Indonesia, there is widespread internal trafficking mainly from rural to urban areas. These victims are used for forced labor, involuntary domestic servitude, and commercial sexual exploitation. Traffickers recruit girls and women under false pretenses; popular tactics include offering young women and girls in rural area jobs as waitresses or hotel employees in distant regions. Once the new recruits arrive at their destination they are horrified to discover that they have incurred high debts to their traffickers and they are expected to pay off their debts by working as prostitutes.

The Indonesian government has been showing progress in its battle on human trafficking for the past several years. Immediately following the tsunami which devastated the Aceh province, the government rapidly responded to reduce the potential for trafficking. Many children had been orphaned during this catastrophic event and needed to be accounted for and protected from the unsavory opportunists. The Indonesian government has limited financial resources and is not able to fund many prevention programs, however they have worked with NGO's on anti-trafficking and education initiatives. Indonesia has cooperated with other nations as part of their effort to fight the trafficking of persons. These efforts include working with the Malaysian government in arresting and prosecuting a major trafficking network responsible for commercial sexual exploitation in Malaysia. Indonesia also worked with Australia in an investigation of a trafficking ring sending Indonesian women into sexual servitude in Australia. Indonesia is currently on the Tier 2 Watch list.

Following the release of the 2006 Trafficking in Persons report, Indonesia has made some progress in their battle against human trafficking. October 2006, the national police trafficking unit has ninety suspects in twenty-four cases under investigation for trafficking crimes involving 437 victims.

Mongolia

Mongolia is a source and transit country for men and women who trafficked for the purpose of forced labor and sexual exploitation. Mongolia also has an internal problem with child trafficking for the purpose of commercial sexual exploitation. The law in Mongolia specifically prohibits the trafficking of women and children. The primary targets of human trafficking schemes were middle-class girls and young women who have been lured abroad by offers to study or work in other nations. These girls and young women range in age from fourteen to twenty-eight years of age. Unfortunately preventive measures, such as increased law enforcement, has remained limited; thereby making it easy to traffic victims across the country's borders. Mongolia had failed to provide anti-trafficking campaigns to help educate its citizens about the dangers of trafficking. In the past year, Mongolia has begun working with the travel industry and UNICEF to establish a voluntary code of conduct to prevent the sexual exploitation of children. While the Mongolian government has recognized that trafficking is a problem, it has failed to place a priority on prevention programs. Some NGO experts believe that members of the police have been involved in the trafficking of young women, to the point of facilitating their movement across borders. Mongolia was placed on the Tier 2 list in the 2006 Trafficking in Persons report.

Columbia

Columbia introduced a new law in June 2002 against human trafficking. This law stipulates that *"anyone who promotes, induces, constrains, enables, finances, co-operates or participates in a person's transfer within the national territory or abroad by resorting to any form of violence, ruse, deception for exploitation purposes, to lead such person to work in prostitution, pornography, debt bondage, begging, forced labor, servile marriage, slavery for the purposes of obtaining financial profit or any other benefit either for himself [sic] or for another person shall incur 10 to 15 years' imprisonment and a fine..."* This wide-ranging law replaced the previous trafficking law which focused only on cross border involvement into prostitution. Offences are aggravated if committed against someone with temporary or permanent physical or psychological injury, causing temporary or permanent physical or psychological injury, trafficking of minors, trafficking of family members or if the offender is a public servant. Penalties thereby increase by one third to one half. Columbia is a Tier 1 nation.

Argentina

Argentina ratified the United Nation Protocol to Prevent, Suppress, and Punish Trafficking in Persons, Especially Women and Children in 2002 however it wasn't until December 2006 that the Senate unanimously approved an anti-trafficking bill to criminalize and punish human trafficking on a federal level. A similar bill was introduced in the Lower House in early October 2006. Government passage and enactment of anti-trafficking legislation is not expected to occur until sometime in 2007. Currently human trafficking is not an offense in Argentina however the penal code does allow traffickers to be prosecuted for related crimes. The lack of a specific anti-trafficking law suggests that traffickers may be identified and successfully prosecuted, yet only receive light sentences. Argentina was placed on the Tier 2 Watch list in 2006 Trafficking in Persons report.

India

India is a source, transit and destination country. Men, women, and children, numbering in the millions, are trafficked for the purpose of bonded labor, forced labor, and commercial exploitation. Indebted servitude and indebted bondage has been recorded to go on for generations. Traffickers place an ever increasing financial obligation on the victims, charge them for food and lodgings, and pass the burden on to their children and grandchildren. Victims can be found working in rice mills, brick kilns, and zari embroidery factories. India is a destination country for women and girls from Nepal and Bangladesh who are trafficked for commercial sexual exploitation. The Ministry of Home Affairs estimates that ninety percent of India's sex trafficking is internal. India was placed on the 2006 Trafficking in Persons Tier 2 Watch list for the third year in a row. This is due to the fact that India does not fully comply with the minimum standards for the elimination of human trafficking.

India's laws criminalizing labor trafficking, such as bonded labor or forced labor are weak and insufficient. Currently their law does not prescribe more than three years of imprisonment. India currently does not have a national law enforcement response to trafficking. Prevalent corruption throughout India's law enforcement community impedes their ability to successfully fight human trafficking. Corrupt officials have been implemental in protecting brothel owners, facilitating the movement of sex trafficking victims, and assisting in the return of those who have run away from the brothels. The same corruption holds true for traffickers involved in forced labor.

The government has continued to fail in the provision of services to trafficking victims. India's government relies heavily on NGO's to assist trafficking victims, which they have been supplying with funding for shelters and services. Reports of inefficiency and corruption continue to surface from those trying to help trafficking victims. In June 2006, two former state ministers in Jammu and Kashmir were arrested, along with several other senior government officials for the trafficking of minor girls for the purpose of commercial sexual exploitation. In September 2006 the central government responded to the need for anti-trafficking law enforcement and created a two person federal team. This team is responsible for collecting and analyzing data on state level law enforcement efforts, monitoring action taken by state governments, and organizing coordination meetings with law enforcement officials responsible for trafficking crimes.

Kenya

Kenya is a source, transit and destination country for trafficking in persons. Men, women, and children are trafficked for forced labor and sexual exploitation. Children are trafficked within the country for the purpose of domestic servitude and commercial sexual exploitation. Kenyan children are also trafficked for agricultural labor and street vending. Kenyans, including children are trafficked into other African nations, the Middle East, Western Europe, and North America for domestic servitude, manual labor, and the commercial sex industry. A lack of awareness by law enforcement officials continues to weaken efforts to combat the trafficking of persons. The United States government has provided financial and training assistance to Kenya's law enforcement, and yet the Human Trafficking Police Unit has not conducted any investigation into human trafficking cases. This is a contributing factor to Kenya being placed on the Tier 2 Watch list.

Kenya has a vast sex tourism problem, which their government has publicly acknowledged. Numerous local and national officials have spoken out against trafficking and sex tourism. This has led to the Ministries of Home Affairs and Tourism to develop a code of conduct geared towards protecting children from commercial sexual exploitation and child sex tourism. February 2006, thirty hoteliers and caterers signed the code. A study by UNICEF and the Kenyan government found that approximately 15,000 girls in four districts on the Kenyan Coast were engaged in commercial the sex industry. The study, 'The Report on the Extent and Effect of Sex Tourism and Sexual Exploitation of Children on the Kenyan Coast' reports that these girls range in ages between twelve to eighteen, and make up thirty percent of the total population of girls from these districts in this age range. The four regions are Mombasa, Kilifi, Malindi and Kwale. UNICEF also reports that two to three thousand girls and boys are involved in full-time sex-for cash. Some of them are paid to perform the most horrific and abnormal acts."

Nigeria

Nigeria is a source, transit, and destination country. Approximately twenty-five percent of Nigerians are victims of human trafficking. Men, women, and children are trafficked for the purpose of forced labor and sexual exploitation. Within Nigeria, women and children are trafficked from rural areas to urban locations. Trafficking victims are used for domestic servitude, street hawking, agricultural labor, and commercial sexual exploitation. Nigeria does not fully comply with the minimum standards for the elimination of human trafficking, but they are beginning to strengthen and institutionalize their response to the trafficking of persons. Nigeria has sixty dedicated anti-trafficking investigators who are actively investigating cases. Unfortunately the coordination efforts between these investigators and other law enforcement agencies are weak and not up to par. Nigeria has been conducting training sessions on human trafficking for investigators and prosecutors; Nigeria is also maintaining a computerized trafficking crime database. There have been reports of police corruption and recently one police officer was arrested for child trafficking. This case is currently under investigation. The Nigerian government is making efforts to educate the public about the dangers of trafficking by broadcasting anti-trafficking television spots and through public awareness events held in motor parks.

Nigeria was placed on the Tier 2 list in the June 2006 Trafficking in Persons report. The government has been strengthening their laws against human trafficking this past year and implemented penalties which include fourteen years in prison for pimps who use underage prostitutes. Last year, the police in Lagos intercepted a refrigerated fish truck carrying sixty-seven children whose ages ranged between six years old and fourteen years old. Two days prior to that incident, the police had arrested four people on the Nigerian-Benin border for smuggling fifty-two children into the country. Last August, a Nigerian father received a disturbing call from his daughter who had been kidnapped along with many other Nigerian girls. She told her father that they were on board a ship bound for an unknown destination; she did not know the name of the vessel or where they heading. She begged him to alert the authorities for help. The young woman told her father that there were so many girls on board and that they were all suffering. The phone call was interrupted by a lost signal. To date, the location of this young woman and the other girls onboard that vessel is unknown. According to human rights groups throughout Nigeria, this is not an uncommon practice.

Ghana

Ghana is a source, transit, and destination country for women and children who are trafficked for the purpose of sexual exploitation and forced labor. Children who are trafficked within the country are forced to work in the fishing villages, on cocoa plantations, as street vendors, porters, in domestic servitude, and for commercial sexual exploitation. International Organization for Migration (IOM) estimates that thousands of children have been trafficked to the fishing villages along the Volta Lake. IOM rescued thirty-nine children from fishing villages in 2006; however the government of Ghana has not taken any legal action against the traffickers. Ghana is currently operating two victim care facilities, which are stretched beyond capacity. The government needs to provide additional services and shelters for victims of human trafficking. The June 2006 Trafficking in Persons report listed Ghana as a Tier 2 nation.

History of International Laws Against Slavery and Forced Labor

1926 – League of Nations Slavery Convention
1930 – ILO Forced Labor Convention
1948 – Universal Declaration of Human Rights
1949 – Geneva Conventions

1956 – United Nations Supplementary Convention on the
Abolition of Slavery, the Slave Trade, and Institutions and
Practices Similar to Slavery

1957 – ILO Abolition of Forced Labor Convention

1966 - International Covenant on Civil and Political Rights

1966 - International Covenant on Economic, Social and
Cultural Rights

1999 – ILO Worst Forms of Child Labor Convention

2000 – United Nations Convention Against Transnational
Organized Crime

United Nations Response to Human Trafficking

UN Protocol against Trafficking in Persons

The United Nations Convention against Transnational Organized Crime has implemented the Protocol to Prevent, Suppress and Punish Trafficking in Persons, especially Women and Children. In accordance with this commitment, the United Nations Office on Drug and Crime (UNODC) urges all countries to work on producing greater information on trafficking in persons. The Convention against Transnational Organized Crime along with its two protocols was signed in Palermo, Italy in December 2000. The two protocols are referred to as the Palermo Protocol. These are the protocol against the trafficking in human beings, especially women and children, and the protocol on migrant smuggling. The Palermo Protocol calls for member nations to adopt measures that will:

- prevent the trafficking of persons, especially women and children.
- hunt down and punish international traffickers
- increase cooperation between nations to become more effective in combating human trafficking
- protect trafficking victims and facilitate their safe return to their country or to a third country
- inform the public about the dangers of human trafficking and the consequences to traffickers

The Trafficking Protocol recognizes the need for a combined approach that integrates effective prevention of trafficking with the prosecution of traffickers and the protection of human rights and assistance to victims of trafficking. In December 2000, the protocols were signed by 120 of the 148 nations present in Palermo, Italy.

The United Nations Office on Drugs and Crime (UNODC) recently released their April 2006 report entitled *Trafficking in Persons Global Patterns*. The 127 page report covers a variety of topics including background information; human trafficking global patterns; regional flows; data, methodology and coding of data; and references. Many people around the world have mixed emotions, as well as some very strong emotions when it comes to the United Nations. No matter how one feels about the United Nations, we should not allow that to stop us from reviewing the data and available resources put forth by the UN.

Excerpt from Trafficking in Persons Global Patterns:

When implementing the Trafficking Protocol, Member States should consider the following recommendations:

Prevention

1. To establish, together with NGOs and civil society, comprehensive regional and national policies and programs to prevent and combat human trafficking and to protect the victims.

2. To implement, together with NGOs and civil society, research, information and media campaigns and social and economic initiatives to prevent and combat trafficking in persons.

3. To undertake measures to alleviate the vulnerability of people (women and children in particular) to human trafficking, such as poverty, underdevelopment and lack of equal opportunity.

4. To undertake measures to discourage demand that fosters exploitation that leads to trafficking in persons.

5. To provide training to relevant officials in the prevention, prosecution of trafficking in persons and protection of the rights of the victims.

6. To exchange information on human trafficking routes, modus operandi, traffickers' profiles and victims identification.

7. To undertake measures to prevent means of transport operated by commercial carriers to be used in the commission of human trafficking offences.

8. To strengthen cooperation among border control agencies by, inter alia, establishing and maintaining direct channels of communication.

Prosecution

9. To undertake measures to ensure that travel and identity documents cannot easily be misused, falsified, unlawfully altered, replicated or issued; and to ensure the integrity and security of travel and identity documents and to prevent their unlawful creation, issuance and use.

10. To enact domestic laws making human trafficking a criminal offence. Such laws should also establish as criminal offences attempting to commit, participating as an accomplice, and organizing or directing other persons to commit human trafficking.

11. To ensure such legislation applies to victims of all ages and both sexes; and clearly distinguish between trafficking in persons and other forms of irregular migration.

12. To ensure that the system of penalties is adequate, given the severity of the crime.

13. To protect the privacy and identity of victims in appropriate cases.

14. To establish measures to protect victims from re-victimization.

15. To implement measures providing to victims information on proceedings, assistance to enable their views and concerns to be presented and considered at appropriate stages of criminal proceedings.

16. *To implement measures that offer victims the possibility of obtaining compensation.*

Protection

17. *To implement measures to provide for the physical, psychological and social recovery of victims. This should include housing and counseling in a language the victims can understand medical, psychological and material assistance as well as employment, educational and training opportunities. The special needs of victims, in particular children, are to be taken into account.*

18. *To provide for the physical safety of victims following rescue.*

19. *To adopt measures that permit victims to remain in the territory, temporarily or permanently, in appropriate cases, giving consideration to humanitarian and compassionate factors.*

20. *To facilitate preferably voluntary return of the victim without undue or unreasonable delay, with due regard for the safety of the victim.*

To fully implement the Trafficking Protocol and to enable effective oversight of that implementation, Member States are encouraged to also consider the following recommendations:

Information

21. *To devote resources to create the infrastructure necessary to collect information about all aspects of human trafficking.*

22. To develop methods at the national level to organize data collection through a comprehensive system of data classification.

23. To assign responsibility for information collection to a centralized agency or some equivalent coordinated statistics system.

24. To gather more information in particular on: victims of trafficking; offenders; organized crime groups; and internal trafficking.

25. To collect information regarding victim identification, referral, assistance and repatriation.

26. To collect qualitative as well as quantitative information.

27. To engage in greater multilateral collaboration to ensure more intensive gathering and analysis of primary data.

28. To report such information to the Conference of the State Parties to the United Nations Convention Against Transnational Crime.

The Global Program against Trafficking in Human Beings, otherwise referred to as GPAT was designed by the United Nations Office on Drugs and Crime (UNODC) in collaboration with the United Nations Interregional Crime and Justice Research Institute (UNICRI). GPAT assists member states in their fight against human trafficking, highlights the involvement of organized criminal organizations, and promotes the development of effective ways to crack down on the perpetrators. The goal of GPAT is to promote awareness of trafficking in human beings and to strengthen institutional capacity; to train law enforcement officers, prosecutors and judges; to advise on drafting and revising relevant legislation; to provide advice and assistance on establishing and strengthening anti-trafficking elements; and to strengthen victim and witness support. GPAT also aims to provide assistance to agencies, institutions and governments as part of their effort to create effective measures against human trafficking.

Other United Nations programs and organizations involved in the battle against human trafficking are United Nations High Commissioner for Refugees (UNHCR), International Child Development Centre (UNICEF), United Nations Development Fund for Women (UNIFEM), International Labor Organization (ILO), World Health Organization (WHO), and the United Nations Human Settlements Program (UNHABITAT).

Interpol

Interpol has 186 member organizations and is the world's largest policing organization which dates back to 1923. Interpol is a contraction of International Police; the organization officially changed its name in 1953 to International Criminal Police Organization-Interpol (ICPO-Interpol). Interpol facilitates cross-border police co-operation, and supports and assists all organizations, authorities and services whose mission is to prevent or combat international crime. Their aim is to facilitate international police co-operation even where diplomatic relations do not exist between particular countries. Police action is taken within the limits of existing laws in different countries and in the spirit of the Universal Declaration of Human Rights. Each member country maintains a National Central Bureau (NCB) staffed by national law enforcement officers. The NCB is the designated contact point for the General Secretariat, regional offices and other member countries requiring assistance with overseas investigations and the location and apprehension of fugitives.

Interpol is involved in the ongoing effort to eliminate human trafficking. As an international law enforcement agency, Interpol has the ability to cross international borders in pursuit of traffickers. Child sexual exploitation on the Internet ranges from posed photos to video recordings of brutal sex crimes. One of their most important tools for helping police fight this sort of crime is the Interpol Child Abuse Image Database (ICAID). This database was created back in 2001 and contains hundreds of thousands of images of child sexual abuse which has been submitted by member countries. The ICAID facilitates the sharing of images and information which assists law enforcement agencies with the identification of new victims. Interpol is committed to eradicating the sexual abuse of children and has passed several resolutions making crimes against children one of international policing top priorities. Their Specialist Group on Crimes against Children focuses on four different arenas: commercial exploitation and trafficking in children; sex offenders; serious violent crimes against children, and child pornography.

Interpol derives its actions from conventions such as the United Nations Convention against Transnational Organized Crime, and the additional Protocol to Prevent, Suppress and Punish Trafficking in Persons, as well as the Council of Europe Convention on Action against Trafficking in Human Beings.

The summary of the European Convention states:

"The Convention is a comprehensive treaty mainly focused on the protection of victims of trafficking and the safeguard of their rights. It also aims at preventing trafficking as well as prosecuting traffickers.

The Convention applies to all forms of trafficking; whether national or transnational, whether or not related to organized crime. It applies whoever the victim: women, men or children and whatever the form of exploitation: sexual exploitation, forced labor or services, etc.

The Convention provides for the setting up of an independent monitoring mechanism guaranteeing parties' compliance with its provisions."

Human Trafficking Cases

The following human trafficking cases are from the years 2001 – 2005. Background information is included with each case along with the final outcome as of this publication.

United States v. Gasanov (Texas)

On March 15, 2002, a Russian couple named Sardar and Nadira Gasanov were convicted of recruiting women from Uzbekistan and bringing them into the United States under false pretenses and forcing them to work in strip clubs and bars in El Paso, Texas. Gasanov, a researcher at the University of Texas at El Paso, falsely represented each woman as coming to the United States to conduct academic research. Gasanov completed the necessary paperwork for their J-1 Visas. The women had been promised modeling careers after each one had raised $300,000 from topless dancing to cover their smuggling fees. The women lived with the Gasanovs and handed over all of their earnings from the topless bars and strip clubs. The Gasanovs charged them living fees and gave the women meager allowances for personal items.

The defendants confiscated the victims' passports, required them to work seven days each week, and threatened their families in Uzbekistan to coerce compliance with the Gasanovs' demands. The couple was indicted on six counts in August 2001.

Count 1: Conspiracy to commit document fraud
Count 2: Conspiracy to harbor illegal aliens
Count 3: Bringing illegal aliens to the U.S. for financial gain
Count 4: Bringing illegal aliens to the U.S. for financial gain
Count 5: Bringing illegal aliens to the U.S. for financial gain
Count 6: Money laundering

The defendants were found guilty of all charges except for count six. On May 17, 2002, the defendants were sentenced to five years of incarceration and ordered to pay approximately $516,000 in restitution. They forfeited their residence and two vehicles.

United States v. Lee (Hawaii)

Kil Soo Lee, a Korean businessman was convicted in the largest human trafficking prosecution case brought by the United States Department of Justice. The long and challenging investigation resulted in a twenty-two count indictment against five defendants. They were charged with holding workers against their will in a garment factory in America Samoa; the charge being involuntary servitude. The indictment charged that 250 Vietnamese and Chinese nationals were brought into the factory by the defendants. These victims were mostly young women. They were forced to work as sewing machine operators in the Daewoosa garment factory. Some of these victims were held for as long as two years. They were forced to work under inhumane conditions, such as extreme food depravation, physical violence, and physical restraint. The defendants forced the victims to live in barracks on a guarded compound. They lived under constant threat and violence. One woman had her eye gouged out when one of the defendants struck her with a jagged pipe as punishment for failing to obey his orders.

Two of the Samoan defendants who conspired with Kil Soo Lee pled guilty to charges of conspiracy. On February 21, 2002, the lead defendant Kil Soo Lee was convicted of the following:

- One count of conspiracy to violate the civil rights of the worker victims
- eleven counts of involuntary servitude
- one count of extortion
- one count of money laundering.

On June 22, 2005, Lee was sentenced to forty years of incarceration.

The Stormy Nights Cases: United States v. Parsons, United States v. Thomas, United States v. Washington, United States v. Williams and Southwell, United States v. White, Sutherland, United States v. Scott, United States v. Phillips (Oklahoma)

"Stormy Nights" was a large scale nation-wide investigation focused on interstate child prostitution rings operating in truck stops and through call services. The investigation was led out of the FBI Oklahoma City Division. Nine pimps in eight cases were indicted on charges based on the Stormy Nights investigation. The children in this case were all United States citizens and originated from Oklahoma City. The defendants in this case travelled with the juvenile victims to truck stops and known prostitution locations in Denver, Houston, Dallas, Miami, and Pennsylvania for the purpose of child prostitution. Sixteen children were recovered as a result of this investigation.

- Michael Wayne Thomas pled guilty and was sentenced to seventeen and a half years of incarceration for transporting a juvenile to Pennsylvania for purposes of prostitution on two occasions and to committing an act of violence in furtherance of a prostitution enterprise.
- Jermaine Dion Washington pled guilty and was sentenced to nearly nine years of incarceration for transporting a juvenile to Denver for the purpose of prostitution.
- DeCory Williams and Tiffone Southwell pled guilty to the charge of transporting a juvenile to Miami for the purpose of prostitution. Williams was sentenced to ten years of incarceration. Southwell was sentenced to more than three years of incarceration.
- Jacinto White pled guilty to interstate travel to Pennsylvania in furtherance of a prostitution enterprise. White received *six months* of incarceration.
- Greg Phillips pled guilty to coercing a juvenile (person under eighteen years of age) to engage in a sexual act. Phillips was sentenced to more than ten years of incarceration.
- Kelvin Scott pled guilty to transporting for immoral purpose and was sentenced to ten years of incarceration.
- Greg Parson pled guilty to transporting a person under the age of eighteen with intent to engage in criminal sexual activity. Parson was sentenced to nearly five years of incarceration.

- Troy Sutherland was convicted at trial on charges of child sex trafficking. The girls were sixteen, fifteen, and thirteen years old. He received two concurrent terms of 240 months imprisonment and two three year supervised released terms. Sutherland appealed his sentences; however the Appellate Court upheld his sentencing.

Unites States v. Satia (Maryland)

On December 20, 2001, the defendants in this case were convicted of involuntary servitude, conspiracy, and harboring the victim for their own monetary gain. The victim in this case was a fourteen year old Cameroonian female national. She was recruited under the false promise of receiving an American education; however once the victim arrived in the U.S., she was isolated in the defendants' home and forced to work for them for several years as their servant. The young girl suffered from physical abuse, sexual assaults, and lived with constant threat of further violence and punishment. On March 27, 2002 the defendants received nine years of incarceration and ordered to pay $105,300 to the victim.

United States v. Virchenko (Alaska)

The first case to be prosecuted under TVPA, involves three defendants: Victor Nikolayevich Virchenko, Pavel Vasilievich Agafonov, and Tony Kennard. They each pled guilty to the charges of transporting minors for illegal sexual activity and six counts of immigration fraud. The defendants fraudulently obtained visas for two teenage Russian girls along with four other Russian women. They told the women and girls that they would be coming to America to perform Russian folk dances in a cultural festival.

When they brought the victims to Alaska, the women and girls the defendants confiscated their passports, visas, and return plane tickets. They were forced to dance in two strip clubs in Anchorage and the victims were always accompanied by one or more of the defendants. They were not allowed to talk to any of the customers Virchenko was sentenced to thirty months in prison, to be followed by deportation.

United States v. Blackwell (Maryland)

Barbara Coleman-Blackwell and her husband Kenneth Blackwell were convicted of conspiring to smuggle a woman from Ghana to the United States, and forcing her to work as a domestic servant and nanny for their child. The victim, who was kept isolated and worked for little or no pay. In order to keep her in this situation, the defendants hid her passport and threatened her with deportation and imprisonment. The victim provided around the clock child care; cooked the family's meals; cleaned the home; and did the family's laundry. Coleman-Blackwell also forced the victim to perform many other unpleasant duties, such as cleaning up vomit, washing between the toes of her of her "employer".

Barbara Coleman-Blackwell was sentenced to more than four years of incarceration while her husband Kenneth Blackwell to supervised release for three years. Grace Coleman, Coleman-Blackwell's mother, who is a powerful member of the Ghanaian Parliament, faces similar charges and extradition to the United

States for aiding the Blackwells. So far, Grace Coleman has not been extradited to the United States.

United States v. Garcia (New York)

In 2002, Maria Garcia, a labor contractor from the Buffalo area, and five other defendants were charged in an 18-count indictment for recruiting undocumented Mexican aliens from the Arizona border, transporting them to Albion, New York. The victims were forced to work in agricultural fields for little or no money and held in conditions of involuntary servitude. The victims were housed in overcrowded and filthy conditions. The charges included conspiracy, trafficking workers into forced labor, transporting and harboring aliens, and violating provisions of the Migrant and Seasonal Worker Protection Act. Garcia and the other defendants forced the migrant workers to perform agricultural work in western New York and threatened them with physical harm, deportation, and arrest if they did not cooperate.

Prior to the trial, the defendants in this case challenged the constitutionality of the Trafficking Victims Protection Act's criminalization of labor trafficking. They argued that TVPA was void for vagueness because the terms within it were not clearly defined. They were referring to: *obtains; threats of serious harm to or physical restraint;* and *means of the abuse or threatened abuse of law or the legal process.* Their defense motion was denied as the magistrate judge declared that terms were common words and likely to be understood by anyone.

Four of the defendants were convicted of force labor and related charges. Two of the remaining defendants are fugitives.

United States v. Curtis (District of Columbia)

A seven-count indictment was returned charging Carlos Curtis
with sex trafficking, transporting a minor in interstate commerce
for prostitution, and production of child pornography. Curtis and
other associates recruited a twelve year old girl in Times Square in
New York City, brought her to a hotel room in Brooklyn, and
photographed the girl engaged in sexually explicit conduct with
an adult. He and his associates enticed the twelve year old
runaway child to become a prostitute by offering her food,
clothing, and shelter. In November 2002, Curtis and his
accomplices transported the twelve year old and a twenty-six year
old woman from Queens, New York, and a seventeen year old
runaway child from Maryland to the District of Columbia so that
the children and woman could engage in prostitution.

Following a two-week jury trial, Curtis was convicted on
July 2, 2004. A federal jury found Curtis guilty of sex trafficking of
children, specifically prostituting a twelve year old and a
seventeen year old girl; transportation of minors for prostitution;
transportation of a person for prostitution; and possession of child
pornography. On March 17, 2006, Carlos Curtis was sentenced to
life in prison for the sex trafficking of minors.

United States v. Jimenez-Calderon (New Jersey)

On September 26, 2002 eight defendants were charged with
conspiring to lure and transport young Mexican girls into the
United States under false pretenses then forcing them into
prostitution. Librada and Antonia Jimenez-Calderon lured young

Mexican girls with promises of legitimate jobs. The girls arrived in Plainfield, New Jersey were confined to a brothel and forced to perform acts of prostitution six to eight times per day. They were not allowed to leave the house or speak to each other. The young victims were subjected to threats of harm, force, and psychological coercion.

- On August 7, 2003, Librada and Antonia Jimenez-Calderon were sentenced to 210 months in prison for conspiracy and sex trafficking. In May 2004, they also were ordered to pay a total of $135,240 to four of their victims.
- Sergio Farfan, Angel Ruiz, Pedro Garcia Burgos, and Maritzana Diaz Lopez were charged with various crimes, including obstruction of justice and sex trafficking. Pedro Garcia Burgos was sentenced to ninety-six months for his involvement in the Jimenez-Calderon sex trafficking ring in Plainfield. Angel Ruiz was sentenced to forty-four months in prison and Sergio Farfan was sentenced to sixteen months in prison for their involvement.
- Delfino and Luis Jimenez-Calderon are still at large and considered fugitives.

United States v. Trakhtenberg (New Jersey and New York)

Charges of conspiring to commit forced labor, document fraud, and inducing aliens to unlawfully enter the United States were brought against Sergey Malchikov, Lev Trakhtenberg, and his wife, Viktoriya I'lina, in the District of New Jersey. The defendants induced over twenty-five women to come from Russia to the United States, under the pretenses of performing cultural folk dance shows. Upon arrival in the United States the defendants confiscated the women's passports and their return airline tickets. The victims were forced to dance nude in strip clubs ten hours per day, six days a week. The defendants threatened the women with serious harm and physical restraint if they did not perform.

- Sergey Malchikov pled guilty to charges of conspiracy to commit forced labor, visa fraud, immigration violations, and extortion. He was sentenced to nearly four years of incarceration.
- Lev Trakhtenberg pled guilty in the District Court of New Jersey to conspiring to commit forced labor, immigration offenses, and visa fraud. He was sentenced to five years of incarceration. He also pled guilty in the Southern District of New York to conspiring to commit extortion. Trakhtenberg threatened a victim's family in Russia with physical harm unless they paid him money he claimed the victim owed for escaping prostitution. He was sentenced to more than three years of incarceration for that offense. Trakhtenberg was ordered to pay approximately $66,300 in restitution to four of his victims.
- I'lina Trakhtenberg pled guilty to conspiring to commit extortion and visa fraud. She was sentenced to sixty months in prison which is the maximum sentenced allowed.

United States v. Guzman (Georgia)

On January 30, 2003, Samuel Mendez Romero and three other defendants were charged in a twenty count indictment. The charges include conspiring to bring Mexican women to the United

States to engage in prostitution, forced prostitution, immigration offenses, and Mann Act violations. According to the indictment, the defendants smuggled at least three victims into the United States, housed them in apartments in the Atlanta area, and forced them to participate in prostitution. Case documentation includes a claim that one of the defendants threatened to kill a victim and her family if she refused to engage in prostitution. The victim was frequently criticized for not bringing in enough money and on at least one occassion, physically assaulted her. The victims were forced to service twenty-five men or more per night as part of their enslavement.

- Samuel Mendez Romero pled guilty to conspiracy, and was subsequently sentenced to nearly three years of incarceration.
- The remaining three defendants are fugitives.

United States v. Maka (Hawaii)

Luelani Maka smuggled seven men from Tonga and forced them to work for his landscaping and construction business for less than a hundred dollars a week. Often they received no pay at all. The victims were housed in hovels on the defendant's pig farm and were forced to work more than twelve hours a day, six days a week. The defendant enslaved his victims through the use of threats and force. Case documentation consists of claims that the victims were beat with a fire extinguisher, farm tools, and the blunt end of a machete. Following a month-long trial, the defendant was convicted of slavery and harboring offenses.

- Fifty-four-year-old Luelani Maka was sentenced to twenty-six years in prison for his crimes.

United States v. Reyes-Rojas (Georgia)

On January 27, 2004, Juan Rojas, Jose Reyes-Rojas, and Raul Reyes-Rojas were charged with:

1. conspiracy
2. sex trafficking
3. importing and harboring aliens for the purpose of prostitution, alien smuggling, and interstate transportation of illegal aliens for smuggling young illegal aliens from Mexico into the United States and forcing them into prostitution.

The defendants are accused of luring their victims with the promise of employment, long-term romance, and marriage. Upon arrival in Atlanta the women were subjected to physical violence, threats, and psychological coercion by the defendants and forced to have sex with numerous men on anightly basis.

- Juan Rojas pled guilty to two sex trafficking counts and was sentenced to nearly six years of incarceration.
- Jose Reyes Rojas pled guilty to one sex trafficking charge and was sentenced to nearly five years in prison.
- The third defendant, Raul Reyes Rojas is a fugitive.

United States v. Russell (California)

On December 3, 2003, Bernard Lawrence Russell was indicted on the following charges:

1. traveling to foreign countries with the intent to engage in sex with a juvenile
2. production of child pornography
3. possession with intent to import child pornography.

Case documentation shows that Russell traveled to the Philippines on multiple instances during a two-year period. His purpose for these trips was to engage in sexual acts with children and to produce child pornography for importation into the United States. To date, three Filipino children have been identified as victims of Russell.

- On April 22, 2005, Russell pled guilty to the charges of traveling in foreign commerce with intent to engage in sex with a juvenile. He was sentenced to more than three years of incarceration.

United States v. Clark (Washington)

In June 2003, Michael Clark was arrested in Cambodia for chils sexual abuse. He was charged with sexually abusing two young Cambodian boys, ages ten and thirteen. On September 24, 2003 Michael Clark was indicted in the United States, for attempting to engage and for engaging in illicit sexual conduct after travelling to foreign country. Clark pled guilty in March 2004, and was sentenced to more than eight years of imprisonment.

United States v. Gates (District of Columbia)

Gary Gates and Tamisha Heyward were charged with multiple counts of sex trafficking and violating the Mann Act. Gates and Heyward operated a sex trafficking and Internet prostitution business from their home. Case documentation shows they were using girls as young as fourteen, to perform sexual acts. Documentation also shows that all of the victims were United States citizens. Gates beat the victims who disobeyed him and sexually assaulted many of them. Gates also provided drugs to some of the girls furthering their addictions and his control on all aspects of their lives.

- Heyward pled guilty to child sex trafficking and unlawful possession of a firearm. Heyward was sentenced to nine years in prison.
- Gates pled guilty to child sex trafficking and first degree child sexual abuse. Gates was sentenced to nearly fifteen years of incarceration.

United States v. Mubang (Maryland)

For two years, Theresa Mubang forced an eleven year old Cameroonian girl to work against her will as a domestic servant. She was brought into the United States illegally and under false pretenses. The eleven year old victim was forced to care for Mubang's two children and to perform all the household chores without pay at Mubang's home in Chevy Chase, Maryland. The young girl was beaten with a broken metal broom stick and a cable cord; she was forbidden to speak of her conditions to anyone; she was prohibited from leaving the house; she was not allowed to open the door to anyone; and Mubang blocked her mail.

- In November 2004, Mubang was convicted on charges of involuntary servitude and harboring an alien. Theresa Mubang fled the country soon after her conviction.
- On February 28, 2005, Mubang was sentenced in absentia to seventeen and a half years of incarceration. Theresa Mubang was also ordered to pay $100,000 to the victim.
- In May 2005, Theresa Mubang was returned to the United States and she is currently serving her sentence.

United States v. Kang (New York)

The Kangs, lured Korean women to New York City by promising them good jobs as hostesses in their nightclub. The victims were subjected to rapes and physical abuse; held for repayment of a $10,000 debt; and the Kangs attempted to force the women into prostitution.

- The Kangs pled guilty to forced labor in November 2005.
- In October 2005, five other defendants pled guilty to alien smuggling, conspiracy to obstruct justice, and obstruction of justice. Two of the five defendants were employees of the Department of Homeland Security.

United States v. Sims (Georgia)

Maurice Sims, a known pimp, was indicted for transporting an American sixteen year-old girl from Arkansas to Georgia for the purpose of prostitution. Sims beat and raped the girl along the way.

- In September 2004, Sims was convicted of:

- o kidnapping
- o trafficking
- o transporting a minor across state lines for criminal sexual purposes
- o persuading an individual to travel interstate for a criminal sexual purpose
- In December 2004, Maurice Sims was sentenced to life in prison.

United States v. Okhotina (California)

January 2003, Alana Okhotina smuggled her eighteen year old Russian niece into the United States. The young woman was forced to work as a prostitute in order to repay the smuggling debt imposed by her aunt. Okhotina threatened to kill the victim and her family if she did not comply with her aunt's demands and work as a prostitute. Okhotina told her niece that she would be arrested as an illegal alien if she went to the police.

- In December 2005, Alana Okhotina entered a guilty plea on the charge of trafficking into slavery. Okhotina's sentencing is still pending.

United States v. Kaufman (Kansas)

Arlen and Linda Kaufman were charged with a thirty-five count indictment for conspiracy, forced labor, and involuntary servitude, health care fraud, mail fraud, making a false representation and writing, obstructing a federal audit, and forfeiture. Case documentation shows that the defendants operated a residential group home for mentally ill adults called

"The Kaufman House." The residents were victimized for more than eighteen years. The Kaufman's engaged in a conspiracy to hold the residents in involuntary servitude and forced labor. According to the indictment, the victims were forced to engage in nudity and sexually explicit acts, and to perform acts of labor and services. These crimes were committed for the Kaufman's entertainment and benefit. All of the victims were United States citizens.

- On November 7, 2005, Arlen and Linda Kaufman were convicted by a jury on the charges of conspiracy, involuntary servitude, forced labor, and multiple health care fraud counts.
- Arlen Kaufman was sentenced to thirty years in prison.
- Linda Kaufman was sentenced to seven years in prison.

United States v. Lozoya (Texas)

Octavio and Joe Lozoya were indicted on immigration charges for holding a Mexican woman as a servant in their trailer home in rural West Texas. They held her with the use of threats and violence against her toddlers. They abused and neglected the child by separating her from her mother's care; kept the child in unsanitary living conditions; bound her legs with duct tape and made her stand for prolonged periods of time; physically abused her; stuffed her underwear in her mouth as punishment for urinating on herself; denied her food as punishment; and forced her mouth shut with duct-tape to prevent her from crying; and forced her to sleep on the floor. In December 1999, the twenty-one month-old girl collapsed and stopped breathing. Joe Lozoya burned the child's body to prevent discovery of their crimes. The defendants refused the mother's pleas to take her daughter to the hospital for medical treatment resulting in the baby's death.

- Octavio Lozoya pled guilty to one count of conspiracy to harbor illegal aliens with death resulting, and one count of harboring an illegal alien with death resulting. He received a sentence of fifteen years of incarceration on these charges. He received five years of incarceration for harboring the mother. The sentences are being served consecutively.
- Joe Lozoya pled guilty to one count of conspiracy to harbor illegal aliens with death resulting. He was sentenced to five years of incarceration.

United States v. Soto-Huarto (Texas)

Eight defendants in Edinburg, Texas were charged with maintaining trailers as safe houses for illegal aliens. Four women victimized in this case, were trafficked from Guatemala, Honduras, and El Salvador; they had agreed to pay the defendants $5000 to be smuggled into the United States. Once they arrived in the United States, the victims were confined to the trailers where they were forced to cook, clean, and do household chores without pay. They were raped repeatedly by the defendants, who were later convicted on federal civil rights violations, extortion, hostage-taking, immigration offenses, involuntary servitude, and human trafficking. In February 2003, two women were found by local law enforcment officers; they had been raped and left for dead. This was punishment for trying to escape from the defendants. Further investigation led federal law enforcement agents to identify and rescue two additional female victims. A joint ICE and FBI initiative brought an end to the trafficking operation and resulted in the arrests of the defendants.

- four defendants pled guilty to transporting aliens
- two defendants pled guilty to involuntary servitude charges
- one defendant pled guilty to conspiracy to commit involuntary servitude
- three of the five defendants were ordered to pay restitution to their victims
- the combined sentences equaled fifty-one years in prison
- ringleader Juan Carlos Soto was sentenced to twenty-three years confinement

United States v. Carreto, et al (New York)

In April 2005, Daniel Perez Alonso, Gerardo Flores Carreto, and Josue Flores Carreto, pleaded guilty to twenty-seven counts of an indictment charging them with various crimes related to their involvement with the Carreto family sex trafficking ring. The three defendants pled guilty to multiple counts of:

1. conspiring to engage in sex trafficking
2. conspiring to import aliens for immoral purposes
3. sex trafficking
4. attempted sex trafficking
5. forced labor
6. violating the Mann Act
7. importing an alien for immoral purposes
8. alien smuggling

They admitted that between 1991 and 2004 they recruited young women from Mexico, smuggled them into the United States, and forced them into prostitution in brothels in the New York City area. The defendants also repeatedly physically and emotionally abused the women. Most of the defendants in this case are related to each other and come from a small town in south-central Mexico. They recruited young, impoverished women in Mexico by forming romantic relationships with them, while planning to smuggle them into the United States for the purpose of forcing them into prostitution.

Three other co-defendants, Eloy Carreto Reyes, Eliu Carreto Fernandez, and Edith Mosquera de Flores, pled guilty to charges related to the trafficking ring during earlier proceedings. Additionally, Consuelo Carreto Valencia and Maria de los Angeles Velasquez Reyes, are being held in prison in Mexico on Mexican federal charges, and they also face extradition to the United States to stand trial on U.S. federal charges.

- Josue Flores Carreto was sentenced to fifty years in prison.
- Gerardo Flores Carreto was sentenced to fifty years incarceration.
- Daniel Perez Alonso was sentenced to twenty-five years imprisonment.
- A co-defendant was sentenced to twenty-seven months imprisonment for benefitting financially from the scheme.

United States v. Salazar (Texas)

Case documentation shows that six defendants in this case were charged with conspiring to sex traffic young Mexican women and girls. The defendants lured young girls and women from Mexico into the United States under false pretenses. When the victims arrived in the U.S.A. the defendants forced them into prostitution; they used physical violence and threats to maintain complete control over them.

- Ivan Salazar pled guilty in July 2006.
- Angel Moreno Salazar was sentenced to fifty-one months incarceration.
- Jose Luis Moreno Salazar was sentenced to sixty months in prison.
- Salvador Fernando Molina Garcia was sentenced to sixty months in jail.
- Juan Carlos Salazar was sentenced to sixty months imprisonment.
- The alleged ringleader, Gerardo Salazar is currently a fugitive.

United States v. Molina (Texas)

Case documentation shows that nine defendants were charged with conspiring to smuggle and harbor illegal aliens. The victims were brought to Texas from Honduras under false pretenses; promising they would be employed as waitresses in restaurants. In January 2003, six of the defendants were sentenced in connection with the trafficking scheme which brought the young Honduran women into Texas. They were sent to work in Fort Worth bars and nightclubs controlled by the defendants. The victims were forced to entertain men in order to pay off their debts. The women were kept in apartments and houses where guards were posted to keep track of the women and to monitor their conversations.

- Dino Antonio Molina, Dilicia Suyapa Aguilar-Galindo and Ena Susana Aguilar-Galindo were each sentenced to fifty-two months in prison after pleading guilty to one count each of conspiracy to smuggle, transport, and harbor illegal aliens.
- Maria De Los Angeles Galindo-Carrasco was sentenced to thirty-four months in prison for the same charge.
- Marco Antonio Sanchez was sentenced to sixty-three months in prison.
- Steven Flores was sentenced to twenty-seven months in prison.
- Three remaining defendants in this case are fugitives

United States v. Trisanti & Nasution (California)

Mariska Trisanti and her husband Herri Naustion were charged with trafficking two victims from Indonesia into the United States. The victims were forced to work as domestic servants against their will. The defendants used threats and physical violence in order to coerce these women into complying. The victims were forced to work seven days a week for seventeen hours a day. Mariska Trisanti pled guilty to involuntary servitude, and her husband pled guilty to harboring an illegal alien.

- Trisanti was sentenced to forty-six months in prison and ordered to pay the victims over $205,000 in restitution.
- Nasution was sentenced to six months of home detention and three years of supervised release.

United States v. Alamin and Akhter (California)

Nur Alamin and his wife Rabiya Akhter were convicted of bringing a young woman from Bangladesh into the United States. They held her against her will in involuntary servitude and forced her to work as their nanny and housekeeper. The victim was repeatedly beaten and threatened in an attempt to keep her under control.

- Rabiya Akhter was sentenced to sixteen months incarceration on an immigration violation.
- Nur Alamin was sentenced to eleven years in prison on an involuntary servitude conviction.
- Both offenders were ordered to pay over $125,000 in restitution to the victim.

United States v. Boehm, et al (Alaska)

Josef F. Boehm was charged with conspiring to commit sex trafficking of children; possession of a controlled substance with intent to distribute; being a felon in possession of a firearm; and unlawful use of a controlled substance in possession of a firearm and ammunition. The eighteen count indictment was brought against Boehm in March 2004. All eight of Boehm's victims are United States citizens. Three additional defendants were charged with conspiracy to commit sex trafficking; sex trafficking of children; and conspiracy to distribute cocaine and crack to persons under the age of twenty-one.

- All four defendants pled guilty.

- Boehm pled guilty to child sex trafficking and drug charges.
- The sentences ranged from three years to thirteen years of incarceration.
- Part of Boehm's plea agreement was forfeiture of his residence in order to establish a $1.2 million trust fund for his victims.

United States v. Valle-Maldonado (California)

Maria de Jesus Valle-Maldonado pled guilty to conspiracy to import and harbor illegal aliens for the purpose of prostitution; importation of aliens for the purpose of prostitution; and bringing illegal aliens into the United States. Valle-Maldonado admitted to the court that she recruited young women and girls in Mexico, arranged to smuggle them into the United States, and forced them to work as prostitutes in her brothel. Some of the women were also transported to massage parlors and other locations for the purpose of sexual exploitation. Javier Sandoval-Garcia, Jose Velasquez-Garcia, and Juan Gregorio Martinez-Vasquez have also been convicted on charged related to this case.

- Maria de Jesus Valle-Maldonado received fifty-four years in the penitentiary and ordered to pay over $135,000 in restitution to nine victims.
- Velasquez-Garcia was sentenced to six months in prison.
- Martinez-Vazquez was sentenced to six months incarceration.

United States v. Bradley and O'Dell (New Hampshire)

Timothy Bradley and Kathleen O'Dell were charged and convicted with holding two Jamaican immigrants of forced labor, human trafficking, domestic servitude, wire fraud, and conspiracy. The defendants lured the victims by means of false promises of good work and pay. Upon arrival in the United States, the defendants confiscated their visas and passports. The victims were housed in deplorable conditions, denied medical care, and threatened with violence on a regular basis. The victims were physically abused, and the defendants restricted their ability to travel.

- they were both sentenced to seventy months of imprisonment
- fined $12,500
- ordered to pay $13,000 in restitution

United States v. Adaobi and Udeozor (Maryland)

Dr. Adaobi Stella Udeozor and George Chidebe Udeozor were indicted on conspiracy, involuntary servitude, and harboring an alien for financial gain. The couple held a fourteen year old Nigerian girl in involuntary servitude, forcing her to work for little or no pay, taking care of their six children, working long hours at their home and in the wife's medical practice, sexually assaulting her, and physically abusing her on a regular basis. George Udeozor fled to Nigeria prior to the trail. Dr. Udeozor was convicted of conspiracy and harboring an alien for financial gain. She was acquitted of holding the girl in involuntary servitude. George Udeozor is currently in a Nigerian jail awaiting extradition to the United States.

- Dr. Udeozor was sentenced to eighty-seven months of incarceration. She will be deported to Nigeria upon completion of her sentence.
- Dr. Udeozor was ordered to over $110,000 to the victim.

United States v. Valdma (Massachusetts)

Roman Valdma pled guilty to charges of importing aliens for immoral purposes; transportation for illegal sexual activity; persuading and enticing illegal sexual activity; encouraging and inducing aliens to come to the United States in violation of the law; bringing an alien to the United States without official authorization for commercial advantage; and visa fraud. Valdma recruited his victims from Estonia and offered them work in his massage business. It was not until the victims arrived in the United States that they learned the true nature of Valdma's massage business.

- Valdma was sentenced to forty-one months in prison and three years of supervised release.
- Valdma was ordered to pay a $75,000 fine and he had to forfeit $80,000 in cash, an automobile, and a condominium to the United States government.

United States v. Gonzalez-Garcia (New Jersey)

Evodio Gonzalez-Garcia, Oscar Romero-Gonzalez, and Domingo Gonzalez-Garcia smuggled a woman into the United States and forced her into prostitution. The victim was the common law wife of Domingo Gonzalez-Garcia. The three men pled guilty to charges of sex trafficking in New Jersey, New York, and Pennsylvania.

- On May 25, 2004 the three men were sentenced to three years imprisonment, followed by three years of supervised release.

United States v. Romero-Flores & Ventura (California)

Guillermo Romero-Flores and Guadalupe Ventura were indicted and charged with transporting women across the border for the purpose of commercial sexual exploitation along with various smuggling offenses. The defendants brought two Mexican women into the United States and kept them in Vista, California apartments as part of their scheme to profit financially from forced prostitution. A federal jury returned guilty verdicts convicting Guillermo Romero-Flores and Guadalupe Ventura on two counts of harboring aliens and two counts of harboring aliens for purposes of prostitution. Ventura was also convicted of one count of bringing in an alien for financial gain and one count of transporting an alien for purposes of prostitution.

- Guillermo Romero-Flores was sentenced to twenty-seven months of incarceration
- Guadalupe Ventura was sentenced to forty-one of imprisonment

United States v. Reddy (California)

Lakireddy Bali Reddy, a wealthy landlord in Berkley California pled guilty to charges of transporting minors for illegal sexual activity and conspiring to commit immigration fraud. The defendant admitted that he arranged to bring between twenty-five and ninety-nine Indian nationals into the United States using fraudulent visa between 1986 and 2000. Reddy also admitted that some of the illegal aliens were vulnerable young women and girls who were dependant on him for employment, housing, and sustenance both here in the United States and in India. Victims as young as thirteen years of age were sexually abused by Lakireddy Bali Reddy. The case was discovered when two young victims, sisters, suffered from carbon monoxide poisoning at one of Reddy's buildings. One of the victims died from the carbon monoxide; the surviving sister told the authorities of Reddy's abuse and exploitation.

- Lakireddy Bali Reddy was sentenced to ninety-seven months in prison and ordered to pay two million dollars in restitution to the victims.
- Prasad Lakireddy, Reddy's son, was sentenced to one year of home detention, five years probation, 300 hours of community service, and he was ordered to pay a $20,000 fine for his participation in his father's human trafficking ring.
- Jayaprakash Lakireddy, Reddy's brother, was convicted of importing underage Indian girls for sex and labor. He was sentenced to twelve months at a half-way house, followed by three years of supervised release, and ordered to pay a $30,000 fine.
- Annapurna Lakireddy, Jayaprakash's wife, pled guilty to conspiracy to commit immigration fraud. She was sentenced to six months home detention with an electronic monitoring device and ordered to pay a $2,000 fine.

Annapurna was also granted permission to participate in her children's sporting events with prior consent.

United States v. Cadena-Sosa (Florida)

The Cadena-Sosa case involves four brothers, their mother, two uncles, and at least one of their wives. The family of traffickers preyed upon victims from their hometown in Mexico. The women would arrive, well dressed and offer employment opportunities in America to their victims. The women would offer waitressing jobs in their restaurants in Florida to the victims, as well as nanny positions for some of the girls. The female recruiters would talk to both the young girls and to their parents. They explained that the girls would earn $400 a week, not including tips. With such salaries, the girls would be able to pay off their $2,000 smuggling fees in a very short time. A home visit with the girl and her family, a small advance of wages, and the Cadenas family promise that the girl would be well taken care of, along with the assurance that she could return home if she was unhappy working for the family, was how the trafficker normally closed the deal.

Hugo Cadena-Sosa was charged with conspiracy to lure Mexican women and girls into the United States under false pretenses. Cadena-Sosa, a citizen of Mexico, promised his victims jobs upon their arrival in America. When the victims arrived, they were forced by Cadena-Sosa into prostitution. He held them in brothels and prostituted them in the Carolinas and in Florida. The victims were forced to service between twenty-five to thirty men a day, six days a week. Failure to do so resulted in severe beatings, and in some cases, being locked in a closet for fifteen days, only being let out to use the bathroom. The women were moved every two weeks to prevent them from forming attachments with their "johns". Fourteen other defendants were also charged in connection with this case.

- Cadena-Sosa was sentenced to sixty months incarceration, two years of supervised release, and ordered to pay $1,000,000 in restitution to his victims.
- Rogerio Cadena, Hug Cadena-Sosa's uncle, pled guilty to federal slavery and prostitution charges. He was sentenced to fifteen years incarceration and ordered to pay $1,000,000 in restitution to his victims.

United States v. Tecum (Florida)

Jose Tecum kidnapped a teenage girl from a village in Guatemala near where he lived. He spent years stalking the girl before kidnapping, raping, and smuggling her into the United States. Tecum tried to persuade the girl to marry him; however both she and her family were resistant to the idea. The family said he was too old for her. He went so far as to threaten to kill the girl and her family unless she agreed to the marriage. He eventually gave up and resorted to kidnapping her and bringing her illegally into the United States. Tecum brought her to his home in South Florida. Along the way he told his victim that was already married and had three children living in the house with him. When he arrived home with the girl, he told his wife that she was his daughter-in-law. Tecum forced the girl to work in agricultural fields during the day to pay off her $1,000 smuggling debt; at night he would enter her room and rape her. His wife caught him one night and flew into a rage which resulted in a domestic violence incident when Tecum beat his wife. Following a police investigation, it was discovered that the young girl cowering in a corner had been kidnapped, raped and held in debt bondage by Jose Tecum.

- Jose Tecum was convicted of kidnapping, immigration violations, slavery, and conspiracy to manufacture false documents. He was sentenced to nine years of imprisonment. During the trial, Tecum threatened his victim in the court, using their native K'iche dialect.
- The young girl was one of the first human trafficking victims to receive a T visa.

United States v. Zavala and Ibanez (New York)

Maruluz Zavala and Jorge Ibanez pled guilty to conspiring to commit forced labor; document servitude; recruiting, harboring, transporting, and housing undocumented workers; transferring false alien registration cards, and other charges. Zavala and Ibanez devised an illegal scheme to obtain visas for Peruvians wishing to come to the United States. The defendants charged the victims smuggling fees which ranged between $6,000 and $13,000. Once on U.S. soil, the victims were relieved of their documents by the defendants and forced to work in factories and turn over their pay, under threat of being turned over to the immigration authorities. The defendants kept most of the money, leaving only fifty dollars a week for the victims to live on. Zavala and Ibanez victimized over sixty Peruvians, including thirteen children. The families were forced to live in squalid conditions.

- Maruluz Zavala was sentenced to fifteen years incarceration.
- Jorge Ibanez was sentenced to 135 months in prison.

- The couple was forced to forfeit their $175,000 residence and bank accounts containing approximately $30,000.

United States v. Gouw and Komala (Virginia)

Hans Gouw and Harjanto Komala pled guilty to conspiracy to commit sex trafficking. Additional charges included conspiring to recruit juvenile females to engage in a commercial sex act, immigration fraud, identification document fraud, and money laundering. The defendants conspired to recruit teenage girls and young Indonesian women to come to the United States and work as prostitutes and nude dancers. Ringleader Hans Gouw admitted that the victims were not allowed to leave their employment for at least one year, lived under constant monitoring, and he confiscated their passports.

- Harjanto Komala was sentenced on May 27, 2005 to one year and one day in prison and ordered to forfeit $50,000.
- Hans Gouw was sentenced on September 9, 2005 to serve five and a half years in prison.

United States v. Lopez-Torres (Texas)

Maria Magdalena Lopez-Torres pled guilty to importing aliens for immoral purposes, possession of a firearm by a convicted felon, and possession of a stolen firearm. Lopez-Torres managed a criminal enterprise that smuggled girls and young women from Mexico into the United States. Once they arrived in America, the victims were forced into prostitution and commercial sex acts. Lopes-Torres admitted to running this operation from April 2001 until May 2003.

- Maria Magdalena Lopez-Torres was sentenced to 151 months of imprisonment.

United States v. Schmidt (Maryland)

Baltimore resident, Richard Arthur Schmidt, age 61, pled guilty to one count of traveling overseas to engage in illicit sexual conduct with a minor; and one count of traveling overseas and engaging in illicit sexual molestation of a minor. Schmidt was arrested in Cambodia for child sex tourism. Schmidt, a former school teacher had previously served thirteen years of an eighteen year prison sentence for prior child molestation acts on young boys. Schmidt was charged under the PROTECT Act.

- Richard Schmidt was sentenced to fifteen years in prison and lifetime supervised release upon completion of his incarceration.

Rescue and Restore Campaign

The U.S. Department of Health and Human Services (HHS) is the designated agency responsible for helping victims of human trafficking. HHS created the Rescue and Restore Victims of Human Trafficking campaign in order to help identify and assist human trafficking victims in the United States. Rescue and Restore focuses on outreach programs geared towards the individuals and agencies most likely to encounter victims of human trafficking, such as law enforcement, social service providers, and health care professionals. HHS aims to educate as many individuals in these fields as possible in order to increase awareness and identification of trafficking victims. Rescue and Restore created the National Human Trafficking Resource Center which connects trafficking victims with service providers in their area. The resource center helps with the identification and certification of trafficking victims and has a twenty-four hour hotline 1-888-373-7888. Their website provides information on human trafficking; information and resources for health care providers, law enforcement, and social service providers. The site also provides fact sheets, educational brochures and posters, trafficking information and referral cards, and pocket assessment cards for service providers and law enforcement.

Rescue and Restore has developed local and national coalitions in their ongoing effort to implement the campaign in communities around the country. Coalition partners include local government, faith based organizations, non-profit organizations, women's organizations, Churches, civic groups, labor organizations, social service providers, immigration organizations, and community health care providers. Coalition partners share campaign information and resources throughout their communities as part of the ongoing effort to identify trafficking victim. Raising public awareness on human trafficking is the primary objective of the Rescue and Restore. Coalition partners are encouraged to implement any or all of the following action steps:

- include information about trafficking, its victims and perpetrators in organization newsletters, on websites and through other communication vehicles

- provide orientation and training sessions, or join with other organizations, including nonprofits, in hosting information forums on the trafficking problem and the national resolve to counter it

- request and disseminate, both internally and in appropriate public places, posters, brochures and other materials now being produced and distributed by the U.S. Department of Health and Human Services

- take part in a new national network that has been established by Capital City Partners to keep local organizations and their members abreast of developments in the awareness campaign as well as ways to address the trafficking challenge

- encourage other organizations, and health and law enforcement officials with whom you come in contact, to access the growing body of information and resources available to rescue and restore the victims of this hideous trade in human beings

Organizations interested in becoming partnered with the Rescue and Restore Campaign should visit their website and complete the "Request to Join the Campaign to Rescue and Restore Victims of Human Trafficking form."

Resource Guide

United States Immigration & Customs Enforcement (ICE)
www.ice.gov

United States Department of Labor - www.dol.gov
- Wage & Hour Division

United States Department of State - www.usdos.gov
- The Office to Monitor and Combat Trafficking in Persons
- TIP Report
- Bureau of Diplomatic Security

United States Health & Human Services Administration for Families and Children - www.acf.hhs.gov
- The Unaccompanied Refugee Minors Program
- Office of Refugee Resettlement (ORR)
- The Campaign to Rescue and Restore

Federal Bureau of Investigation - www.fbi.gov

United States Department of Justice - www.usdoj.gov

Interpol - www.interpol.int

United Nations Office for Drug Control and Crime Prevention
www.unodc.org

UNICEF www.unicef.org

Women In Need Network - www.WomenInNeedNetwork.org

First Internet Global Human Trafficking (FIGHT) Task Force
www.ModernDaySlavery.org

Anti-Slavery International - www.antislavery.org

Ansar Burney Trust International - www.ansarburney.com

Campaign Against Child Exploitation (CACE) - www.caceusa.org

Center for the Advancement of Human Rights (CAHR)
www.cahr.fsu.edu

Coalition Against Trafficking of Women (CATW)
www.catwinternational.org

Coalition to Abolish Slavery and Trafficking (CAST)
www.castla.org

Children's Rights Information Network (CRIN) - www.crin.org

End Child Prostitution, Child Pornography, and Child Trafficking for Sexual Purpose (ECPAT-USA) - www.ecpatusa.org

European Network Against Child Trafficking (ENACT) www.enact.it

Florida Freedom Partnership - www.floridafreedom.org

iAbolish – The American Anti-Slavery Group - www.iabolish.org

International Labor Organization (ILO) - www.ilo.org

International Organization for Migration (IOM) - www.iom.int

Polaris Project - www.polarisproject.org

Protection Project - www.protectionproject.org

Rutherford Institute - www.rutherford.org

SAANLAP India - www.saanlapindia.org

The Emancipation Network - www.wmancipationnetwork.org

Appendix

The Appendix contains federal statutes, U.S. Code, legislation, and model statutes in an effort to provide you with the information necessary to enable your work as an advocate on behalf of human trafficking victims. The Emancipation Proclamation led to the Thirteenth Amendment to the United States Constitution. From there our legislators have enacted various Acts and laws to protect those who have victimized by criminals, slave traders, and human traffickers.

The Emancipation Proclamation
January 1, 1863

By the President of the United States of America:

A Proclamation.

Whereas, on the twenty-second day of September, in the year of our Lord one thousand eight hundred and sixty-two, a proclamation was issued by the President of the United States, containing, among other things, the following, to wit:

"That on the first day of January, in the year of our Lord one thousand eight hundred and sixty-three, all persons held as slaves within any State or designated part of a State, the people whereof shall then be in rebellion against the United States, shall be then, thenceforward, and forever free; and the Executive Government of the United States, including the military and naval authority thereof, will recognize and maintain the freedom of such persons, and will do no act or acts to repress such persons, or any of them, in any efforts they may make for their actual freedom.

"That the Executive will, on the first day of January aforesaid, by proclamation, designate the States and parts of States, if any, in which the people thereof, respectively, shall then be in rebellion against the United States; and the fact that any State, or the people thereof, shall on that day be, in good faith, represented in the Congress of the United States by members chosen thereto at elections wherein a majority of the qualified voters of such State shall have participated, shall, in the absence of strong countervailing testimony, be deemed conclusive evidence that such State, and the people thereof, are not then in rebellion against the United States."

Now, therefore I, Abraham Lincoln, President of the United States, by virtue of the power in me vested as Commander-in-Chief, of the Army and Navy of the United States in time of actual armed rebellion against the authority and government of the United States, and as a fit and necessary war measure for suppressing said rebellion, do, on this first day of January, in the year of our Lord one thousand eight hundred and sixty-three, and in accordance with my purpose so to do publicly proclaimed for the full period of one hundred days, from the day first above mentioned, order and designate as the States and parts of States wherein the people thereof respectively, are this day in rebellion against the United States, the following, to wit:

Arkansas, Texas, Louisiana, (except the Parishes of St. Bernard, Plaquemines, Jefferson, St. John, St. Charles, St. James Ascension, Assumption, Terrebonne, Lafourche, St. Mary, St. Martin, and Orleans, including the City of New Orleans) Mississippi, Alabama, Florida, Georgia, South Carolina, North Carolina, and Virginia, (except the forty-eight counties designated as West Virginia, and also the counties of Berkley, Accomac, Northampton, Elizabeth City, York, Princess Ann, and Norfolk, including the cities of Norfolk and Portsmouth[)], and which excepted parts, are for the present, left precisely as if this proclamation were not issued.

And by virtue of the power, and for the purpose aforesaid, I do order and declare that all persons held as slaves within said designated States, and parts of States, are, and henceforward shall be free; and that the Executive government of the United States, including the military and naval authorities thereof, will recognize and maintain the freedom of said persons.

And I hereby enjoin upon the people so declared to be free to abstain from all violence, unless in necessary self-defence; and I recommend to them that, in all cases when allowed, they labor faithfully for reasonable wages.

And I further declare and make known, that such persons of suitable condition, will be received into the armed service of the

United States to garrison forts, positions, stations, and other places, and to man vessels of all sorts in said service.

And upon this act, sincerely believed to be an act of justice, warranted by the Constitution, upon military necessity, I invoke the considerate judgment of mankind, and the gracious favor of Almighty God.

In witness whereof, I have hereunto set my hand and caused the seal of the United States to be affixed.

Done at the City of Washington, this first day of January, in the year of our Lord one thousand eight hundred and sixty three, and of the Independence of the United States of America the eighty-seventh.

By the President: ABRAHAM LINCOLN
WILLIAM H. SEWARD, Secretary of State.

AMENDMENT XIII

Passed by Congress January 31, 1865. Ratified December 6, 1865.

Note: A portion of Article IV, section 2, of the Constitution was superseded by the 13th amendment.

Section 1.

Neither slavery nor involuntary servitude, except as a punishment for crime whereof the party shall have been duly convicted, shall exist within the United States, or any place subject to their jurisdiction.

Section 2.

Congress shall have power to enforce this article by appropriate legislation.

THE MANN ACT

Full text of the White-Slave Traffic Act, as passed by the Sixty-First Congress on June 25, 1910:

CHAP. 395 — An Act to further regulate interstate commerce and foreign commerce by prohibiting the transportation therein for immoral purposes of women and girls, and for other purposes.

Be it enacted by the Senate and House of Representatives of the United States of America in Congress assembled, That the term "interstate commerce," as used in this Act, shall include transportation from any State or Territory or the District of Columbia, and the term "foreign commerce," as used in this Act, shall include transportation from any State or Territory or the District of Columbia to any foreign country and from any foreign country to any State or Territory or the District of Columbia.

SEC. 2 That any person who shall knowingly transport or cause to be transported, or aid or assist in obtaining transportation for, or in transporting, in interstate or foreign commerce, or in any Territory or in the District of Columbia, any woman or girl for the purpose of prostitution or debauchery, or for any other immoral purpose, or with the intent and purpose to induce, entice, or compel such woman or girl to become a prostitute or to give herself up to debauchery, or to engage in any other immoral practice; or who shall knowingly procure or obtain, or cause to be procured or obtained, or aid or assist in procuring or obtaining, any ticket or tickets, or any form of transportation or evidence of the right thereto, to be used by any woman or girl in interstate or foreign commerce, or in any Territory or the District of Columbia, in going to any place for the purpose of prostitution or debauchery, or for any other immoral purpose, or with the intent or purpose on the part of such person to induce, entice, or compel her to give herself up to the practice of prostitution, or to give herself up to the practice of debauchery, or any other immoral practice, whereby any such woman or girl shall be transported in interstate or foreign commerce, or in any Territory or the District of Columbia, shall be deemed guilty of a felony, and upon conviction thereof shall be punished by a fine not exceeding five thousand dollars, or by imprisonment of not more than five years, or by both such fine and imprisonment, in the discretion of the court.

SEC. 3 That any person who shall knowingly persuade, induce, entice, or coerce, or cause to be persuaded, induced, enticed, or coerced, or aid or assist in persuading, inducing, enticing or coercing any woman or girl to go from one place to another in interstate or foreign commerce, or in any Territory or the District of Columbia, for the purpose of prostitution or debauchery, or for any other immoral purpose, or with the intent and purpose on the part of such person that such woman or girl shall engage in the practice of prostitution or debauchery, or any other immoral practice, whether with or without her consent, and who shall thereby knowingly cause or aid or assist in causing such woman or girl to go and be carried or transported as a passenger upon the line or route of any common carrier or carriers in interstate or foreign commerce, or any Territory or the District of Columbia, shall be deemed guilty of a felony and on conviction thereof shall be punished by a fine of not more than five thousand dollars, or by imprisonment for a term not exceeding five years, or by both fine and imprisonment, in the discretion of the court.

SEC. 4 That any person who shall knowingly persuade, induce, entice or coerce any woman or girl under the age of eighteen years from any State or Territory or the District of Columbia to any other State or Territory or the District of Columbia, with the purpose and intent to induce or coerce her, or that she shall be induced or coerced to engage in prostitution or debauchery, or any other immoral practice, and shall in furtherance of such purpose knowingly induce or cause her to go and to be carried or transported as a passenger in interstate commerce upon the line or route of any common carrier or carriers, shall be deemed guilty of a felony, and in conviction there of shall be punished by a fine of not more than ten thousand dollars, or by imprisonment for a term not exceeding ten years, or by both such fine and imprisonment, in the discretion of the court.

SEC. 5 That any violation of any of the above sections two, three, and four shall be prosecuted in any court having jurisdiction of crimes within the district in which said violation was committed, or from, through, or into which any such woman or girl may have been carried or transported as a passenger in interstate or foreign commerce, or in any Territory or the District of Columbia, contrary to the provisions of any of said sections.

SEC. 6 That for the purpose of regulating and preventing the transportation in foreign commerce of alien women and girls for purposes of prostitution and debauchery, and in pursuance of and for the purpose of carrying out the terms of the agreement of project of arrangement for the suppression of the white-slave traffic, adopted July twenty-fifth, nineteen hundred and two, for submission to their respective governments by the delegates of various powers represented at the Paris conference and confirmed by a formal agreement signed at Paris on May eighteenth, nineteen hundred and four, and adhered to by the United States on June sixth, nineteen hundred and eight, as shown by the proclamation of the President of the United States, dated June fifteenth, nineteen hundred and eight, the Commissioner-General of Immigration is hereby designated as the authority of the United States to receive and centralize information concerning the procuration of alien women and girls with a view to their debauchery, and to exercise supervision over such alien women and girls, receive their declarations, establish their identity, and ascertain from them who induced them to leave their native countries, respectively; and it shall be the duty of said Commissioner-General of Immigration to receive and keep on file in his office the statements and declarations which may be made by such alien women and girls, and those which are hereinafter required pertaining to such alien women and girls engaged in prostitution and debauchery in this country, and to furnish receipts for such statements and declarations provided for in this act to the persons, respectively, making and filing them.

Every person who shall keep, maintain, control, support or harbor in any house or place for the purpose of prostitution, or for any other immoral purpose, any alien woman or girl within three years after she shall have entered the United States from any country, party to the said arrangement for the suppression of the white-slave traffic, shall file with the Commissioner- General of Immigration a statement in writing setting forth the name of such alien woman or girl, the place at which she is kept, and all facts as to the date of her entry into the United States, the port through which she entered, her age, nationality, and parentage, and concerning her procuration to come to this country within the knowledge of such person, and any person who shall fail within thirty days after such person shall commence to keep, maintain, control, support, or harbor in any house or place for the purpose of prostitution, or for any other immoral purpose, any alien woman or girl within three years after she shall have entered the United States from any of the countries, party to the said arrangement for the suppression of the white-slave traffic, to file such statement concerning such alien woman or girl with the Commissioner-General of Immigration, or who shall knowingly and willfully state falsely or fail to disclose in such statement any fact within his knowledge or belief with reference, to the age, nationality, or parentage of any such alien woman or girl, or concerning her procuration to come to this country, shall be deemed guilty of a misdemeanor, and on conviction shall be punished by a fine of not more than two thousand dollars, or by imprisonment for a term not exceeding two years, or by both such fine and imprisonment, in the discretion of the court.

In any prosecution brought under this section, if it appear that any such statement required is not on file in the office of the Commissioner- General of Immigration, the person whose duty it shall be to file such statement shall be presumed to have failed to file said statement, as herein required, unless such person or persons shall prove otherwise. No person shall be excused from furnishing the statement, as required by this section, on the ground or for the reason that the statement so required by him, or the information therein contained, might tend to criminate him or subject him to a penalty or forfeiture, but no person shall be prosecuted or subjected to any penalty or forfeiture under any law of the United States for or on account of any transaction, matter, or thing, concerning which he may truthfully report in such statement, as required by the provisions of this section.

SEC. 7 That the term "Territory," as used in this Act, shall include the district of Alaska, the insular possessions of the United States, and the Canal Zone. The word "person," as used in this Act, shall be construed to import both the plural and the singular, as the case demands, and shall include corporations, companies, societies, and associations. When construing and enforcing the provisions of this Act, the act, omission, or failure of any officer, agent, or other person, acting for or employed by any other person or by any corporation, company, society, or association, within the scope of his employment or office, shall in every case be also deemed to be the act, omission, or failure of such other person, or of such company, society, or association as well of that of the person himself.

SEC. 8 That this Act shall be known and referred to as the "White-slave traffic Act."

Approved, Sixty-First Congress, June 25, 1910.

HOBBS ANTI-RACKETEERING ACT (1946)

18 USCA Section 1951 Interference with commerce by threats or violence

(a) Whoever in any way or degree obstructs, delays, or affects commerce or the movement of any article or commodity in commerce, by robbery or extortion or attempts or conspires so to do, or commits or threatens physical violence to any person or property in furtherance of a plan or purpose to do anything in violation of this section shall be fined under this title or imprisoned not more than twenty years, or both.

(b) As used in this section -

> (1) The term "robbery" means the unlawful taking or obtaining of personal property from the person or in the presence of another, against his will, by means of actual or threatened force, or violence, or fear of injury, immediate or future, to his person or property, or property in his custody or possession, or the person or property of a relative or member of his family or of anyone in his company at the time of the taking or obtaining.

> (2) The term "extortion" means the obtaining of property from another, with his consent, induced by wrongful use of actual or threatened force, violence, or fear, or under color of official right.

> (3) The term "commerce" means commerce within the District of Columbia, or any Territory or Possession of the

United States; all commerce between any point in a State, Territory, Possession, or the District of Columbia and any point outside thereof; all commerce between points within the same State through any place outside such State; and all other commerce over which the United States has jurisdiction.

(c) This section shall not be construed to repeal, modify or affect section 17 of Title 15, sections 52, 101-115, 151-166 of Title 29 or sections 151-188 of Title 45.

The "Model State Anti-Trafficking Criminal Statute" listed below is a complete excerpt from the *Report on Activities to Combat Human Trafficking Fiscal Years 2001- 2005* provided by the U. S. Department of Justice Civil Rights Division.

MODEL STATE ANTI-TRAFFICKING CRIMINAL STATUTE
****

An ACT relating to criminal consequences of conduct that involves certain trafficking of persons and involuntary servitude.

BE IT ENACTED BY THE LEGISLATURE OF THE STATE OF _____:

(A) TITLE _____, PENAL CODE, is amended by adding Article

    XXX to read as follows: ARTICLE XXX: TRAFFICKING OF

    PERSONS AND INVOLUNTARY SERVITUDE SEC.

    XXX.01. DEFINITIONS. In this Article:

(1) "Blackmail" is to be given its ordinary meaning as defined by [state blackmail statute, if any] and includes but is not limited to a threat to expose any secret tending to subject any person to hatred, contempt, or ridicule.

(2) "Commercial sexual activity" means any sex act on account of which anything of value is given, promised to, or received by any person.

(3) "Financial harm" includes credit extortion as defined by [state extortion statute, if any], criminal violation of the usury laws as defined by [state statutes defining usury], or employment contracts that violate the Statute of Frauds as defined by [state statute of frauds].

(4) "Forced labor or services" means labor, as defined in paragraph

(5), _infra_, or services, as defined in paragraph (8), _infra_, that are performed or provided by another person and are obtained or maintained through an actor's:

(A) causing or threatening to cause serious harm to any person;

(B) physically restraining or threatening to physically restrain another person;

(C) abusing or threatening to abuse the law or legal process;

(D) knowingly destroying, concealing, removing, confiscating or possessing any actual or purported passport or other immigration document, or any other actual or purported government identification document, of another person;

(E) blackmail; or

(F) causing or threatening to cause financial harm to [using financial control over] any person.

(5) "Labor" means work of economic or financial value.

(6) "Maintain" means, in relation to labor or services, to secure continued performance thereof, regardless of any initial agreement on the part of the victim to perform such type of service.

(7) "Obtain" means, in relation to labor or services, to secure performance thereof.

(8) "Services" means an ongoing relationship between a person and the actor in which the person performs activities under the supervision of or for the benefit of the actor. Commercial sexual activity and sexually-explicit performances are forms of "services" under this Section. Nothing in this provision should be construed to legitimize or legalize prostitution.

(9) "Sexually-explicit performance" means a live or public act or show intended to arouse or satisfy the sexual desires or appeal to the prurient interests of patrons.

(10) "Trafficking victim" means a person subjected to the practices set forth in Sections XXX.02(1) (involuntary servitude) or XXX.02(2) (sexual servitude of a minor), or transported in violation of Section XXX.02(3) (trafficking of persons for forced labor or services).

SEC. XXX.02. CRIMINAL PROVISIONS.

(1) INVOLUNTARY SERVITUDE. Whoever knowingly subjects, or attempts to subject, another person to forced labor or services

shall be punished by imprisonment as follows, subject to Section (4), infra:

> (A) by causing or threatening to cause physical harm to any person, not more than 20 years;
>
> (B) by physically restraining or threatening to physically restrain another person, not more than 15 years;
>
> (C) by abusing or threatening to abuse the law or legal process, not more than 10 years;
>
> (D) by knowingly destroying, concealing, removing, confiscating or possessing any actual or purported passport or other immigration document, or any other actual or purported government identification document, of another person, not more than 5 years,
>
> (E) by using blackmail, or using or threatening to cause financial harm to [using financial control over] any person, not more than 3 years.

(2) SEXUAL SERVITUDE OF A MINOR. Whoever knowingly recruits, entices, harbors, transports, provides, or obtains by any means, or attempts to recruit, entice, harbor, provide, or obtain by any means, another person under 18 years of age, knowing that the minor will engage in commercial sexual activity, sexually-explicit performance, or the production of pornography (see [relevant state statute] (defining pornography)), or causes or attempts to cause a minor to engage in commercial sexual activity, sexually-explicit performance, or the production of pornography,

shall be punished by imprisonment as follows, subject to the provisions of Section (4), infra:

> (A) in cases involving a minor between the ages of [age of consent] and 18 years, not involving overt force or threat, for not more than 15 years;

> (B) in cases in which the minor had not attained the age of [age of consent] years, not involving overt force or threat, for not more than 20 years;

> (C) in cases in which the violation involved overt force or threat, for not more than 25 years.

(3) TRAFFICKING OF PERSONS FOR FORCED LABOR OR SERVICES. Whoever knowingly (a) recruits, entices, harbors, transports, provides, or obtains by any means, or attempts to recruit, entice, harbor, transport, provide, or obtain by any means, another person, intending or knowing that the person will be subjected to forced labor or services; or (b) benefits, financially or by receiving anything of value, from participation in a venture which has engaged in an act described in violation of Sections XXX.02(1) or (2) of this Title, shall, subject to the provisions of Section (4) infra, be imprisoned for not more than 15 years.

(4) SENTENCING ENHANCEMENTS.

> (A) Statutory Maximum - Rape, Extreme Violence, and Death. If the violation of this Article involves kidnapping or an attempt to kidnap, aggravated sexual abuse or the attempt to commit aggravated sexual abuse, or an attempt

to kill, the defendant shall be imprisoned for any term of years or life, or if death results, may be sentenced to any term of years or life [or death].

(B) <u>Sentencing Considerations Within Statutory Maximums</u>.

(1) <u>Bodily Injury</u>. If, pursuant to a violation of this Article, a victim suffered bodily injury, the sentence may be enhanced as follows:

(1) Bodily injury, an additional ____ years of imprisonment; (2) Serious Bodily Injury, an additional ____ years of imprisonment; (3) Permanent or Life-Threatening Bodily Injury, an additional ____ years of imprisonment; or (4) If death results, defendant shall be sentenced in accordance with Homicide statute for relevant level of criminal intent).

(2) <u>Time in Servitude</u>. In determining sentences within statutory maximums, the sentencing court should take into account the time in which the victim was held in servitude, with increased penalties for cases in which the victim was held for between 180 days and one year, and increased penalties for cases in which the victim was held for more than one year.

(3) <u>Number of Victims</u>. In determining sentences within statutory maximums, the sentencing court should take into account the number of victims, and may provide for substantially-increased sentences in cases involving more than 10 victims.

(5)   RESTITUTION. Restitution is mandatory under this
        Article. In addition to any other amount of loss
        identified, the court shall order restitution including the
        greater of 1) the gross income or value to the defendant
        of the victim's labor or services or 2) the value of the
        victim's labor as guaranteed under the minimum wage
        and overtime provisions of the Fair Labor Standards
        Act (FLSA) and [corresponding state statutes if any].

(B) TRAFFICKING VICTIM PROTECTION

1) ASSESSMENT OF VICTIM PROTECTION NEEDS

        (A) The Attorney General, in consultation with the
        [Department of Health and Social Services] shall, no later
        than one year from the effective date of this statute, issue a
        report outlining how existing victim/witness laws and
        regulations respond to the needs of trafficking victims, as
        defined in XXX.01(8) of the Criminal Code, and suggesting
        areas of improvement and modification.

        (B) The [Department of Health and Social Services], in
        consultation with the Attorney General, shall, no later than
        one year from the effective date of this statute, issue a
        report outlining how existing social service programs
        respond or fail to respond to the needs of trafficking
        victims, as defined in XXX.01(8) of the Criminal Code, and
        the interplay of such existing programs with federally-
        funded victim service programs, and suggesting areas of
        improvement and modification. [Such inquiry shall

include, but not be limited to, the ability of state programs and licensing bodies to recognize federal T non-immigrant status for the purposes of benefits, programs, and licenses.]

Explanatory Notes

Purpose

This Model Law is offered to help criminal law policymakers at the state level address the phenomenon of modern-day slavery, often termed "trafficking in persons." In the course of researching this proposal, it became clear that many states already have laws on their books that directly address this crime problem. For instance, many trafficking-like crimes may be codified in seemingly-unrelated parts of a state code, such as the kidnapping or prostitution sections. Unfortunately, by being codified in disparate parts of the criminal code, it may unclear to prosecutors that the behaviors are trafficking in persons crimes and may be charged as such. Research into these existing state statutes revealed that they are often archaic, little-known, or underutilized, and do not necessarily reflect the current understanding of slavery and trafficking in persons.

The Thirteenth Amendment to the U.S. Constitution mandates that:

Neither slavery nor involuntary servitude, except as a punishment for crime whereof the party shall have been duly convicted, shall exist within the United States, or any place subject to their jurisdiction....

Under the Trafficking Victims Protection Act of 2000, Pub. L. 106-386 ("TVPA"), a "severe form of trafficking in persons" is defined as:

(A) sex trafficking in which a commercial sex act is induced by force, fraud, or coercion, or in which the person induced to perform such act has not attained 18 years of age; or
(B) the recruitment, harboring, transportation, provision, or obtaining of a person for labor or services, through the use of force, fraud, or coercion for the purpose of subjection to involuntary servitude, peonage, debt bondage, or slavery.

In the international arena, the United Nations Convention Against Transnational Organized Crime, supplemental Protocol to Prevent, Suppress and Punish Trafficking in Persons, especially Women and Children defines trafficking in persons as:

[T]he recruitment, transportation, transfer, harboring or receipt of persons, by means of the threat or use of force or other forms of coercion, of abduction, of fraud, of deception, of the abuse of power or of a position of vulnerability or of the giving or receiving of payments or benefits to achieve the consent of a person having control over another person, for the purpose of exploitation. Exploitation shall include, at a minimum, the exploitation of the prostitution of others or other forms of sexual exploitation, forced labor or services, slavery or practices similar to slavery, servitude or the removal of organs[.]

Federal criminal provisions specific to trafficking in persons are codified at Title 18, United States Code, Chapter 77, Peonage, Slavery, and Trafficking in Persons. Some of these statutes are newly-enacted provisions of the TVPA; some of these statutes date from the Civil War era. All of these federal criminal civil rights statutes are rooted in the 13th Amendment's guarantee of freedom. The other federal criminal civil rights statutes, such as 42 U.S.C. §3631 (Interference with Housing Rights) and 18 U.S.C. §242 (Deprivation of Rights Under Color of Law), have corresponding state statutes. E.g., Indiana Code, § 22-9.5-10-1 (criminalizing interference with another's rights) and Texas Penal Code §39.03 (criminalizing official oppression). Such federal/state overlap allows for more prosecutions to be brought and allows local prosecutors to respond most appropriately to crime problems in their own jurisdictions. State prosecutors' increased prosecution of racial violence cases in the last 20 years can serve as a model for increased enforcement of the U.S. Constitution's guarantee of freedom from involuntary servitude.

Many state constitutions mirror the federal constitutional prohibition against involuntary servitude, see, e.g, Arkansas Const. Art. 2, § 27, and some states have involuntary servitude statutes on their books. See, e.g., Cal. Penal Code § 181 (Slavery, Infringement of personal liberty; purchase of custody). Other states have similar statutes. North Carolina adopted a state involuntary servitude statute in the wake of several high-profile federal migrant labor prosecutions. See N.C.G.S.A. § 14-43.2. Arizona's criminal code, for example, includes kidnapping for involuntary servitude in its kidnapping statute, A.R.S. §13-1304, and a crime of taking a child for prostitution in its prostitution statutes. A.R.S. §13-3206. It is unclear whether such statutes are well-known by police and prosecutors, and to what extent they are being used to combat trafficking in persons.

The Model Penal Code recommends creation of an involuntary servitude crime as part of its overall kidnapping chapter. MPC 212.3(b), Felonious Restraint (third degree felony for holding a person in involuntary servitude). While the U.S. Department of Justice has not surveyed the field to determine how many states adopted this proposal, Nebraska is an example of one state that has this Model Penal Code provision on the books. See Neb.Rev.St. §28-314.

Certainly, experience at the federal level indicates that more comprehensive trafficking in persons statutes are needed to address the wide range of coercive tactics that traffickers use to obtain and maintain the labor and services of their victims. The proposed Model Law seeks to provide a tool for drafting modern anti-trafficking crimes, based on the Justice Department's experience in investigating and litigating these cases. Additionally, there is a strong need for uniformity in definitions and concepts across state lines to minimize confusion as trafficking victims in state prosecutions begin to seek the victim protections available through the federal Departments of Health and Human Services and of Homeland Security.

States and territories interested in adopting anti-trafficking legislation should survey their existing criminal codes to determine whether they include prohibitions on involuntary servitude, kidnapping, or false imprisonment, which have simply not been brought to bear against trafficking in persons. Such a survey will assist in incorporating relevant portions of a modern anti-trafficking statute into existing law, and could result in increased use of such statutes. Bundling of appropriate statutes into a Slavery/Trafficking chapter, as in the federal criminal code, will make it more likely that such crimes are recognized and charged.

Definitions

The heart of the concept of "trafficking in persons" is the denial of the liberty of another. Accordingly, the transportation of a person is a secondary inquiry, the apparent meaning of "trafficking" aside. Thus, the definitions section and the criminal provisions focus on the coercive nature of the service, rather than the movement of the victim or the type of underlying service.

The definitions are in alphabetical order.

Section XXX.01(1) defines blackmail in a manner identical to the Model Penal Code's Criminal Coercion statute, Section 212.5(1)(c).

Section XXX.01(2), "commercial sexual activity," tracks the definition of commercial sexual activity in the TVPA.

Section XXX.01(3) defines "financial harm" to reflect the TVPA and the UN Protocol's inclusion of "debt bondage" as a form of trafficking in persons. In order to differentiate a debt that has the effect of coercion, as opposed to simply a bad bargain, the proposal adopts the usury laws of the relevant jurisdiction to illustrate debts that contravene public policy and may thus appropriately be considered to be coercive. On the federal level, an example of this type of law can be found at 18 U.S.C. § 892 (Making Extortionate Extension of Credit).

Section XXX.01(4) defines "forced labor or services" as those obtained or maintained through coercion, and lists the forms of coercion that would, if used to compel forced labor or services, justify a finding that the labor or service was involuntary.

Section XXX.01(5), which defines "labor," covers work activities which would, but for the coercion, be otherwise legitimate and legal. The legitimacy or legality of the work is to be determined by focusing on the job, rather than on the legal status or work authorization status of the worker.

Section XXX.01(6)'s "maintain" builds upon the Model Penal Code's definition of "obtain" and incorporates the principle in federal anti-slavery caselaw that a person's initial agreement to perform a particular activity or type of service is not a waiver of any coercion aimed at keeping that person from leaving the service.

Section XXX.01(7), "obtain" tracks the definition set forth at Model Penal Code's Theft statute, Section 223.0(5)(b).

Section XXX.01(8), which defines "services," incorporates activities that are akin to an employment relationship but are in market sectors that are not legitimate forms of "labor." Notable in this area is commercial sexual activity, which is criminalized in almost every jurisdiction in the United States. Differentiation between "labor" and "services" makes it clear that this Model Law does not legitimize or legalize prostitution.

The notion that commercial sexual activity or concubinage can be "service" for the purposes of involuntary servitude statutes is reflected in case law. See, e.g. Pierce v. United States, 146 F.2d 84, 85 86 (5th Cir. 1944) (upholding conviction for forcing women to commit "immoral acts" at roadhouse to pay off debts); Bernal v. United States, 241 F. 339, 341 (5th Cir. 1917) (outlining as a crime when a woman was lured to house of prostitution under false pretenses and required to serve as prostitute or maid to pay debt); and the recent prosecutions, U.S. v. Cadena (SD FL 1998); U.S. v. Kwon (D. CNMI 1999); U.S. v. Pipkins (ND GA 2000); and U.S. v. Soto (SD TX 2003). See also Neal Kumar Katyal, Men Who Own Women: A Thirteenth Amendment Critique of Forced Prostitution, 103 YALE L.J. 791 (1993). Non-sexual forms of "service" might include rings that hold children for street begging or petty theft.

Section XXX.01(9) introduces the concept of "sexually-explicit performance." A number of recent federal cases have involved persons being held in servitude for purposes of sexually-explicit performances such as "exotic dancing." Unlike prostitution, which is typically illegal and involves commercial sexual activity, sexually-explicit performance may be legal, absent any coercion. Inclusion of sexually-explicit performance in this Model Law recognizes that such activity can have an impact on victims similar to sexual abuse, and reflects federal experience in which international traffickers are increasingly placing their victims into strip clubs rather than prostitution. The proposed criminal statutes provide expanded coverage for minors who are held in sexual performance as opposed to prostitution.

Section XXX.01(10) defines "trafficking victim," not for the purposes of the criminal statutes so much as to provide a working definition for state and local agencies who subsequently establish or modify programs to serve victims of these crimes.

Trafficking/Servitude Chapter

The Slavery/Trafficking crimes in this Article are arranged in a particular order that reflects the Department of Justice's experiences and understanding of the interplay between slavery/involuntary servitude and the transportation of persons for illicit purposes.

First, Involuntary Servitude, which focuses on the denial of a victim's liberty, applies to all persons held in compelled service, regardless of age, type of service, and whether they are transported or not. This approach de-links the crime from the nationality of the victim or the underlying morality of the service. All adults in coerced service are protected by this Section.

Second, a provision specific to minors in sexually-related activities sets forth a lesser standard of coercion – recognizing that sexual activities are conceptually different when minors are involved – by casting as Sexual Servitude those activities which involve minors but are not the result of coercion. This Section is the equivalent of Statutory Rape laws, which obviate the need to prove coercion when a victim is under the age of legal consent.

This Section would allow for trafficking prosecutions in cases in which minors are kept in prostitution because of their circumstances but overt force is not used, such as is common in cases involving runaway U.S. citizen youth. As noted above, this provision extends the concept of proving sexual exploitation without a concomitant need to find coercion to include sexually-explicit performance and child pornography, as well as sexual acts.

Finally, Trafficking of Persons for Forced Labor or Services punishes the trade in coerced labor or services, but focuses on the recruiting, moving, and harboring for these practices. Conceptually, these actions are illegal if done for the purpose of the exploitation captured by the servitude offenses previously set forth.

Section XXX.02(1) (Involuntary Servitude) provides a baseline offense that is graded according to the severity of the coercion used against the victim. Rather than the federal approach, in which there are separate crimes based on the level of coercion (a function of the development of the federal anti-slavery laws over the course of almost 200 years), the proposed offense – the obtaining or maintaining another person in service through coercion – outlines different statutory maximums for cases involving force, threats, document confiscation, blackmail, etc. For drafting purposes, jurisdictions that prefer to codify each crime separately could easily do so by referring to Appendix A, Optional Servitude Offenses, which sets the proposed crimes out in a different manner. States with guidelines sentencing may want to adopt a simple involuntary servitude statute with a 20-year statutory maximum and then incorporate gradations by level of coercion within their guidelines instead of adopting a multi-part statute or multiple servitude statutes. Such a statute is set forth in Appendix B, Alternative Servitude Offense.

Statutory maximums are provided as an illustration of a graduated approach based on the type and level of coercion used against the victim. Many jurisdictions simply designate particular levels of a crime as a Class A, B, or C Felony or as a First, Second, or Third Degree Felony, rather than assigning a specific statutory maximum within the actual offense. Statutory maximums are provided in this Model Law as an example of relative culpability. The statutory maximums should be reviewed and incorporated in keeping with the sentencing structure of the criminal code of the particular state or territory.

Each of the crimes punishes attempts as well as completed offenses. Criminalizing attempts allows prosecutors to focus on a defendant's objectively observable intent to use coercion for compulsory service rather than on a victim's subjective response to the coercion. For instance, a victim flees after a beating intended to hold her, rather than staying and submitting to the "master"; in this instance, the enslavement is attempted but not completed. Nonetheless, by criminalizing the attempt, a prosecutor may charge the defendant with his intended enslavement instead of having to wait for the victim actually to be enslaved (or to feel coerced). Such an approach has obvious benefits from the perspective of public safety: no victim should have to remain in a dangerous situation in order for the wrong done to him or her to be prosecutable. Note that the particular attempt language in the Model Law should be reviewed to ensure that it reflects an individual state's approach to attempts.

Penalties

The proposal's sentencing section sets forth two main concepts. First, the proposal reflects the notion that statutory maximum sentences should be increased in particularly violent instances of trafficking in persons, especially where the crime involves sexual abuse. Second, the actual sentences should reflect the time the victim was held and the various levels of injury suffered by a victim, as well as the number of victims harmed in a particular case. Additionally, gradation in sentences is appropriate among situations involving minors, especially those involving minors under the age of consent.

In the federal system these offense characteristics are incorporated into the U.S. Sentencing Guidelines, see U.S.S.G. §2H4.1, and have different effects depending on the other adjustments that are applied. Thus, the Model Law sets out offense characteristics which should be considered, but does not assign them values.

All of the offense characteristics offered for particular consideration should be reviewed and incorporated in keeping with the sentencing structure of the criminal code of a particular state or territory.

Restitution

The proposed measure of restitution tracks the federal restitution provision of the TVPA, codified at 18 U.S.C. §1594. Mandatory restitution allows prosecutors to recover money that the victims can use to assist them in their recovery. Unlike theft cases, there is typically little identifiable out-of-pocket loss in a trafficking case – the victims themselves are the objects that are stolen. Accordingly, this provision fixes the actual loss to the victim as either 1) the value of their services to the trafficker, or 2) the minimum wage for hours worked. The first measure of restitution, the value to the trafficker of the victim's labor or services, not only prevents the traffickers from profiting from their crime, but also avoids the unpalatable situation of assigning a wage valuation to instances of forced prostitution. The second measure of loss, the minimum wage calculation, is a handy tool in cases where victims did not receive any pay for their work, or sub-minimum wage, or in certain sex trafficking cases where the defendants hold their victims in concubinage rather than selling them as prostitutes (in which there is therefore no other identifiable measure of the value of the sexual services to the traffickers).

Trafficking Victim Protection

Federal experience has shown that prosecution without victim protection is unworkable. At the federal level, there is a variety of benefits and services available to trafficking victims.

Accordingly, this Model Law provides a mechanism through which a state could determine how well current state programs serve the needs of trafficking victims. In addition, a state may want to consider optional Model Law language regarding the incorporation of federal T non-immigrant status as a basis through which certain state benefits, programs, and licenses could be accessed by alien trafficking victims.

The "Model State Anti-Trafficking Criminal Statute, Appendix A" listed below is a complete excerpt from the *Report on Activities to Combat Human Trafficking Fiscal Years 2001- 2005* provided by the U. S. Department of Justice Civil Rights Division.

MODEL STATE ANTI-TRAFFICKING CRIMINAL STATUTE
APPENDIX A - Optional Servitude Offenses

[This formulation would also obviate the need for Section (4)(A), statutory maximum sentences.]

SEC. XXX.02. CRIMINAL PROVISIONS.

(1) INVOLUNTARY SERVITUDE OFFENSES.

(A) INVOLUNTARY SERVITUDE. Whoever knowingly subjects, or attempts to subject, another person to forced labor or services by causing or threatening to cause physical harm to any person shall be punished by imprisonment for not more than 20 years; but if the violation involves kidnapping or an attempt to kidnap, aggravated sexual abuse or the attempt to commit aggravated sexual abuse, or an attempt to kill, the defendant shall be imprisoned for any term of years or life, or if death results, may be sentenced to any term of years or life [or death].

(B) UNLAWFUL RESTRAINT FOR FORCED LABOR. Whoever knowingly subjects, or attempts to subject, another person to forced labor or services by physically restraining or threatening to physically restrain another person, shall be punished by imprisonment for not more than 15 years; but if the violation involves kidnapping or an attempt to kidnap, aggravated sexual abuse or the attempt to commit aggravated sexual abuse, or an attempt to kill, the defendant shall be imprisoned for any term of years or life, or if death results, may be sentenced to any term of years or life, [or death].

(C) LEGAL COERCION FOR FORCED LABOR. Whoever knowingly subjects, or attempts to subject, another person to forced labor or services by abusing or threatening to abuse the law or legal process shall be punished by imprisonment for not more than 10 years; but if the violation involves kidnapping or an attempt to kidnap, aggravated sexual abuse or the attempt to commit aggravated sexual abuse, or an attempt to kill, the defendant shall be imprisoned for any term of years or life, or if death results, may be sentenced to any term of years or life, [or death].

(D) DOCUMENT SERVITUDE. Whoever knowingly subjects, or attempts to subject, another person to forced labor or services by knowingly destroying, concealing, removing, confiscating or possessing any actual or purported passport or other immigration document, or any other actual or purported government identification document, of another person, shall be punished by imprisonment for not more than 5 years; but if the violation involves kidnapping or an attempt to kidnap, aggravated sexual abuse or the attempt to commit aggravated sexual abuse, or an attempt to kill, the defendant shall be imprisoned for any term of years or life, or if death results, may be sentenced to any term of years or life, [or death].

(E) DEBT BONDAGE. Whoever knowingly subjects, or attempts to subject, another person to forced labor or services by blackmail, or by using or threatening to cause financial harm to [using financial control over] any person, shall be punished by imprisonment for not more than 3 years; but if the violation involves kidnapping or an attempt to kidnap, aggravated sexual abuse or the attempt to commit aggravated sexual abuse, or an attempt to kill, the defendant shall be imprisoned for any term of years or life, or if death results, may be sentenced to any term of years or life, [or death].

The "Model State Anti-Trafficking Criminal Statute, Appendix B"
listed below is a complete excerpt from the *Report on Activities to
Combat Human Trafficking Fiscal Years 2001- 2005* provided by the
U. S. Department of Justice Civil Rights Division.

MODEL STATE ANTI-TRAFFICKING CRIMINAL STATUTE
Appendix B - Alternative Servitude Offense

[Use sentencing guidelines to differentiate among levels of
coercion and other aggravating factors.]

SEC. XXX.02. CRIMINAL PROVISIONS.

(1) INVOLUNTARY SERVITUDE. Whoever knowingly subjects,
or attempts to subject, another person to forced labor or services
shall be punished by imprisonment for not more than 20 years;
but if the violation involves kidnapping or an attempt to kidnap,
aggravated sexual abuse or the attempt to commit aggravated
sexual abuse, or an attempt to kill, the defendant shall be
imprisoned for any term of years or life, or if death results, may be
sentenced to any term of years or life, [or death].

TRAFFICKING VICTIMS PROTECTION ACT — MINIMUM STANDARDS FOR THE ELIMINATION OF TRAFFICKING IN PERSONS

Trafficking Victims Protection Act of 2000, Div. A of Pub. L. No. 106-386, § 108, as amended.

(A) Minimum standards

For purposes of this chapter, the minimum standards for the elimination of trafficking applicable to the government of a country of origin, transit, or destination for a significant number of victims of severe forms of trafficking are the following:

(1) The government of the country should prohibit severe forms of trafficking in persons and punish acts of such trafficking.

(2) For the knowing commission of any act of sex trafficking involving force, fraud, coercion, or in which the victim of sex trafficking is a child incapable of giving meaningful consent, or of trafficking which includes rape or kidnapping or which causes a death, the government of the country should prescribe punishment commensurate with that for grave crimes, such as forcible sexual assault.

(3) For the knowing commission of any act of a severe form of trafficking in persons, the government of the country should prescribe punishment that is sufficiently stringent to deter and that adequately reflects the heinous nature of the offense.

(4) The government of the country should make serious and sustained efforts to eliminate severe forms of trafficking in persons.

(B) Criteria
In determinations under subsection (A)(4) of this section, the following factors should be considered as indicia of serious and sustained efforts to eliminate severe forms of trafficking in persons:

(1) Whether the government of the country vigorously investigates and prosecutes acts of severe forms of trafficking in persons, and convicts and sentences persons responsible for such acts, that take place wholly or partly within the territory of the country. After reasonable requests from the Department of State for data regarding investigations, prosecutions, convictions, and sentences, a government, which does not provide such data, consistent with the capacity of such government to obtain such data, shall be presumed not to have vigorously investigated, prosecuted, convicted or sentenced such acts. During the periods prior to the annual report submitted on June 1, 2004, and on June 1, 2005, and the periods afterwards until September 30 of each such year, the Secretary of State may disregard the presumption contained in the preceding sentence if the government has provided some data to the Department of State regarding such acts and the Secretary has determined that the government is making a good faith effort to collect such data.

(2) Whether the government of the country protects victims of severe forms of trafficking in persons and encourages their assistance in the investigation and prosecution of such trafficking,

including provisions for legal alternatives to their removal to countries in which they would face retribution or hardship, and ensures that victims are not inappropriately incarcerated, fined, or otherwise penalized solely for unlawful acts as a direct result of being trafficked.

(3) Whether the government of the country has adopted measures to prevent severe forms of trafficking in persons, such as measures to inform and educate the public, including potential victims, about the causes and consequences of severe forms of trafficking in persons, *measures to reduce the demand for commercial sex acts and for participation in international sex tourism by nationals of the country, measures to ensure that its nationals who are deployed abroad as part of a peacekeeping or other similar mission do not engage in or facilitate severe forms of trafficking in persons or exploit victims of such trafficking, and measures to prevent the use of forced labor or child labor in violation of international standards* (added in the reauthorization of the TVPRA of 2005, will become effective January 10, 2008).

(4) Whether the government of the country cooperates with other governments in the investigation and prosecution of severe forms of trafficking in persons.

(5) Whether the government of the country extradites persons charged with acts of severe forms of trafficking in persons on substantially the same terms and to substantially the same extent as persons charged with other serious crimes (or, to the extent such extradition would be inconsistent with the laws of such country or with international agreements to which the country is a party, whether the government is taking all appropriate measures

to modify or replace such laws and treaties so as to permit such extradition).

(6) Whether the government of the country monitors immigration and emigration patterns for evidence of severe forms of trafficking in persons and whether law enforcement agencies of the country respond to any such evidence in a manner that is consistent with the vigorous investigation and prosecution of acts of such trafficking, as well as with the protection of human rights of victims and the internationally recognized human right to leave any country, including one's own, and to return to one's own country.

(7) Whether the government of the country vigorously investigates, prosecutes, convicts, and sentences public officials who participate in or facilitate severe forms of trafficking in persons, *including nationals of the country who are deployed abroad as part of a peacekeeping or other similar mission who engage in or facilitate severe forms of trafficking in persons or exploit victims of such trafficking* (added in the reauthorization of the TVPRA of 2005, will become effective January 10, 2008), and takes all appropriate measures against officials who condone such trafficking. After reasonable requests from the Department of State for data regarding such investigations, prosecutions, convictions, and sentences, a government which does not provide such data consistent with its resources shall be presumed not to have vigorously investigated, prosecuted, convicted, or sentenced such acts. During the periods prior to the annual report submitted on June 1, 2004, and on June 1, 2005, and the periods afterwards until September 30 of each such year, the Secretary of State may disregard the presumption contained in the preceding sentence if

the government has provided some data to the Department of State regarding such acts and the Secretary has determined that the government is making a good faith effort to collect such data.

(8) Whether the percentage of victims of severe forms of trafficking in the country that are non-citizens of such countries is insignificant.

(9) Whether the government of the country, consistent with the capacity of such government, systematically monitors its efforts to satisfy the criteria described in paragraphs (1) through (8) and makes available publicly a periodic assessment of such efforts.

(10) Whether the government of the country achieves appreciable progress in eliminating severe forms of trafficking when compared to the assessment in the previous year.

The PROTECT Act 2003 is a comprehensive law intended to prevent child abuse and child exploitation. It strengthens law enforcements ability to prevent, investigate, prosecute and punish violent crimes against children. President Bush signed the PROTECT Act on April 30, 2003.

One Hundred Eighth Congress
of the
United States of America
AT THE FIRST SESSION

Begun and held at the City of Washington on Tuesday, the seventh day of January, two thousand and three

An Act

To prevent child abduction and the sexual exploitation of children, and for other purposes.

Be it enacted by the Senate and House of Representatives of the United States of America in Congress assembled,

SECTION 1. SHORT TITLE; TABLE OF CONTENTS.

(a) SHORT TITLE- This Act may be cited as the `Prosecutorial Remedies and Other Tools to end the Exploitation of Children Today Act of 2003' or `PROTECT Act'.
(b) TABLE OF CONTENTS- The table of contents for this Act is as follows:
Sec. 1. Short title; table of contents.

Sec. 2. Severability.

TITLE I--SANCTIONS AND OFFENSES

Sec. 101. Supervised release term for sex offenders.
Sec. 102. First degree murder for child abuse and child torture murders.
Sec. 103. Sexual abuse penalties.
Sec. 104. Stronger penalties against kidnapping.
Sec. 105. Penalties against sex tourism.
Sec. 106. Two strikes you're out.
Sec. 107. Attempt liability for international parental kidnapping.
Sec. 108. Pilot program for national criminal history background checks and feasibility study.

TITLE II--INVESTIGATIONS AND PROSECUTIONS

Sec. 201. Interceptions of communications in investigations of sex offenses.
Sec. 202. No statute of limitations for child abduction and sex crimes.
Sec. 203. No pretrial release for those who rape or kidnap children.
Sec. 204. Suzanne's law.

TITLE III--PUBLIC OUTREACH

Subtitle A--AMBER Alert

Sec. 301. National coordination of AMBER alert communications network.

Sec. 302. Minimum standards for issuance and dissemination of alerts through AMBER alert communications network.

Sec. 303. Grant program for notification and communications systems along highways for recovery of abducted children.

Sec. 304. Grant program for support of AMBER alert communications plans.

Sec. 305. Limitation on liability.

Subtitle B--National Center for Missing and Exploited Children

Sec. 321. Increased support.

Sec. 322. Forensic and investigative support of missing and exploited children.

Sec. 323. Creation of cyber tipline.

Subtitle C--Sex Offender Apprehension Program

Sec. 341. Authorization.

Subtitle D--Missing Children Procedures in Public Buildings

Sec. 361. Short title.

Sec. 362. Definitions.

Sec. 363. Procedures in public buildings regarding a missing or lost child.

Subtitle E--Child Advocacy Center Grants

Sec. 381. Information and documentation required by Attorney General under Victims of Child Abuse Act of 1990.

TITLE IV--SENTENCING REFORM

Sec. 401. Sentencing reform.

TITLE V--OBSCENITY AND PORNOGRAPHY

Subtitle A--Child Obscenity and Pornography Prevention

Sec. 501. Findings.
Sec. 502. Improvements to prohibition on virtual child pornography.
Sec. 503. Certain activities relating to material constituting or containing child pornography.
Sec. 504. Obscene child pornography.
Sec. 505. Admissibility of evidence.
Sec. 506. Extraterritorial production of child pornography for distribution in the United States.
Sec. 507. Strengthening enhanced penalties for repeat offenders.
Sec. 508. Service provider reporting of child pornography and related information.
Sec. 509. Investigative authority relating to child pornography.
Sec. 510. Civil remedies.
Sec. 511. Recordkeeping requirements.
Sec. 512. Sentencing enhancements for interstate travel to engage in sexual act with a juvenile.

Sec. 513. Miscellaneous provisions.

Subtitle B--Truth in Domain Names

Sec. 521. Misleading domain names on the Internet.

TITLE VI--MISCELLANEOUS PROVISIONS

Sec. 601. Penalties for use of minors in crimes of violence.
Sec. 602. Sense of Congress.
Sec. 603. Communications Decency Act of 1996.
Sec. 604. Internet availability of information concerning registered sex offenders.
Sec. 605. Registration of child pornographers in the national sex offender registry.
Sec. 606. Grants to States for costs of compliance with new sex offender registry requirements.
Sec. 607. Safe ID Act.
Sec. 608. Illicit Drug Anti-Proliferation Act.
Sec. 609. Definition of vehicle.
Sec. 610. Authorization of John Doe DNA indictments.
Sec. 611. Transitional housing assistance grants for child victims of domestic violence, stalking, or sexual assault.

SEC. 2. SEVERABILITY.

If any provision of this Act, or the application of such provision to any person or circumstance, is held invalid, the remainder of this Act, and the application of such provision to other persons not similarly situated or to other circumstances, shall not be affected by such invalidation.

TITLE I--SANCTIONS AND OFFENSES

SEC. 101. SUPERVISED RELEASE TERM FOR SEX OFFENDERS.

Section 3583 of title 18, United States Code, is amended--
    (1) in subsection (e)(3), by inserting `on any such revocation' after `required to serve';
    (2) in subsection (h), by striking `that is less than the maximum term of imprisonment authorized under subsection (e)(3)'; and
    (3) by adding at the end the following:
`(k) Notwithstanding subsection (b), the authorized term of supervised release for any offense under section 1201 involving a minor victim, and for any offense under section 1591, 2241, 2242, 2244(a)(1), 2244(a)(2), 2251, 2251A, 2252, 2252A, 2260, 2421, 2422, 2423, or 2425, is any term of years or life.'.

SEC. 102. FIRST DEGREE MURDER FOR CHILD ABUSE AND CHILD TORTURE MURDERS.

Section 1111 of title 18, United States Code, is amended--
    (1) in subsection (a)--
        (A) by inserting `child abuse,' after `sexual abuse,'; and

(B) by inserting `or perpetrated as part of a pattern or practice of assault or torture against a child or children;' after `robbery;'; and

(2) by inserting at the end the following:

(c) For purposes of this section--

(1) the term `assault' has the same meaning as given that term in section 113;

(2) the term `child' means a person who has not attained the age of 18 years and is--

(A) under the perpetrator's care or control; or

(B) at least six years younger than the perpetrator;

(3) the term `child abuse' means intentionally or knowingly causing death or serious bodily injury to a child;

(4) the term `pattern or practice of assault or torture' means assault or torture engaged in on at least two occasions;

(5) the term `serious bodily injury' has the meaning set forth in section 1365; and

(6) the term `torture' means conduct, whether or not committed under the color of law, that otherwise satisfies the definition set forth in section 2340(1).

SEC. 103. SEXUAL ABUSE PENALTIES.

(a) MAXIMUM PENALTY INCREASES- (1) Chapter 110 of title 18, United States Code, is amended--

(A) in section 2251(d)--

(i) by striking `20' and inserting `30'; and

(ii) by striking `30' the first place it appears and inserting `50';

(B) in section 2252(b)(1)--

   (i) by striking `15' and inserting `20'; and

   (ii) by striking `30' and inserting `40';

  (C) in section 2252(b)(2)--

   (i) by striking `5' and inserting `10'; and

   (ii) by striking `10' and inserting `20';

  (D) in section 2252A(b)(1)--

   (i) by striking `15' and inserting `20'; and

   (ii) by striking `30' and inserting `40'; and

  (E) in section 2252A(b)(2)--

   (i) by striking `5' and inserting `10'; and

   (ii) by striking `10' and inserting `20'.

(2) Chapter 117 of title 18, United States Code, is amended--

  (A) in section 2422(a), by striking `10' and inserting `20';

  (B) in section 2422(b), by striking `15' and inserting `30'; and

  (C) in section 2423(a), by striking `15' and inserting `30'.

(3) Section 1591(b)(2) of title 18, United States Code, is amended by striking `20' and inserting `40'.

(b) MINIMUM PENALTY INCREASES- (1) Chapter 110 of title 18, United States Code, is amended--

  (A) in section 2251(d)--

   (i) by striking `or imprisoned not less than 10' and inserting `and imprisoned not less than 15';

   (ii) by striking `and both,';

   (iii) by striking `15' and inserting `25'; and

   (iv) by striking `30' the second place it appears and inserting `35';

  (B) in section 2251A (a) and (b), by striking `20' and inserting `30';

  (C) in section 2252(b)(1)--

(i) by striking `or imprisoned' and inserting `and imprisoned not less than 5 years and';

(ii) by striking `or both,'; and

(iii) by striking `5' and inserting `15';

(D) in section 2252(b)(2), by striking `2' and inserting `10';

(E) in section 2252A(b)(1)--

(1) by striking `or imprisoned' and inserting `and imprisoned not less than 5 years and';

(ii) by striking `or both,'; and

(iii) by striking `5' and inserting `15'; and

(F) in section 2252A(b)(2), by striking `2' and inserting `10'.

(2) Chapter 117 of title 18, United States Code, is amended--

(A) in section 2422(b)--

(i) by striking `, imprisoned' and inserting `and imprisoned not less than 5 years and'; and

(ii) by striking `, or both'; and

(B) in section 2423(a)--

(i) by striking `, imprisoned' and inserting `and imprisoned not less than 5 years and'; and

(ii) by striking `, or both'.

SEC. 104. STRONGER PENALTIES AGAINST KIDNAPPING.

(a) SENTENCING GUIDELINES- Notwithstanding any other provision of law regarding the amendment of Sentencing Guidelines, the United States Sentencing Commission is directed to amend the Sentencing Guidelines, to take effect on the date that is 30 days after the date of the enactment of this Act--

(1) so that the base offense level for kidnapping in section 2A4.1(a) is increased from level 24 to level 32;

(2) so as to delete section 2A4.1(b)(4)(C); and

(3) so that the increase provided by section 2A4.1(b)(5) is 6 levels instead of 3.

(b) MINIMUM MANDATORY SENTENCE- Section 1201(g) of title 18, United States Code, is amended by striking `shall be subject to paragraph (2)' in paragraph (1) and all that follows through paragraph (2) and inserting `shall include imprisonment for not less than 20 years.'.

SEC. 105. PENALTIES AGAINST SEX TOURISM.

(a) IN GENERAL- Section 2423 of title 18, United States Code, is amended by striking subsection (b) and inserting the following:

(b) TRAVEL WITH INTENT TO ENGAGE IN ILLICIT SEXUAL CONDUCT- A person who travels in interstate commerce or travels into the United States, or a United States citizen or an alien admitted for permanent residence in the United States who travels in foreign commerce, for the purpose of engaging in any illicit sexual conduct with another person shall be fined under this title or imprisoned not more than 30 years, or both.

(c) ENGAGING IN ILLICIT SEXUAL CONDUCT IN FOREIGN PLACES- Any United States citizen or alien admitted for permanent residence who travels in foreign commerce, and engages in any illicit sexual conduct with another person shall be fined under this title or imprisoned not more than 30 years, or both.

(d) ANCILLARY OFFENSES- Whoever, for the purpose of commercial advantage or private financial gain, arranges, induces, procures, or facilitates the travel of a person knowing that such a person is traveling in interstate commerce or foreign commerce for the purpose of engaging in illicit sexual conduct shall be fined under this title, imprisoned not more than 30 years, or both.

(e) ATTEMPT AND CONSPIRACY- Whoever attempts or conspires to violate subsection (a), (b), (c), or (d) shall be punishable in the same manner as a completed violation of that subsection.

(f) DEFINITION- As used in this section, the term `illicit sexual conduct' means (1) a sexual act (as defined in section 2246) with a person under 18 years of age that would be in violation of chapter 109A if the sexual act occurred in the special maritime and territorial jurisdiction of the United States; or (2) any commercial sex act (as defined in section 1591) with a person under 18 years of age.

(g) DEFENSE- In a prosecution under this section based on illicit sexual conduct as defined in subsection (f)(2), it is a defense, which the defendant must establish by a preponderance of the evidence, that the defendant reasonably believed that the person with whom the defendant engaged in the commercial sex act had attained the age of 18 years.'.

(b) CONFORMING AMENDMENT- Section 2423(a) of title 18, United States Code, is amended by striking `or attempts to do so,

SEC. 106. TWO STRIKES YOU'RE OUT.

(a) IN GENERAL- Section 3559 of title 18, United States Code, is amended by adding at the end the following new subsection:

(e) MANDATORY LIFE IMPRISONMENT FOR REPEATED SEX OFFENSES AGAINST CHILDREN-

(1) IN GENERAL- A person who is convicted of a Federal sex offense in which a minor is the victim shall be sentenced to life imprisonment if the person has a prior sex conviction in which a minor was the victim, unless the sentence of death is imposed.

(2) DEFINITIONS- For the purposes of this subsection--

(A) the term `Federal sex offense' means an offense under section 2241 (relating to aggravated sexual abuse), 2242 (relating to sexual abuse), 2244(a)(1) (relating to abusive sexual contact), 2245 (relating to sexual abuse resulting in death), 2251 (relating to sexual exploitation of children), 2251A (relating to selling or buying of children), 2422(b) (relating to coercion and enticement of a minor into prostitution), or 2423(a) (relating to transportation of minors);

(B) the term `State sex offense' means an offense under State law that is punishable by more than one year in prison and consists of conduct that would be a Federal sex offense if, to the extent or in the manner specified in the applicable provision of this title--

(i) the offense involved interstate or foreign commerce, or the use of the mails; or

(ii) the conduct occurred in any commonwealth, territory, or possession of the United States, within the special maritime and territorial jurisdiction of the United States, in a Federal prison, on any land or building owned by, leased to, or otherwise used by or under the control of the Government of the United States, or in the Indian country (as defined in section 1151);

(C) the term `prior sex conviction' means a conviction for which the sentence was imposed before the conduct occurred constituting the subsequent Federal sex offense, and which was for a Federal sex offense or a State sex offense;

(D) the term `minor' means an individual who has not attained the age of 17 years; and

(E) the term `State' has the meaning given that term in subsection (c)(2).

(3) NONQUALIFYING FELONIES- An offense described in section 2422(b) or 2423(a) shall not serve as a basis for sentencing under this subsection if the defendant establishes by clear and convincing evidence that--

(A) the sexual act or activity was consensual and not for the purpose of commercial or pecuniary gain;

(B) the sexual act or activity would not be punishable by more than one year in prison under the law of the State in which it occurred; or

(C) no sexual act or activity occurred.'.

(b) CONFORMING AMENDMENT- Sections 2247(a) and 2426(a) of title 18, United States Code, are each amended by inserting `, unless section 3559(e) applies' before the final period.

SEC. 107. ATTEMPT LIABILITY FOR INTERNATIONAL PARENTAL KIDNAPPING.

Section 1204 of title 18, United States Code, is amended--
　　　(1) in subsection (a), by inserting `, or attempts to do so,' before `or retains'; and
　　　(2) in subsection (c)--
　　　　　(A) in paragraph (1), by inserting `or the Uniform Child Custody Jurisdiction and Enforcement Act' before `and was'; and
　　　　　(B) in paragraph (2), by inserting `or' after the semicolon.

SEC. 108. PILOT PROGRAM FOR NATIONAL CRIMINAL HISTORY BACKGROUND CHECKS AND FEASIBILITY STUDY.

(a) ESTABLISHMENT OF PILOT PROGRAM-
　　　(1) IN GENERAL- Not later than 90 days after the date of the enactment of this Act, the Attorney General shall establish a pilot program for volunteer groups to obtain national and State criminal history background checks through a 10-fingerprint check to be conducted utilizing State criminal records and the Integrated Automated Fingerprint Identification System of the Federal Bureau of Investigation.
　　　(2) STATE PILOT PROGRAM-
　　　　　(A) IN GENERAL- The Attorney General shall designate 3 States as participants in an 18-month State pilot program.

(B) VOLUNTEER ORGANIZATION REQUESTS- A volunteer organization in one of the 3 States participating in the State pilot program under this paragraph that is part of the Boys and Girls Clubs of America, the National Mentoring Partnerships, or the National Council of Youth Sports may submit a request for a 10-fingerprint check from the participating State. A volunteer organization in a participating State may not submit background check requests under paragraph (3).

(C) STATE CHECK- The participating State under this paragraph after receiving a request under subparagraph (B) shall conduct a State background check and submit a request that a Federal check be performed through the Integrated Automated Fingerprint Identification System of the Federal Bureau of Investigation, to the Attorney General, in a manner to be determined by the Attorney General.

(D) INFORMATION PROVIDED- Under procedures established by the Attorney General, any criminal history record information resulting from the State and Federal check under subparagraph (C) shall be provided to the State or National Center for Missing and Exploited Children consistent with the National Child Protection Act.

(E) COSTS- A State may collect a fee to perform a criminal background check under this paragraph which may not exceed the actual costs to the State to perform such a check.

(F) TIMING- For any background check performed under this paragraph, the State shall provide the State criminal record information to the Attorney General within 7 days after receiving the request from the organization, unless the Attorney General determines during the feasibility study that such a check cannot reasonably be performed within that time period. The Attorney General shall provide the criminal history records information to the National Center for Missing and Exploited Children within 7 business days after receiving the request from the State.

(3) CHILD SAFETY PILOT PROGRAM-

(A) IN GENERAL- The Attorney General shall establish an 18-month Child Safety Pilot Program that shall provide for the processing of 100,000 10-fingerprint check requests from organizations described in subparagraph (B) conducted through the Integrated Automated Fingerprint Identification System of the Federal Bureau of Investigation.

(B) ELIGIBLE ORGANIZATIONS- An organization described in this subparagraph is an organization in a State not designated under paragraph (2) that has received a request allotment pursuant to subparagraph (C).

(C) REQUEST ALLOTMENTS- The following organizations may allot requests as follows:

(i) 33,334 for the Boys and Girls Clubs of America.

(ii) 33,333 for the National Mentoring Partnership.

(iii) 33,333 for the National Council of Youth Sports.

(D) PROCEDURES- The Attorney General shall notify the organizations described in subparagraph (C) of a process by which the organizations may provide fingerprint cards to the Attorney General.

(E) VOLUNTEER INFORMATION REQUIRED- An organization authorized to request a background check under this paragraph shall--

(i) forward to the Attorney General the volunteer's fingerprints; and

(ii) obtain a statement completed and signed by the volunteer that--

(I) sets out the provider or volunteer's name, address, date of birth appearing on a valid identification document as defined in section 1028 of title 18, United States Code, and a photocopy of the valid identifying document;

(II) states whether the volunteer has a criminal record, and, if so, sets out the particulars of such record;

(III) notifies the volunteer that the Attorney General may perform a criminal history background check and that the volunteer's signature to the statement constitutes an acknowledgment that such a check may be conducted;

(IV) notifies the volunteer that prior to and after the completion of the background check, the organization may choose to deny the provider access to children; and

(V) notifies the volunteer of his right to correct an erroneous record held by the Attorney General.

(F) TIMING- For any background checks performed under this paragraph, the Attorney General shall provide the criminal history records information to the National Center for Missing and Exploited Children within 14 business days after receiving the request from the organization.

(G) DETERMINATIONS OF FITNESS-

(i) IN GENERAL- Consistent with the privacy protections delineated in the National Child Protection Act (42 U.S.C. 5119), the National Center for Missing and Exploited Children may make a determination whether the criminal history record information received in response to the criminal history background checks conducted under this paragraph indicates that the provider or volunteer has a criminal history record that renders the provider or volunteer unfit to provide care to children based upon criteria established jointly by, the National Center for Missing and Exploited Children, the Boys and Girls Clubs of America, the National Mentoring Partnership, and the National Council of Youth Sports.

(ii) CHILD SAFETY PILOT PROGRAM- The National Center for Missing and Exploited

Children shall convey that determination to the organizations making requests under this paragraph.

(4) FEES COLLECTED BY ATTORNEY GENERAL- The Attorney General may collect a fee which may not exceed $18 to cover the cost to the Federal Bureau of Investigation to conduct the background check under paragraph (2) or (3).

(b) RIGHTS OF VOLUNTEERS- Each volunteer who is the subject of a criminal history background check under this section is entitled to contact the Attorney General to initiate procedures to--

(1) obtain a copy of their criminal history record report; and

(2) challenge the accuracy and completeness of the criminal history record information in the report.

(c) AUTHORIZATION OF APPROPRIATIONS-

(1) IN GENERAL- There is authorized to be appropriated such sums as may be necessary to the National Center for Missing and Exploited Children for fiscal years 2004 and 2005 to carry out the requirements of this section.

(2) STATE PROGRAM- There is authorized to be appropriated such sums as may be necessary to the Attorney General for the States designated in subsection (a)(1) for fiscal years 2004 and 2005 to establish and enhance fingerprint technology infrastructure of the participating State.

(d) FEASIBILITY STUDY FOR A SYSTEM OF BACKGROUND CHECKS FOR EMPLOYEES AND VOLUNTEERS-

(1) STUDY REQUIRED- The Attorney General shall conduct a feasibility study within 180 days after the date of

the enactment of this Act. The study shall examine, to the extent discernible, the following:

(A) The current state of fingerprint capture and processing at the State and local level, including the current available infrastructure, State system capacities, and the time for each State to process a civil or volunteer print from the time of capture to submission to the Federal Bureau of Investigation (FBI).

(B) The intent of the States concerning participation in a nationwide system of criminal background checks to provide information to qualified entities.

(C) The number of volunteers, employees, and other individuals that would require a fingerprint-based criminal background check.

(D) The impact on the Integrated Automated Fingerprint Identification System (IAFIS) of the Federal Bureau of Investigation in terms of capacity and impact on other users of the system, including the effect on Federal Bureau of Investigation work practices and staffing levels.

(E) The current fees charged by the Federal Bureau of Investigation, States and local agencies, and private companies to process fingerprints and conduct background checks.

(F) The existence of `model' or best practice programs which could easily be expanded and duplicated in other States.

(G) The extent to which private companies are currently performing background checks and the possibility of using private companies in the future to perform any of the background check process, including, but not limited to, the capture and transmission of fingerprints and fitness determinations.

(H) The cost of development and operation of the technology and the infrastructure necessary to establish a nationwide fingerprint-based and other criminal background check system.

(I) The extent of State participation in the procedures for background checks authorized in the National Child Protection Act (Public Law 103-209), as amended by the Volunteers for Children Act (sections 221 and 222 of Public Law 105-251).

(J) The extent to which States currently provide access to nationwide criminal history background checks to organizations that serve children.

(K) The extent to which States currently permit volunteers to appeal adverse fitness determinations, and whether similar procedures are required at the Federal level.

(L) The implementation of the 2 pilot programs created in subsection (a).

(M) Any privacy concerns that may arise from nationwide criminal background checks.

(N) Any other information deemed relevant by the Department of Justice.

(2) INTERIM REPORT- Based on the findings of the feasibility study under paragraph (1), the Attorney General shall, not later than 180 days after the date of the enactment of this Act, submit to Congress an interim report, which may include recommendations for a pilot

project to develop or improve programs to collect fingerprints and perform background checks on individuals that seek to volunteer with organizations that work with children, the elderly, or the disabled.

(3) FINAL REPORT- Based on the findings of the pilot project, the Attorney General shall, not later than 60 days after completion of the pilot project under this section, submit to Congress a final report, including recommendations, which may include a proposal for grants to the States to develop or improve programs to collect fingerprints and perform background checks on individuals that seek to volunteer with organizations that work with children, the elderly, or the disabled, and which may include recommendations for amendments to the National Child Protection Act and the Volunteers for Children Act so that qualified entities can promptly and affordably conduct nationwide criminal history background checks on their employees and volunteers.

TITLE II--INVESTIGATIONS AND PROSECUTIONS

SEC. 201. INTERCEPTIONS OF COMMUNICATIONS IN INVESTIGATIONS OF SEX OFFENSES.

Section 2516(1) of title 18, United States Code, is amended--
(1) in paragraph (a), by inserting after `chapter 37 (relating to espionage),' the following: `chapter 55 (relating to kidnapping),'; and
(2) in paragraph (c)--
(A) by inserting `section 1591 (sex trafficking of children by force, fraud, or coercion),' after `section

1511 (obstruction of State or local law enforcement),'; and

(B) by inserting `section 2251A (selling or buying of children), section 2252A (relating to material constituting or containing child pornography), section 1466A (relating to child obscenity), section 2260 (production of sexually explicit depictions of a minor for importation into the United States), sections 2421, 2422, 2423, and 2425 (relating to transportation for illegal sexual activity and related crimes),' after `sections 2251 and 2252 (sexual exploitation of children),'.

SEC. 202. NO STATUTE OF LIMITATIONS FOR CHILD ABDUCTION AND SEX CRIMES.

Section 3283 of title 18, United States Code, is amended to read as follows:

`Sec. 3283. Offenses against children

`No statute of limitations that would otherwise preclude prosecution for an offense involving the sexual or physical abuse, or kidnaping, of a child under the age of 18 years shall preclude such prosecution during the life of the child.'.

SEC. 203. NO PRETRIAL RELEASE FOR THOSE WHO RAPE OR KIDNAP CHILDREN.

Section 3142(e) of title 18, United States Code, is amended--

(1) by striking `1901 et seq.), or' and inserting `1901 et seq.),'; and

(2) by striking `of title 18 of the United States Code' and inserting `of this title, or an offense involving a minor victim under section 1201, 1591, 2241, 2242, 2244(a)(1), 2245, 2251, 2251A, 2252(a)(1), 2252(a)(2), 2252(a)(3), 2252A(a)(1), 2252A(a)(2), 2252A(a)(3), 2252A(a)(4), 2260, 2421, 2422, 2423, or 2425 of this title'.

SEC. 204. SUZANNE'S LAW.

Section 3701(a) of the Crime Control Act of 1990 (42 U.S.C. 5779(a)) is amended by striking `age of 18' and inserting `age of 21'.

TITLE III--PUBLIC OUTREACH

Subtitle A--AMBER Alert

SEC. 301. NATIONAL COORDINATION OF AMBER ALERT COMMUNICATIONS NETWORK.

(a) COORDINATION WITHIN DEPARTMENT OF JUSTICE- The Attorney General shall assign an officer of the Department of Justice to act as the national coordinator of the AMBER Alert communications network regarding abducted children. The officer so designated shall be known as the AMBER Alert Coordinator of the Department of Justice.

(b) DUTIES- In acting as the national coordinator of the AMBER Alert communications network, the Coordinator shall--

(1) seek to eliminate gaps in the network, including gaps in areas of interstate travel;

(2) work with States to encourage the development of additional elements (known as local AMBER plans) in the network;

(3) work with States to ensure appropriate regional coordination of various elements of the network; and

(4) act as the nationwide point of contact for--

    (A) the development of the network; and

    (B) regional coordination of alerts on abducted children through the network.

(c) CONSULTATION WITH FEDERAL BUREAU OF INVESTIGATION- In carrying out duties under subsection (b), the Coordinator shall notify and consult with the Director of the Federal Bureau of Investigation concerning each child abduction for which an alert is issued through the AMBER Alert communications network.

(d) COOPERATION- The Coordinator shall cooperate with the Secretary of Transportation and the Federal Communications Commission in carrying out activities under this section.

(e) REPORT- Not later than March 1, 2005, the Coordinator shall submit to Congress a report on the activities of the Coordinator and the effectiveness and status of the AMBER plans of each State that has implemented such a plan. The Coordinator shall prepare the report in consultation with the Secretary of Transportation.

SEC. 302. MINIMUM STANDARDS FOR ISSUANCE AND DISSEMINATION OF ALERTS THROUGH AMBER ALERT COMMUNICATIONS NETWORK.

(a) ESTABLISHMENT OF MINIMUM STANDARDS- Subject to subsection (b), the AMBER Alert Coordinator of the Department of Justice shall establish minimum standards for--

    (1) the issuance of alerts through the AMBER Alert communications network; and

    (2) the extent of the dissemination of alerts issued through the network.

(b) LIMITATIONS- (1) The minimum standards established under subsection (a) shall be adoptable on a voluntary basis only.

(2) The minimum standards shall, to the maximum extent practicable (as determined by the Coordinator in consultation with State and local law enforcement agencies), provide that appropriate information relating to the special needs of an abducted child (including health care needs) are disseminated to the appropriate law enforcement, public health, and other public officials.

(3) The minimum standards shall, to the maximum extent practicable (as determined by the Coordinator in consultation with State and local law enforcement agencies), provide that the dissemination of an alert through the AMBER Alert communications network be limited to the geographic areas most likely to facilitate the recovery of the abducted child concerned.

(4) In carrying out activities under subsection (a), the Coordinator may not interfere with the current system of voluntary coordination between local broadcasters and State and local law enforcement agencies for purposes of the AMBER Alert communications network.

(c) COOPERATION- (1) The Coordinator shall cooperate with the Secretary of Transportation and the Federal Communications Commission in carrying out activities under this section.

(2) The Coordinator shall also cooperate with local broadcasters and State and local law enforcement agencies in establishing minimum standards under this section.

SEC. 303. GRANT PROGRAM FOR NOTIFICATION AND COMMUNICATIONS SYSTEMS ALONG HIGHWAYS FOR RECOVERY OF ABDUCTED CHILDREN.

(a) PROGRAM REQUIRED- The Secretary of Transportation shall carry out a program to provide grants to States for the development or enhancement of notification or communications systems along highways for alerts and other information for the recovery of abducted children.

(b) DEVELOPMENT GRANTS-

(1) IN GENERAL- The Secretary may make a grant to a State under this subsection for the development of a State program for the use of changeable message signs or other motorist information systems to notify motorists about abductions of children. The State program shall provide for the planning, coordination, and design of systems, protocols, and message sets that support the coordination and communication necessary to notify motorists about abductions of children.

(2) ELIGIBLE ACTIVITIES- A grant under this subsection may be used by a State for the following purposes:

(A) To develop general policies and procedures to guide the use of changeable message signs or other motorist information systems to notify motorists about abductions of children.

(B) To develop guidance or policies on the content and format of alert messages to be conveyed on changeable message signs or other traveler information systems.

(C) To coordinate State, regional, and local plans for the use of changeable message signs or other transportation related issues.

(D) To plan secure and reliable communications systems and protocols among public safety and transportation agencies or modify existing communications systems to support the notification of motorists about abductions of children.

(E) To plan and design improved systems for communicating with motorists, including the capability for issuing wide area alerts to motorists.

(F) To plan systems and protocols to facilitate the efficient issuance of child abduction notification and other key information to motorists during off-hours.

(G) To provide training and guidance to transportation authorities to facilitate appropriate use of changeable message signs and other traveler information systems for the notification of motorists about abductions of children.

(c) IMPLEMENTATION GRANTS-

(1) IN GENERAL- The Secretary may make a grant to a State under this subsection for the implementation of a program for the use of changeable message signs or other motorist information systems to notify motorists about abductions of children. A State shall be eligible for a grant under this subsection if the Secretary determines that the

State has developed a State program in accordance with subsection (b).

(2) ELIGIBLE ACTIVITIES- A grant under this subsection may be used by a State to support the implementation of systems that use changeable message signs or other motorist information systems to notify motorists about abductions of children. Such support may include the purchase and installation of changeable message signs or other motorist information systems to notify motorists about abductions of children.

(d) FEDERAL SHARE- The Federal share of the cost of any activities funded by a grant under this section may not exceed 80 percent.

(e) DISTRIBUTION OF GRANT AMOUNTS- The Secretary shall, to the maximum extent practicable, distribute grants under this section equally among the States that apply for a grant under this section within the time period prescribed by the Secretary.

(f) ADMINISTRATION- The Secretary shall prescribe requirements, including application requirements, for the receipt of grants under this section.

(g) DEFINITION- In this section, the term `State' means any of the 50 States, the District of Columbia, or Puerto Rico.

(h) AUTHORIZATION OF APPROPRIATIONS- There is authorized to be appropriated to the Secretary to carry out this section $20,000,000 for fiscal year 2004. Such amounts shall remain available until expended.

(i) STUDY OF STATE PROGRAMS-

(1) STUDY- The Secretary shall conduct a study to examine State barriers to the adoption and implementation of State programs for the use of communications systems along

highways for alerts and other information for the recovery of abducted children.

(2) REPORT- Not later than 1 year after the date of enactment of this Act, the Secretary shall transmit to Congress a report on the results of the study, together with any recommendations the Secretary determines appropriate.

SEC. 304. GRANT PROGRAM FOR SUPPORT OF AMBER ALERT COMMUNICATIONS PLANS.

(a) PROGRAM REQUIRED- The Attorney General shall carry out a program to provide grants to States for the development or enhancement of programs and activities for the support of AMBER Alert communications plans.

(b) ACTIVITIES- Activities funded by grants under the program under subsection (a) may include--

(1) the development and implementation of education and training programs, and associated materials, relating to AMBER Alert communications plans;

(2) the development and implementation of law enforcement programs, and associated equipment, relating to AMBER Alert communications plans;

(3) the development and implementation of new technologies to improve AMBER Alert communications; and

(4) such other activities as the Attorney General considers appropriate for supporting the AMBER Alert communications program.

(c) FEDERAL SHARE- The Federal share of the cost of any activities funded by a grant under the program under subsection (a) may not exceed 50 percent.

(d) DISTRIBUTION OF GRANT AMOUNTS ON GEOGRAPHIC BASIS- The Attorney General shall, to the maximum extent practicable, ensure the distribution of grants under the program under subsection (a) on an equitable basis throughout the various regions of the United States.

(e) ADMINISTRATION- The Attorney General shall prescribe requirements, including application requirements, for grants under the program under subsection (a).

(f) AUTHORIZATION OF APPROPRIATIONS- (1) There is authorized to be appropriated for the Department of Justice $5,000,000 for fiscal year 2004 to carry out this section and, in addition, $5,000,000 for fiscal year 2004 to carry out subsection (b)(3).

(2) Amounts appropriated pursuant to the authorization of appropriations in paragraph (1) shall remain available until expended.

SEC. 305. LIMITATION ON LIABILITY.

(a) Except as provided in subsection (b), the National Center for Missing and Exploited Children, including any of its officers, employees, or agents, shall not be liable for damages in any civil action for defamation, libel, slander, or harm to reputation arising out of any action or communication by the National Center for Missing and Exploited Children, its officers, employees, or agents, in connection with any clearinghouse, hotline or complaint intake or forwarding program or in connection with activity that is wholly or partially funded by the United States and undertaken in cooperation with, or at the direction of a Federal law enforcement agency.

(b) The limitation in subsection (a) does not apply in any action in which the plaintiff proves that the National Center for Missing and Exploited Children, its officers, employees, or agents acted with actual malice, or provided information or took action for a purpose unrelated to an activity mandated by Federal law. For purposes of this subsection, the prevention, or detection of crime, and the safety, recovery, or protection of missing or exploited children shall be deemed, per se, to be an activity mandated by Federal law.

Subtitle B--National Center for Missing and Exploited Children

SEC. 321. INCREASED SUPPORT.

(a) IN GENERAL- Section 408(a) of the Missing Children's Assistance Act (42 U.S.C. 5777(a)) is amended by striking `fiscal years 2000 through 2003' and inserting `fiscal years 2004 through 2005.'.

(b) ANNUAL GRANT TO NATIONAL CENTER FOR MISSING AND EXPLOITED CHILDREN- Section 404(b)(2) of the Missing Children's Assistance Act (42 U.S.C. 5773(b)(2)) is amended by striking `$10,000,000 for each of fiscal years 2000, 2001, 2002, and 2003' and inserting `$20,000,000 for each of the fiscal years 2004 through 2005'.

SEC. 322. FORENSIC AND INVESTIGATIVE SUPPORT OF MISSING AND EXPLOITED CHILDREN.

Section 3056 of title 18, United States Code, is amended by adding at the end the following:

`(f) Under the direction of the Secretary of Homeland Security, officers and agents of the Secret Service are authorized, at the request of any State or local law enforcement agency, or at the request of the National Center for Missing and Exploited Children, to provide forensic and investigative assistance in support of any investigation involving missing or exploited children.'.

SEC. 323. CREATION OF CYBER TIPLINE.

Section 404(b)(1) of the Missing Children's Assistance Act (42 U.S.C. 5773(b)(1)) is amended--

(1) in subparagraph (F), by striking `and' at the end;

(2) in subparagraph (G), by striking the period at the end and inserting `; and'; and

(3) by adding at the end the following:

`(H) coordinate the operation of a cyber tipline to provide online users an effective means of reporting Internet-related child sexual exploitation in the areas of--

`(i) distribution of child pornography;

`(ii) online enticement of children for sexual acts; and

`(iii) child prostitution.'.

Subtitle C--Sex Offender Apprehension Program

SEC. 341. AUTHORIZATION.

Section 1701(d) of part Q of title I of the Omnibus Crime Control and Safe Streets Act of 1968 (42 U.S.C. 3796dd(d)) is amended--

> (1) by redesignating paragraphs (10) and (11) as (11) and (12), respectively; and
>
> (2) by inserting after paragraph (9) the following:
>
> `(10) assist a State in enforcing a law throughout the State which requires that a convicted sex offender register his or her address with a State or local law enforcement agency and be subject to criminal prosecution for failure to comply;'.

Subtitle D--Missing Children Procedures in Public Buildings

SEC. 361. SHORT TITLE.

This subtitle may be cited as the `Code Adam Act of 2003'.

SEC. 362. DEFINITIONS.

In this subtitle, the following definitions apply:

> (1) CHILD- The term `child' means an individual who is 17 years of age or younger.
>
> (2) CODE ADAM ALERT- The term `Code Adam alert' means a set of procedures used in public buildings to alert employees and other users of the building that a child is missing.
>
> (3) DESIGNATED AUTHORITY- The term `designated authority' means--
>
> > (A) with respect to a public building owned or leased for use by an Executive agency--

(i) except as otherwise provided in this paragraph, the Administrator of General Services;

(ii) in the case of the John F. Kennedy Center for the Performing Arts, the Board of Trustees of the John F. Kennedy Center for the Performing Arts;

(iii) in the case of buildings under the jurisdiction, custody, and control of the Smithsonian Institution, the Board of Regents of the Smithsonian Institution; or

(iv) in the case of another public building for which an Executive agency has, by specific or general statutory authority, jurisdiction, custody, and control over the building, the head of that agency;

(B) with respect to the Supreme Court Building, the Marshal of the Supreme Court; with respect to the Thurgood Marshall Federal Judiciary Building, the Director of the Administrative Office of United States Courts; and with respect to all other public buildings owned or leased for use by an establishment in the judicial branch of government, the General Services Administration in consultation with the United States Marshals Service; and

(C) with respect to a public building owned or leased for use by an establishment in the legislative branch of government, the Capitol Police Board.

(4) EXECUTIVE AGENCY- The term `Executive agency' has the same meaning such term has under section 105 of title 5, United States Code.

(5) FEDERAL AGENCY- The term `Federal agency' means any Executive agency or any establishment in the legislative or judicial branches of the Government.
(6) PUBLIC BUILDING- The term `public building' means any building (or portion thereof) owned or leased for use by a Federal agency.

SEC. 363. PROCEDURES IN PUBLIC BUILDINGS REGARDING A MISSING OR LOST CHILD.

(a) IN GENERAL- Not later than 180 days after the date of enactment of this Act, the designated authority for a public building shall establish procedures for locating a child that is missing in the building.
(b) NOTIFICATION AND SEARCH PROCEDURES- Procedures established under this section shall provide, at a minimum, for the following:

(1) Notifying security personnel that a child is missing.
(2) Obtaining a detailed description of the child, including name, age, eye and hair color, height, weight, clothing, and shoes.
(3) Issuing a Code Adam alert and providing a description of the child, using a fast and effective means of communication.
(4) Establishing a central point of contact.
(5) Monitoring all points of egress from the building while a Code Adam alert is in effect.
(6) Conducting a thorough search of the building.
(7) Contacting local law enforcement.
(8) Documenting the incident.

Subtitle E--Child Advocacy Center Grants

SEC. 381. INFORMATION AND DOCUMENTATION REQUIRED BY ATTORNEY GENERAL UNDER VICTIMS OF CHILD ABUSE ACT OF 1990.

(a) REGIONAL CHILDREN'S ADVOCACY CENTERS- Section 213 of the Victims of Child Abuse Act of 1990 (42 U.S.C. 13001b) is amended--

(1) in subsection (c)(4)--

(A) by striking `and' at the end of subparagraph (B)(ii);

(B) in subparagraph (B)(iii), by striking `Board' and inserting `board'; and

(C) by redesignating subparagraphs (C) and (D) as clauses (iv) and (v), respectively, of subparagraph (B), and by realigning such clauses so as to have the same indentation as the preceding clauses of subparagraph (B); and

(2) in subsection (e), by striking `Board' in each of paragraphs (1)(B)(ii), (2)(A), and (3), and inserting `board'.

(b) AUTHORIZATION OF APPROPRIATIONS- The text of section 214B of such Act (42 U.S.C. 13004) is amended to read as follows:

`(a) SECTIONS 213 AND 214- There are authorized to be appropriated to carry out sections 213 and 214, $15,000,000 for each of fiscal years 2004 and 2005.

`(b) SECTION 214A- There are authorized to be appropriated to carry out section 214A, $5,000,000 for each of fiscal years 2004 and 2005.'.

TITLE IV--SENTENCING REFORM

SEC. 401. SENTENCING REFORM.

(a) ENFORCEMENT OF SENTENCING GUIDELINES FOR CHILD ABDUCTION AND SEX OFFENSES- Section 3553(b) of title 18, United States Code is amended--

    (1) by striking `The court' and inserting the following:

    `(1) IN GENERAL- Except as provided in paragraph (2), the court'; and

    (2) by adding at the end the following:

    `(2) CHILD CRIMES AND SEXUAL OFFENSES-

        `(A) SENTENCING- In sentencing a defendant convicted of an offense under section 1201 involving a minor victim, an offense under section 1591, or an offense under chapter 71, 109A, 110, or 117, the court shall impose a sentence of the kind, and within the range, referred to in subsection (a)(4) unless--

            `(i) the court finds that there exists an aggravating circumstance of a kind, or to a degree, not adequately taken into consideration by the Sentencing Commission in formulating the guidelines that should result in a sentence greater than that described;

            `(ii) the court finds that there exists a mitigating circumstance of a kind or to a degree, that--

                `(I) has been affirmatively and specifically identified as a

permissible ground of downward
departure in the sentencing
guidelines or policy statements
issued under section 994(a) of title
28, taking account of any
amendments to such sentencing
guidelines or policy statements by
Congress;

`(II) has not been taken into
consideration by the Sentencing
Commission in formulating the
guidelines; and

`(III) should result in a sentence
different from that described; or

`(iii) the court finds, on motion of the
Government, that the defendant has
provided substantial assistance in the
investigation or prosecution of another
person who has committed an offense and
that this assistance established a mitigating
circumstance of a kind, or to a degree, not
adequately taken into consideration by the
Sentencing Commission in formulating the
guidelines that should result in a sentence
lower than that described.

In determining whether a circumstance was adequately taken into
consideration, the court shall consider only the sentencing
guidelines, policy statements, and official commentary of the
Sentencing Commission, together with any amendments thereto
by act of Congress. In the absence of an applicable sentencing

guideline, the court shall impose an appropriate sentence, having due regard for the purposes set forth in subsection (a)(2). In the absence of an applicable sentencing guideline in the case of an offense other than a petty offense, the court shall also have due regard for the relationship of the sentence imposed to sentences prescribed by guidelines applicable to similar offenses and offenders, and to the applicable policy statements of the Sentencing Commission, together with any amendments to such guidelines or policy statements by act of Congress.'.

(b) CONFORMING AMENDMENTS TO GUIDELINES MANUAL- The Federal Sentencing Guidelines are amended--
    (1) in section 5K2.0--
        (A) by striking `Under' and inserting the following: `(a) DOWNWARD DEPARTURES IN CRIMINAL CASES OTHER THAN CHILD CRIMES AND SEXUAL OFFENSES- Under'; and
        (B) by adding at the end the following:
`(b) DOWNWARD DEPARTURES IN CHILD CRIMES AND SEXUAL OFFENSES-
`Under 18 U.S.C. Sec. 3553(b)(2), the sentencing court may impose a sentence below the range established by the applicable guidelines only if the court finds that there exists a mitigating circumstance of a kind, or to a degree, that--

> `(1) has been affirmatively and specifically identified as a permissible ground of downward departure in the sentencing guidelines or policy statements issued under section 994(a) of title 28, United States Code, taking account of any amendments to such sentencing guidelines or policy statements by act of Congress;

`(2) has not adequately been taken into consideration by the Sentencing Commission in formulating the guidelines; and

`(3) should result in a sentence different from that described.

The grounds enumerated in this Part K of chapter 5 are the sole grounds that have been affirmatively and specifically identified as a permissible ground of downward departure in these sentencing guidelines and policy statements. Thus, notwithstanding any other reference to authority to depart downward elsewhere in this Sentencing Manual, a ground of downward departure has not been affirmatively and specifically identified as a permissible ground of downward departure within the meaning of section 3553(b)(2) unless it is expressly enumerated in this Part K as a ground upon which a downward departure may be granted.'.

(2) At the end of part K of chapter 5, add the following:

`Sec. 5K2.22 Specific Offender Characteristics as Grounds for Downward Departure in child crimes and sexual offenses (Policy Statement)

`In sentencing a defendant convicted of an offense under section 1201 involving a minor victim, an offense under section 1591, or an offense under chapter 71, 109A, 110, or 117 of title 18, United States Code, age may be a reason to impose a sentence below the applicable guideline range only if and to the extent permitted by Sec. 5H1.1.

`An extraordinary physical impairment may be a reason to impose a sentence below the applicable guideline range only if and to the extent permitted by Sec. 5H1.4. Drug, alcohol, or gambling dependence or abuse is not a reason for imposing a sentence below the guidelines.

     (3) Section 5K2.20 is amended by striking `A' and inserting `Except where a defendant is convicted of an offense under section 1201 involving a minor victim, an offense under section 1591, or an offense under chapter 71, 109A, 110, or 117 of title 18, United States Code, a'.

     (4) Section 5H1.6 is amended by inserting after the first sentence the following: `In sentencing a defendant convicted of an offense under section 1201 involving a minor victim, an offense under section 1591, or an offense under chapter 71, 109A, 110, or 117 of title 18, United States Code, family ties and responsibilities and community ties are not relevant in determining whether a sentence should be below the applicable guideline range.'.

     (5) Section 5K2.13 is amended by--

          (A) striking `or' before `(3)'; and

          (B) replacing `public' with `public; or (4) the defendant has been convicted of an offense under chapter 71, 109A, 110, or 117 of title 18, United States Code.'.

(c) STATEMENT OF REASONS FOR IMPOSING A SENTENCE- Section 3553(c) of title 18, United States Code, is amended--

     (1) by striking `described.' and inserting `described, which reasons must also be stated with specificity in the written order of judgment and commitment, except to the extent that the court relies upon statements received in camera in accordance with Federal Rule of Criminal Procedure 32. In the event that the court relies upon statements received in camera in accordance with Federal Rule of Criminal

Procedure 32 the court shall state that such statements were so received and that it relied upon the content of such statements.';

(2) by inserting `, together with the order of judgment and commitment,' after `the court's statement of reasons'; and

(3) by inserting `and to the Sentencing Commission,' after `to the Probation System'.

(d) REVIEW OF A SENTENCE-

(1) REVIEW OF DEPARTURES- Section 3742(e)(3) of title 18, United States Code, is amended to read as follows:

`(3) is outside the applicable guideline range, and

   `(A) the district court failed to provide the written statement of reasons required by section 3553(c);

   `(B) the sentence departs from the applicable guideline range based on a factor that--

      `(i) does not advance the objectives set forth in section 3553(a)(2); or

      `(ii) is not authorized under section 3553(b); or

      `(iii) is not justified by the facts of the case; or

   `(C) the sentence departs to an unreasonable degree from the applicable guidelines range, having regard for the factors to be considered in imposing a sentence, as set forth in section 3553(a) of this title and the reasons for the imposition of the particular sentence, as stated by the district court pursuant to the provisions of section 3553(c); or'.

(2) STANDARD OF REVIEW- The last paragraph of section 3742(e) of title 18, United States Code, is amended by striking `shall give due deference to the district court's

application of the guidelines to the facts' and inserting `, except with respect to determinations under subsection (3)(A) or (3)(B), shall give due deference to the district court's application of the guidelines to the facts. With respect to determinations under subsection (3)(A) or (3)(B), the court of appeals shall review de novo the district court's application of the guidelines to the facts'.

(3) DECISION AND DISPOSITION-

    (A) The first paragraph of section 3742(f) of title 18, United States Code, is amended by striking `the sentence';

    (B) Section 3742(f)(1) of title 18, United States Code, is amended by inserting `the sentence' before `was imposed';

    (C) Section 3742(f)(2) of title 18, United States Code, is amended to read as follows:

`(2) the sentence is outside the applicable guideline range and the district court failed to provide the required statement of reasons in the order of judgment and commitment, or the departure is based on an impermissible factor, or is to an unreasonable degree, or the sentence was imposed for an offense for which there is no applicable sentencing guideline and is plainly unreasonable, it shall state specific reasons for its conclusions and--

    `(A) if it determines that the sentence is too high and the appeal has been filed under subsection (a), it shall set aside the sentence and remand the case for further sentencing proceedings with such instructions as the court considers appropriate, subject to subsection (g);

`(B) if it determines that the sentence is too low and the appeal has been filed under subsection (b), it shall set aside the sentence and remand the case for further sentencing proceedings with such instructions as the court considers appropriate, subject to subsection (g);'; and

(D) Section 3742(f)(3) of title 18, United States Code, is amended by inserting `the sentence' before `is not described'.

(e) IMPOSITION OF SENTENCE UPON REMAND- Section 3742 of title 18, United States Code, is amended by redesignating subsections (g) and (h) as subsections (h) and (i) and by inserting the following after subsection (f):

`(g) SENTENCING UPON REMAND- A district court to which a case is remanded pursuant to subsection (f)(1) or (f)(2) shall resentence a defendant in accordance with section 3553 and with such instructions as may have been given by the court of appeals, except that--

`(1) In determining the range referred to in subsection 3553(a)(4), the court shall apply the guidelines issued by the Sentencing Commission pursuant to section 994(a)(1) of title 28, United States Code, and that were in effect on the date of the previous sentencing of the defendant prior to the appeal, together with any amendments thereto by any act of Congress that was in effect on such date; and

`(2) The court shall not impose a sentence outside the applicable guidelines range except upon a ground that--

`(A) was specifically and affirmatively included in the written statement of reasons required by section 3553(c) in connection with the previous sentencing of the defendant prior to the appeal; and

`(B) was held by the court of appeals, in remanding the case, to be a permissible ground of departure.'.

(f) DEFINITIONS- Section 3742 of title 18, United States Code, as amended by subsection (e), is further amended by adding at the end the following:

`(j) DEFINITIONS- For purposes of this section--

`(1) a factor is a `permissible' ground of departure if it--

`(A) advances the objectives set forth in section 3553(a)(2); and

`(B) is authorized under section 3553(b); and

`(C) is justified by the facts of the case; and

`(2) a factor is an `impermissible' ground of departure if it is not a permissible factor within the meaning of subsection (j)(1).'.

(g) REFORM OF GUIDELINES GOVERNING ACCEPTANCE OF RESPONSIBILITY- Subject to subsection (j), the Guidelines Manual promulgated by the Sentencing Commission pursuant to section 994(a) of title 28, United States Code, is amended--

(1) in section 3E1.1(b)--

(A) by inserting `upon motion of the government stating that' immediately before `the defendant has assisted authorities'; and

(B) by striking `taking one or more' and all that follows through and including `additional level' and insert `timely notifying authorities of his intention to enter a plea of guilty, thereby permitting the government to avoid preparing for trial and permitting the government and the court to allocate their resources efficiently, decrease the offense level by 1 additional level';

(2) in the Application Notes to the Commentary to section 3E1.1, by amending Application Note 6--

(A) by striking `one or both of'; and

(B) by adding the following new sentence at the end: 'Because the Government is in the best position to determine whether the defendant has assisted authorities in a manner that avoids preparing for trial, an adjustment under subsection (b) may only be granted upon a formal motion by the Government at the time of sentencing.'; and

(3) in the Background to section 3E1.1, by striking `one or more of'.

(h) IMPROVED DATA COLLECTION- Section 994(w) of title 28, United States Code, is amended to read as follows:

`(w)(1) The Chief Judge of each district court shall ensure that, within 30 days following entry of judgment in every criminal case, the sentencing court submits to the Commission a written report of the sentence, the offense for which it is imposed, the age, race, sex of the offender, and information regarding factors made relevant by the guidelines. The report shall also include--

`(A) the judgment and commitment order;

`(B) the statement of reasons for the sentence imposed (which shall include the reason for any departure from the otherwise applicable guideline range);

`(C) any plea agreement;

`(D) the indictment or other charging document;

`(E) the presentence report; and

`(F) any other information as the Commission finds appropriate.

`(2) The Commission shall, upon request, make available to the House and Senate Committees on the Judiciary, the written reports and all underlying records accompanying those reports described in this section, as well as other records received from courts.

`(3) The Commission shall submit to Congress at least annually an analysis of these documents, any recommendations for legislation that the Commission concludes is warranted by that analysis, and an accounting of those districts that the Commission believes have not submitted the appropriate information and documents required by this section.

`(4) The Commission shall make available to the Attorney General, upon request, such data files as the Commission may assemble or maintain in electronic form that include any information submitted under paragraph (1). Such data files shall be made available in electronic form and shall include all data fields requested, including the identity of the sentencing judge.'.

(i) SENTENCING GUIDELINES AMENDMENTS- (1) Subject to subsection (j), the Guidelines Manual promulgated by the Sentencing Commission pursuant to section 994(a) of title 28, United States Code, is amended as follows:

(A) Application Note 4(b)(i) to section 4B1.5 is amended to read as follows:

`(i) IN GENERAL- For purposes of subsection (b), the defendant engaged in a pattern of activity involving prohibited sexual conduct if on at least two separate occasions, the defendant engaged in prohibited sexual conduct with a minor.'.

(B) Section 2G2.4(b) is amended by adding at the end the following:

`(4) If the offense involved material that portrays sadistic or masochistic conduct or other depictions of violence, increase by 4 levels.

`(5) If the offense involved--

>`(A) at least 10 images, but fewer than 150, increase by 2 levels;

>`(B) at least 150 images, but fewer than 300, increase by 3 levels;

>`(C) at least 300 images, but fewer than 600, increase by 4 levels; and

>`(D) 600 or more images, increase by 5 levels.'.

(C) Section 2G2.2(b) is amended by adding at the end the following:

`(6) If the offense involved--

>`(A) at least 10 images, but fewer than 150, increase by 2 levels;

>`(B) at least 150 images, but fewer than 300, increase by 3 levels;

>`(C) at least 300 images, but fewer than 600, increase by 4 levels; and

>`(D) 600 or more images, increase by 5 levels.'.

(2) The Sentencing Commission shall amend the Sentencing Guidelines to ensure that the Guidelines adequately reflect the seriousness of the offenses under sections 2243(b), 2244(a)(4), and 2244(b) of title 18, United States Code.

(j) CONFORMING AMENDMENTS-

(1) Upon enactment of this Act, the Sentencing Commission shall forthwith distribute to all courts of the United States and to the United States Probation System

the amendments made by subsections (b), (g), and (i) of this section to the sentencing guidelines, policy statements, and official commentary of the Sentencing Commission. These amendments shall take effect upon the date of enactment of this Act, in accordance with paragraph (5).

(2) On or before May 1, 2005, the Sentencing Commission shall not promulgate any amendment to the sentencing guidelines, policy statements, or official commentary of the Sentencing Commission that is inconsistent with any amendment made by subsection (b) or that adds any new grounds of downward departure to Part K of chapter 5.

(3) With respect to cases covered by the amendments made by subsection (i) of this section, the Sentencing Commission may make further amendments to the sentencing guidelines, policy statements, or official commentary of the Sentencing Commission, except that the Commission shall not promulgate any amendments that, with respect to such cases, would result in sentencing ranges that are lower than those that would have applied under such subsection.

(4) At no time may the Commission promulgate any amendment that would alter or repeal the amendments made by subsection (g) of this section.

(5) Section 3553(a) of title 18, United States Code, is amended--

> (A) by amending paragraph (4)(A) to read as follows:
>
> `(A) the applicable category of offense committed by the applicable category of defendant as set forth in the guidelines--

`(i) issued by the Sentencing Commission pursuant to section 994(a)(1) of title 28, United States Code, subject to any amendments made to such guidelines by act of Congress (regardless of whether such amendments have yet to be incorporated by the Sentencing Commission into amendments issued under section 994(p) of title 28); and

`(ii) that, except as provided in section 3742(g), are in effect on the date the defendant is sentenced; or';

(B) in paragraph (4)(B), by inserting `, taking into account any amendments made to such guidelines or policy statements by act of Congress (regardless of whether such amendments have yet to be incorporated by the Sentencing Commission into amendments issued under section 994(p) of title 28)' after `Code';

(C) by amending paragraph (5) to read as follows:

`(5) any pertinent policy statement--

`(A) issued by the Sentencing Commission pursuant to section 994(a)(2) of title 28, United States Code, subject to any amendments made to such policy statement by act of Congress (regardless of whether such amendments have yet to be incorporated by the Sentencing Commission into amendments issued under section 994(p) of title 28); and

`(B) that, except as provided in section 3742(g), is in effect on the date the defendant is sentenced.'.

(k) COMPLIANCE WITH STATUTE- Section 994(a) of title 28, United States Code, is amended by striking `consistent with all pertinent provisions of this title and title 18, United States Code,' and inserting `consistent with all pertinent provisions of any Federal statute'.

(l) REPORT BY ATTORNEY GENERAL-

(1) DEFINED TERM- For purposes of this section, the term `report described in paragraph (3)' means a report, submitted by the Attorney General, which states in detail the policies and procedures that the Department of Justice has adopted subsequent to the enactment of this Act--

(A) to ensure that Department of Justice attorneys oppose sentencing adjustments, including downward departures, that are not supported by the facts and the law;

(B) to ensure that Department of Justice attorneys in such cases make a sufficient record so as to permit the possibility of an appeal;

(C) to delineate objective criteria, specified by the Attorney General, as to which such cases may warrant consideration of an appeal, either because of the nature or magnitude of the sentencing error, its prevalence in the district, or its prevalence with respect to a particular judge;

(D) to ensure that Department of Justice attorneys promptly notify the designated Department of Justice component in Washington concerning such adverse sentencing decisions; and

(E) to ensure the vigorous pursuit of appropriate and meritorious appeals of such adverse decisions.

(2) REPORT REQUIRED-

(A) IN GENERAL- Not later than 15 days after a district court's grant of a downward departure in any case, other than a case involving a downward departure for substantial assistance to authorities pursuant to section 5K1.1 of the United States Sentencing Guidelines, the Attorney General shall submit a report to the Committees on the Judiciary of the House of Representatives and the Senate containing the information described under subparagraph (B).

(B) CONTENTS- The report submitted pursuant to subparagraph (A) shall set forth--

(i) the case;

(ii) the facts involved;

(iii) the identity of the district court judge;

(iv) the district court's stated reasons, whether or not the court provided the United States with advance notice of its intention to depart; and

(v) the position of the parties with respect to the downward departure, whether or not the United States has filed, or intends to file, a motion for reconsideration.

(C) APPEAL OF THE DEPARTURE- Not later than 5 days after a decision by the Solicitor General regarding the authorization of an appeal of the departure, the Attorney General shall submit a report to the Committees on the Judiciary of the House of Representatives and the Senate that describes the decision of the Solicitor General and the basis for such decision.

(3) EFFECTIVE DATE- Paragraph (2) shall take effect on the day that is 91 days after the date of enactment of this Act, except that such paragraph shall not take effect if not more than 90 days after the date of enactment of this Act the Attorney General has submitted to the Judiciary Committees of the House of Representatives and the Senate the report described in paragraph (3).

(m) REFORM OF EXISTING PERMISSIBLE GROUNDS OF DOWNWARD DEPARTURES- Not later than 180 days after the enactment of this Act, the United States Sentencing Commission shall--

(1) review the grounds of downward departure that are authorized by the sentencing guidelines, policy statements, and official commentary of the Sentencing Commission; and

(2) promulgate, pursuant to section 994 of title 28, United States Code--

(A) appropriate amendments to the sentencing guidelines, policy statements, and official commentary to ensure that the incidence of downward departures are substantially reduced;

(B) a policy statement authorizing a downward departure of not more than 4 levels if the Government files a motion for such departure pursuant to an early disposition program authorized by the Attorney General and the United States Attorney; and

(C) any other conforming amendments to the sentencing guidelines, policy statements, and official commentary of the Sentencing Commission necessitated by this Act, including a revision of paragraph 4(b) of part A of chapter 1 and a revision of section 5K2.0.

(n) COMPOSITION OF SENTENCING COMMISSION-

(1) IN GENERAL- Section 991(a) of title 28, United States Code, is amended by striking `At least three' and inserting `Not more than 3'.

(2) APPLICABILITY- The amendment made under paragraph (1) shall not apply to any person who is serving, or who has been nominated to serve, as a member of the Sentencing Commission on the date of enactment of this Act.

TITLE V--OBSCENITY AND PORNOGRAPHY

Subtitle A--Child Obscenity and Pornography Prevention

SEC. 501. FINDINGS.

Congress finds the following:

(1) Obscenity and child pornography are not entitled to protection under the First Amendment under Miller v. California, 413 U.S. 15 (1973) (obscenity), or New York v.

Ferber, 458 U.S. 747 (1982) (child pornography) and thus may be prohibited.

(2) The Government has a compelling state interest in protecting children from those who sexually exploit them, including both child molesters and child pornographers. `The prevention of sexual exploitation and abuse of children constitutes a government objective of surpassing importance,' New York v. Ferber, 458 U.S. 747, 757 (1982), and this interest extends to stamping out the vice of child pornography at all levels in the distribution chain. Osborne v. Ohio, 495 U.S. 103, 110 (1990).

(3) The Government thus has a compelling interest in ensuring that the criminal prohibitions against child pornography remain enforceable and effective. `The most expeditious if not the only practical method of law enforcement may be to dry up the market for this material by imposing severe criminal penalties on persons selling, advertising, or otherwise promoting the product.' Ferber, 458 U.S. at 760.

(4) In 1982, when the Supreme Court decided Ferber, the technology did not exist to--

> (A) computer generate depictions of children that are indistinguishable from depictions of real children;
>
> (B) use parts of images of real children to create a composite image that is unidentifiable as a particular child and in a way that prevents even an expert from concluding that parts of images of real children were used; or
>
> (C) disguise pictures of real children being abused by making the image look computer-generated.

(5) Evidence submitted to the Congress, including from the National Center for Missing and Exploited Children, demonstrates that technology already exists to disguise depictions of real children to make them unidentifiable and to make depictions of real children appear computer-generated. The technology will soon exist, if it does not already, to computer generate realistic images of children.

(6) The vast majority of child pornography prosecutions today involve images contained on computer hard drives, computer disks, and/or related media.

(7) There is no substantial evidence that any of the child pornography images being trafficked today were made other than by the abuse of real children. Nevertheless, technological advances since Ferber have led many criminal defendants to suggest that the images of child pornography they possess are not those of real children, insisting that the government prove beyond a reasonable doubt that the images are not computer-generated. Such challenges increased significantly after the decision in Ashcroft v. Free Speech Coalition, 535 U.S. 234 (2002).

(8) Child pornography circulating on the Internet has, by definition, been digitally uploaded or scanned into computers and has been transferred over the Internet, often in different file formats, from trafficker to trafficker. An image seized from a collector of child pornography is rarely a first-generation product, and the retransmission of images can alter the image so as to make it difficult for even an expert conclusively to opine that a particular image depicts a real child. If the original image has been scanned from a paper version into a digital format, this task can be even harder since proper forensic assessment

may depend on the quality of the image scanned and the tools used to scan it.

(9) The impact of the Free Speech Coalition decision on the Government's ability to prosecute child pornography offenders is already evident. The Ninth Circuit has seen a significant adverse effect on prosecutions since the 1999 Ninth Circuit Court of Appeals decision in Free Speech Coalition. After that decision, prosecutions generally have been brought in the Ninth Circuit only in the most clear-cut cases in which the government can specifically identify the child in the depiction or otherwise identify the origin of the image. This is a fraction of meritorious child pornography cases. The National Center for Missing and Exploited Children testified that, in light of the Supreme Court's affirmation of the Ninth Circuit decision, prosecutors in various parts of the country have expressed concern about the continued viability of previously indicted cases as well as declined potentially meritorious prosecutions.

(10) Since the Supreme Court's decision in Free Speech Coalition, defendants in child pornography cases have almost universally raised the contention that the images in question could be virtual, thereby requiring the government, in nearly every child pornography prosecution, to find proof that the child is real. Some of these defense efforts have already been successful. In addition, the number of prosecutions being brought has been significantly and adversely affected as the resources required to be dedicated to each child pornography case now are significantly higher than ever before.

(11) Leading experts agree that, to the extent that the technology exists to computer generate realistic images of child pornography, the cost in terms of time, money, and expertise is--and for the foreseeable future will remain--prohibitively expensive. As a result, for the foreseeable future, it will be more cost-effective to produce child pornography using real children. It will not, however, be difficult or expensive to use readily available technology to disguise those depictions of real children to make them unidentifiable or to make them appear computer-generated.

(12) Child pornography results from the abuse of real children by sex offenders; the production of child pornography is a byproduct of, and not the primary reason for, the sexual abuse of children. There is no evidence that the future development of easy and inexpensive means of computer generating realistic images of children would stop or even reduce the sexual abuse of real children or the practice of visually recording that abuse.

(13) In the absence of congressional action, the difficulties in enforcing the child pornography laws will continue to grow increasingly worse. The mere prospect that the technology exists to create composite or computer-generated depictions that are indistinguishable from depictions of real children will allow defendants who possess images of real children to escape prosecution; for it threatens to create a reasonable doubt in every case of computer images even when a real child was abused. This threatens to render child pornography laws that protect real children unenforceable. Moreover, imposing an additional requirement that the Government prove beyond

a reasonable doubt that the defendant knew that the image was in fact a real child--as some courts have done-- threatens to result in the de facto legalization of the possession, receipt, and distribution of child pornography for all except the original producers of the material.

(14) To avoid this grave threat to the Government's unquestioned compelling interest in effective enforcement of the child pornography laws that protect real children, a statute must be adopted that prohibits a narrowly-defined subcategory of images.

(15) The Supreme Court's 1982 Ferber v. New York decision holding that child pornography was not protected drove child pornography off the shelves of adult bookstores. Congressional action is necessary now to ensure that open and notorious trafficking in such materials does not reappear, and even increase, on the Internet.

SEC. 502. IMPROVEMENTS TO PROHIBITION ON VIRTUAL CHILD PORNOGRAPHY.

(a) Section 2256(8) of title 18, United States Code, is amended--

> (1) so that subparagraph (B) reads as follows:
>> `(B) such visual depiction is a digital image, computer image, or computer-generated image that is, or is indistinguishable from, that of a minor engaging in sexually explicit conduct; or';
>
> (2) by striking `; or' at the end of subparagraph (C) and inserting a period; and

(3) by striking subparagraph (D).

(b) Section 2256(2) of title 18, United States Code, is amended to read as follows:

`(2)(A) Except as provided in subparagraph (B), `sexually explicit conduct' means actual or simulated--

`(i) sexual intercourse, including genital-genital, oral-genital, anal-genital, or oral-anal, whether between persons of the same or opposite sex;

`(ii) bestiality;

`(iii) masturbation;

`(iv) sadistic or masochistic abuse; or

`(v) lascivious exhibition of the genitals or pubic area of any person;

`(B) For purposes of subsection 8(B) of this section, `sexually explicit conduct' means--

`(i) graphic sexual intercourse, including genital-genital, oral-genital, anal-genital, or oral-anal, whether between persons of the same or opposite sex, or lascivious simulated sexual intercourse where the genitals, breast, or pubic area of any person is exhibited;

`(ii) graphic or lascivious simulated;

`(I) bestiality;

`(II) masturbation; or

`(III) sadistic or masochistic abuse;

or

`(iii) graphic or simulated lascivious exhibition of the genitals or pubic area of any person;'.

(c) Section 2256 is amended by inserting at the end the following new paragraphs:

`(10) `graphic', when used with respect to a depiction of sexually explicit conduct, means that a viewer can observe any part of the genitals or pubic area of any depicted person or animal during any part of the time that the sexually explicit conduct is being depicted; and

`(11) the term `indistinguishable' used with respect to a depiction, means virtually indistinguishable, in that the depiction is such that an ordinary person viewing the depiction would conclude that the depiction is of an actual minor engaged in sexually explicit conduct. This definition does not apply to depictions that are drawings, cartoons, sculptures, or paintings depicting minors or adults.'.

(d) Section 2252A(c) of title 18, United States Code, is amended to read as follows:

`(c) It shall be an affirmative defense to a charge of violating paragraph (1), (2), (3)(A), (4), or (5) of subsection (a) that--

`(1)(A) the alleged child pornography was produced using an actual person or persons engaging in sexually explicit conduct; and

`(B) each such person was an adult at the time the material was produced; or

`(2) the alleged child pornography was not produced using any actual minor or minors.

No affirmative defense under subsection (c)(2) shall be available in any prosecution that involves child pornography as described in section 2256(8)(C). A defendant may not assert an affirmative defense to a charge of violating paragraph (1), (2), (3)(A), (4), or (5) of subsection (a) unless, within the time provided for filing pretrial motions or at such time prior to trial as the judge may direct, but in no event later than 10 days before the commencement of the trial, the defendant provides the court and the United States with notice of the intent to assert such defense and the substance of any expert or other specialized testimony or evidence upon which the defendant intends to rely. If the defendant fails to comply with this subsection, the court shall, absent a finding of extraordinary circumstances that prevented timely compliance, prohibit the defendant from asserting such defense to a charge of violating paragraph (1), (2), (3)(A), (4), or (5) of subsection (a) or presenting any evidence for which the defendant has failed to provide proper and timely notice.'.

SEC. 503. CERTAIN ACTIVITIES RELATING TO MATERIAL CONSTITUTING OR CONTAINING CHILD PORNOGRAPHY.

Section 2252A of title 18, United States Code, is amended--
    (1) in subsection (a)--
        (A) by striking paragraph (3) and inserting the following:
    `(3) knowingly--

`(A) reproduces any child pornography for distribution through the mails, or in interstate or foreign commerce by any means, including by computer; or

`(B) advertises, promotes, presents, distributes, or solicits through the mails, or in interstate or foreign commerce by any means, including by computer, any material or purported material in a manner that reflects the belief, or that is intended to cause another to believe, that the material or purported material is, or contains--

> `(i) an obscene visual depiction of a minor engaging in sexually explicit conduct; or
> `(ii) a visual depiction of an actual minor engaging in sexually explicit conduct;';

(B) in paragraph (4), by striking `or' at the end;

(C) in paragraph (5), by striking the comma at the end and inserting `; or'; and

(D) by adding after paragraph (5) the following:

`(6) knowingly distributes, offers, sends, or provides to a minor any visual depiction, including any photograph, film, video, picture, or computer generated image or picture, whether made or produced by electronic, mechanical, or other means, where such visual depiction is, or appears to be, of a minor engaging in sexually explicit conduct--

> `(A) that has been mailed, shipped, or transported in interstate or foreign commerce by any means, including by computer;
> `(B) that was produced using materials that have been mailed, shipped, or transported in interstate

or foreign commerce by any means, including by computer; or

`(C) which distribution, offer, sending, or provision is accomplished using the mails or by transmitting or causing to be transmitted any wire communication in interstate or foreign commerce, including by computer, for purposes of inducing or persuading a minor to participate in any activity that is illegal.'; and

(2) in subsection (b)(1), by striking `paragraphs (1), (2), (3), or (4)' and inserting `paragraph (1), (2), (3), (4), or (6)'.

SEC. 504. OBSCENE CHILD PORNOGRAPHY.

(a) IN GENERAL- Chapter 71 of title 18, United States Code, is amended by inserting after section 1466 the following:

`Sec. 1466A. Obscene visual representations of the sexual abuse of children

`(a) IN GENERAL- Any person who, in a circumstance described in subsection (d), knowingly produces, distributes, receives, or possesses with intent to distribute, a visual depiction of any kind, including a drawing, cartoon, sculpture, or painting, that--

`(1)(A) depicts a minor engaging in sexually explicit conduct; and
`(B) is obscene; or
`(2)(A) depicts an image that is, or appears to be, of a minor engaging in graphic bestiality, sadistic or masochistic abuse, or sexual intercourse, including genital-

genital, oral-genital, anal-genital, or oral-anal, whether
between persons of the same or opposite sex; and
    `(B) lacks serious literary, artistic, political, or scientific
    value;
or attempts or conspires to do so, shall be subject to the penalties
provided in section 2252A(b)(1), including the penalties provided
for cases involving a prior conviction.
`(b) ADDITIONAL OFFENSES- Any person who, in a
circumstance described in subsection (d), knowingly possesses a
visual depiction of any kind, including a drawing, cartoon,
sculpture, or painting, that--
    `(1)(A) depicts a minor engaging in sexually explicit
    conduct; and
    `(B) is obscene; or
    `(2)(A) depicts an image that is, or appears to be, of a
    minor engaging in graphic bestiality, sadistic or
    masochistic abuse, or sexual intercourse, including genital-
    genital, oral-genital, anal-genital, or oral-anal, whether
    between persons of the same or opposite sex; and
    `(B) lacks serious literary, artistic, political, or scientific
    value;
or attempts or conspires to do so, shall be subject to the penalties
provided in section 2252A(b)(2), including the penalties provided
for cases involving a prior conviction.
`(c) NONREQUIRED ELEMENT OF OFFENSE- It is not a
required element of any offense under this section that the minor
depicted actually exist.
`(d) CIRCUMSTANCES- The circumstance referred to in
subsections (a) and (b) is that--
    `(1) any communication involved in or made in
    furtherance of the offense is communicated or transported

by the mail, or in interstate or foreign commerce by any means, including by computer, or any means or instrumentality of interstate or foreign commerce is otherwise used in committing or in furtherance of the commission of the offense;

`(2) any communication involved in or made in furtherance of the offense contemplates the transmission or transportation of a visual depiction by the mail, or in interstate or foreign commerce by any means, including by computer;

`(3) any person travels or is transported in interstate or foreign commerce in the course of the commission or in furtherance of the commission of the offense;

`(4) any visual depiction involved in the offense has been mailed, or has been shipped or transported in interstate or foreign commerce by any means, including by computer, or was produced using materials that have been mailed, or that have been shipped or transported in interstate or foreign commerce by any means, including by computer; or

`(5) the offense is committed in the special maritime and territorial jurisdiction of the United States or in any territory or possession of the United States.

`(e) AFFIRMATIVE DEFENSE- It shall be an affirmative defense to a charge of violating subsection (b) that the defendant--

`(1) possessed less than 3 such visual depictions; and

`(2) promptly and in good faith, and without retaining or allowing any person, other than a law enforcement agency, to access any such visual depiction--

`(A) took reasonable steps to destroy each such visual depiction; or

`(B) reported the matter to a law enforcement agency and afforded that agency access to each such visual depiction.

`(f) DEFINITIONS- For purposes of this section--

`(1) the term `visual depiction' includes undeveloped film and videotape, and data stored on a computer disk or by electronic means which is capable of conversion into a visual image, and also includes any photograph, film, video, picture, digital image or picture, computer image or picture, or computer generated image or picture, whether made or produced by electronic, mechanical, or other means;

`(2) the term `sexually explicit conduct' has the meaning given the term in section 2256(2)(A) or 2256(2)(B); and

`(3) the term `graphic', when used with respect to a depiction of sexually explicit conduct, means that a viewer can observe any part of the genitals or pubic area of any depicted person or animal during any part of the time that the sexually explicit conduct is being depicted.'.

(b) TECHNICAL AND CONFORMING AMENDMENT- The table of sections at the beginning of such chapter is amended by inserting after the item relating to section 1466 the following new item:

`1466A. Obscene visual representations of the sexual abuse of children.'.

(c) SENTENCING GUIDELINES-

(1) CATEGORY- Except as provided in paragraph (2), the applicable category of offense to be used in determining the sentencing range referred to in section 3553(a)(4) of title 18, United States Code, with respect to any person convicted under section 1466A of such title, shall be the

category of offenses described in section 2G2.2 of the Sentencing Guidelines.

(2) RANGES- The Sentencing Commission may promulgate guidelines specifically governing offenses under section 1466A of title 18, United States Code, if such guidelines do not result in sentencing ranges that are lower than those that would have applied under paragraph (1).

SEC. 505. ADMISSIBILITY OF EVIDENCE.

Section 2252A of title 18, United States Code, is amended by adding at the end the following:

`(e) ADMISSIBILITY OF EVIDENCE- On motion of the government, in any prosecution under this chapter or section 1466A, except for good cause shown, the name, address, social security number, or other nonphysical identifying information, other than the age or approximate age, of any minor who is depicted in any child pornography shall not be admissible and may be redacted from any otherwise admissible evidence, and the jury shall be instructed, upon request of the United States, that it can draw no inference from the absence of such evidence in deciding whether the child pornography depicts an actual minor.'.

SEC. 506. EXTRATERRITORIAL PRODUCTION OF CHILD PORNOGRAPHY FOR DISTRIBUTION IN THE UNITED STATES.

Section 2251 of title 18, United States Code, is amended--

(1) by striking `subsection (d)' each place that term appears and inserting `subsection (e)';

(2) by redesignating subsections (c) and (d) as subsections (d) and (e), respectively; and

(3) by inserting after subsection (b) the following:

`(c)(1) Any person who, in a circumstance described in paragraph (2), employs, uses, persuades, induces, entices, or coerces any minor to engage in, or who has a minor assist any other person to engage in, any sexually explicit conduct outside of the United States, its territories or possessions, for the purpose of producing any visual depiction of such conduct, shall be punished as provided under subsection (e).

`(2) The circumstance referred to in paragraph (1) is that--

`(A) the person intends such visual depiction to be transported to the United States, its territories or possessions, by any means, including by computer or mail; or

`(B) the person transports such visual depiction to the United States, its territories or possessions, by any means, including by computer or mail.'.

SEC. 507. STRENGTHENING ENHANCED PENALTIES FOR REPEAT OFFENDERS.

Sections 2251(e) (as redesignated by section 506(2)), 2252(b), and 2252A(b) of title 18, United States Code, are each amended--

(1) by inserting `chapter 71,' immediately before each occurrence of `chapter 109A,'; and

(2) by inserting `or under section 920 of title 10 (article 120 of the Uniform Code of Military Justice),' immediately before each occurrence of `or under the laws'.

SEC. 508. SERVICE PROVIDER REPORTING OF CHILD PORNOGRAPHY AND RELATED INFORMATION.

(a) Section 227 of the Victims of Child Abuse Act of 1990 (42 U.S.C. 13032) is amended--

    (1) in subsection (b)(1)--

        (A) by inserting `2252B,' after `2252A,'; and

        (B) by inserting `or a violation of section 1466A of that title,' after `of that title),';

    (2) in subsection (c), by inserting `or pursuant to' after `to comply with';

    (3) by amending subsection (f)(1)(D) to read as follows:

        `(D) where the report discloses a violation of State criminal law, to an appropriate official of a State or subdivision of a State for the purpose of enforcing such State law.';

    (4) by redesignating paragraph (3) of subsection (b) as paragraph (4); and

    (5) by inserting after paragraph (2) of subsection (b) the following new paragraph:

`(3) In addition to forwarding such reports to those agencies designated in subsection (b)(2), the National Center for Missing and Exploited Children is authorized to forward any such report to an appropriate official of a state or subdivision of a state for the purpose of enforcing state criminal law.'.

(b) Section 2702 of title 18, United States Code, is amended--

    (1) in subsection (b)--

        (A) in paragraph (6), by striking subparagraph (B);

(B) by redesignating paragraphs (6) and (7) as paragraphs (7) and (8) respectively;

(C) by striking `or' at the end of paragraph (5); and

(D) by inserting after paragraph (5) the following new paragraph:

`(6) to the National Center for Missing and Exploited Children, in connection with a report submitted thereto under section 227 of the Victims of Child Abuse Act of 1990 (42 U.S.C. 13032);'; and

(2) in subsection (c)--

(A) by striking `or' at the end of paragraph (4);

(B) by redesignating paragraph (5) as paragraph (6); and

(C) by adding after paragraph (4) the following new paragraph:

`(5) to the National Center for Missing and Exploited Children, in connection with a report submitted thereto under section 227 of the Victims of Child Abuse Act of 1990 (42 U.S.C. 13032); or'.

SEC. 509. INVESTIGATIVE AUTHORITY RELATING TO CHILD PORNOGRAPHY.

Section 3486(a)(1)(C)(i) of title 18, United States Code, is amended by striking `the name, address' and all that follows through `subscriber or customer utilized' and inserting `the information specified in section 2703(c)(2)'.

SEC. 510. CIVIL REMEDIES.

Section 2252A of title 18, United States Code, as amended by this Act, is amended by adding at the end the following:

`(f) CIVIL REMEDIES-

> `(1) IN GENERAL- Any person aggrieved by reason of the conduct prohibited under subsection (a) or (b) or section 1466A may commence a civil action for the relief set forth in paragraph (2).

> `(2) RELIEF- In any action commenced in accordance with paragraph (1), the court may award appropriate relief, including--

>> `(A) temporary, preliminary, or permanent injunctive relief;

>> `(B) compensatory and punitive damages; and

>> `(C) the costs of the civil action and reasonable fees for attorneys and expert witnesses.'.

SEC. 511. RECORDKEEPING REQUIREMENTS.

(a) IN GENERAL- Section 2257 of title 18, United States Code, is amended--

> (1) in subsection (d)(2), by striking `of this section' and inserting `of this chapter or chapter 71,';

> (2) in subsection (h)(3), by inserting `, computer generated image, digital image, or picture,' after `video tape'; and

> (3) in subsection (i)--

>> (A) by striking `not more than 2 years' and inserting `not more than 5 years'; and

>> (B) by striking `5 years' and inserting `10 years'.

(b) REPORT- Not later than 1 year after enactment of this Act, the Attorney General shall submit to Congress a report detailing the number of times since January 1993 that the Department of Justice has inspected the records of any producer of materials regulated pursuant to section 2257 of title 18, United States Code, and section 75 of title 28 of the Code of Federal Regulations. The Attorney General shall indicate the number of violations prosecuted as a result of those inspections.

SEC. 512. SENTENCING ENHANCEMENTS FOR INTERSTATE TRAVEL TO ENGAGE IN SEXUAL ACT WITH A JUVENILE.

Pursuant to its authority under section 994(p) of title 28, United States Code, and in accordance with this section, the United States Sentencing Commission shall review and, as appropriate, amend the Federal Sentencing Guidelines and policy statements to ensure that guideline penalties are adequate in cases that involve interstate travel with the intent to engage in a sexual act with a juvenile in violation of section 2423 of title 18, United States Code, to deter and punish such conduct.

SEC. 513. MISCELLANEOUS PROVISIONS.

(a) APPOINTMENT OF TRIAL ATTORNEYS-
> (1) IN GENERAL- Not later than 6 months after the date of enactment of this Act, the Attorney General shall appoint 25 additional trial attorneys to the Child Exploitation and Obscenity Section of the Criminal Division of the Department of Justice or to appropriate United States Attorney's Offices, and those trial attorneys shall have as their primary focus, the investigation and prosecution of Federal child pornography and obscenity laws.

(2) AUTHORIZATION OF APPROPRIATIONS- There are authorized to be appropriated to the Department of Justice such sums as may be necessary to carry out this subsection.

(b) REPORT TO CONGRESSIONAL COMMITTEES-

(1) IN GENERAL- Not later than 9 months after the date of enactment of this Act, and every 2 years thereafter, the Attorney General shall report to the Chairpersons and Ranking Members of the Committees on the Judiciary of the Senate and the House of Representatives on the Federal enforcement actions under chapter 110 or section 1466A of title 18, United States Code.

(2) CONTENTS- The report required under paragraph (1) shall include--

(A) an evaluation of the prosecutions brought under chapter 110 or section 1466A of title 18, United States Code;

(B) an outcome-based measurement of performance; and

(C) an analysis of the technology being used by the child pornography industry.

(c) SENTENCING GUIDELINES- Pursuant to its authority under section 994(p) of title 28, United States Code, and in accordance with this section, the United States Sentencing Commission shall review and, as appropriate, amend the Federal Sentencing Guidelines and policy statements to ensure that the guidelines are adequate to deter and punish conduct that involves a violation of paragraph (3)(B) or (6) of section 2252A(a) of title 18, United States Code, as created by this Act. With respect to the guidelines for section 2252A(a)(3)(B), the Commission shall consider the relative culpability of promoting, presenting, describing, or distributing material in violation of that section as compared with solicitation of such material.

Subtitle B--Truth in Domain Names

SEC. 521. MISLEADING DOMAIN NAMES ON THE INTERNET.

(a) IN GENERAL- Chapter 110 of title 18, United States Code, is amended by inserting after section 2252A the following:

`Sec. 2252B. Misleading domain names on the Internet

`(a) Whoever knowingly uses a misleading domain name on the Internet with the intent to deceive a person into viewing material constituting obscenity shall be fined under this title or imprisoned not more than 2 years, or both.

`(b) Whoever knowingly uses a misleading domain name on the Internet with the intent to deceive a minor into viewing material that is harmful to minors on the Internet shall be fined under this title or imprisoned not more than 4 years, or both.

`(c) For the purposes of this section, a domain name that includes a word or words to indicate the sexual content of the site, such as `sex' or `porn', is not misleading.

`(d) For the purposes of this section, the term `material that is harmful to minors' means any communication, consisting of nudity, sex, or excretion, that, taken as a whole and with reference to its context--

      `(1) predominantly appeals to a prurient interest of minors;

`(2) is patently offensive to prevailing standards in the adult community as a whole with respect to what is suitable material for minors; and
`(3) lacks serious literary, artistic, political, or scientific value for minors.
`(e) For the purposes of subsection (d), the term `sex' means acts of masturbation, sexual intercourse, or physical contact with a person's genitals, or the condition of human male or female genitals when in a state of sexual stimulation or arousal.'.
(b) CLERICAL AMENDMENT- The table of sections at the beginning of chapter 110 of title 18, United States Code, is amended by inserting after the item relating to section 2252A the following new item:
`2252B. Misleading domain names on the Internet.'.

TITLE VI--MISCELLANEOUS PROVISIONS

SEC. 601. PENALTIES FOR USE OF MINORS IN CRIMES OF VIOLENCE.

Chapter 1 of title 18, United States Code, is amended by adding at the end the following:

`Sec. 25. Use of minors in crimes of violence

`(a) DEFINITIONS- In this section, the following definitions shall apply:
`(1) CRIME OF VIOLENCE- The term `crime of violence' has the meaning set forth in section 16.
`(2) MINOR- The term `minor' means a person who has not reached 18 years of age.

`(3) USES- The term `uses' means employs, hires, persuades, induces, entices, or coerces.

`(b) PENALTIES- Any person who is 18 years of age or older, who intentionally uses a minor to commit a crime of violence for which such person may be prosecuted in a court of the United States, or to assist in avoiding detection or apprehension for such an offense, shall--

   `(1) for the first conviction, be subject to twice the maximum term of imprisonment and twice the maximum fine that would otherwise be authorized for the offense; and

   `(2) for each subsequent conviction, be subject to 3 times the maximum term of imprisonment and 3 times the maximum fine that would otherwise be authorized for the offense.'.

(b) CLERICAL AMENDMENT- The table of sections at the beginning of chapter 1 of title 18, United States Code, is amended by adding at the end the following:

   `25. Use of minors in crimes of violence.'.

SEC. 602. SENSE OF CONGRESS.

(a) FOCUS OF INVESTIGATION AND PROSECUTION- It is the sense of Congress that the Child Exploitation and Obscenity Section of the Criminal Division of the Department of Justice should focus its investigative and prosecutorial efforts on major producers, distributors, and sellers of obscene material and child pornography that use misleading methods to market their material to children.

(b) VOLUNTARY LIMITATION ON WEBSITE FRONT PAGES- It is the sense of Congress that the online commercial adult entertainment industry should voluntarily refrain from placing obscenity, child pornography, or material that is harmful to minors on the front pages of their websites to protect juveniles from material that may negatively impact their social, moral, and psychological development.

SEC. 603. COMMUNICATIONS DECENCY ACT OF 1996.

Section 223 of the Communications Act of 1934 (47 U.S.C. 223) is amended--

(1) in subsection (a)(1)--

(A) in subparagraph (A), by striking `, lewd, lascivious, filthy, or indecent' and inserting `or child pornography'; and

(B) in subparagraph (B), by striking `indecent' and inserting `child pornography'; and

(2) in subsection (d)(1), by striking `, in context, depicts or describes, in terms patently offensive as measured by contemporary community standards, sexual or excretory activities or organs' and inserting `is obscene or child pornography'.

SEC. 604. INTERNET AVAILABILITY OF INFORMATION CONCERNING REGISTERED SEX OFFENDERS.

(a) IN GENERAL- Section 170101(e)(2) of the Violent Crime Control and Law Enforcement Act of 1994 (42 U.S.C. 14071(e)(2)) is amended by adding at the end the following: `The release of information under this paragraph shall include the maintenance of an Internet site containing such information that is available to the public and instructions on the process for correcting information that a person alleges to be erroneous.'.

(b) COMPLIANCE DATE- Each State shall implement the amendment made by this section within 3 years after the date of enactment of this Act, except that the Attorney General may grant an additional 2 years to a State that is making a good faith effort to implement the amendment made by this section.

(c) NATIONAL INTERNET SITE- The Crimes Against Children Section of the Criminal Division of the Department of Justice shall create a national Internet site that links all State Internet sites established pursuant to this section.

SEC. 605. REGISTRATION OF CHILD PORNOGRAPHERS IN THE NATIONAL SEX OFFENDER REGISTRY.

(a) JACOB WETTERLING CRIMES AGAINST CHILDREN AND SEXUALLY VIOLENT OFFENDER REGISTRATION PROGRAM- Section 170101 of the Violent Crime Control and Law Enforcement Act of 1994 (42 U.S.C. 14071) is amended--

> (1) by striking the section heading and inserting the following:

`SEC.170101.JACOB WETTERLING CRIMES AGAINST CHILDREN AND SEXUALLY VIOLENT OFFENDER REGISTRATION PROGRAM.';

> and
>
> (2) in subsection (a)(3)--
>> (A) in clause (vii), by striking `or' at the end;
>> (B) by redesignating clause (viii) as clause (ix); and
>> (C) by inserting after clause (vii) the following:

'(viii) production or distribution of child pornography, as described in section 2251, 2252, or 2252A of title 18, United States Code; or'.

(b) AUTHORIZATION OF APPROPRIATIONS- There are authorized to be appropriated to the Department of Justice, for each of fiscal years 2004 through 2007, such sums as may be necessary to carry out the amendments made by this section.

SEC. 606. GRANTS TO STATES FOR COSTS OF COMPLIANCE WITH NEW SEX OFFENDER REGISTRY REQUIREMENTS.

Section 170101(i)(3) of the Violent Crime Control and Law Enforcement Act of 1994 (42 U.S.C. 14071(i)(3)) is amended to read as follows:

'(3) AUTHORIZATION OF APPROPRIATIONS- There is authorized to be appropriated for each of the fiscal years 2004 through 2007 such sums as may be necessary to carry out the provisions of section 1701(d)(10) of the Omnibus Crime Control and Safe Streets Act of 1968 (42 U.S.C. 3796dd(d)(10)), as added by the PROTECT Act.'.

SEC. 607. SAFE ID ACT.

(a) SHORT TITLE- This section may be cited as the 'Secure Authentication Feature and Enhanced Identification Defense Act of 2003' or 'SAFE ID Act'.

(b) FRAUD AND FALSE STATEMENTS-

(1) OFFENSES- Section 1028(a) of title 18, United States Code, is amended--

(A) in paragraph (1), by inserting `, authentication feature,' after `an identification document';

(B) in paragraph (2)--

(i) by inserting `, authentication feature,' after `an identification document'; and

(ii) by inserting `or feature' after `such document';

(C) in paragraph (3), by inserting `, authentication features,' after `possessor)';

(D) in paragraph (4)--

(i) by inserting `, authentication feature,' after `possessor)'; and

(ii) by inserting `or feature' after `such document';

(E) in paragraph (5), by inserting `or authentication feature' after `implement' each place that term appears;

(F) in paragraph (6)--

(i) by inserting `or authentication feature' before `that is or appears';

(ii) by inserting `or authentication feature' before `of the United States';

(iii) by inserting `or feature' after `such document'; and

(iv) by striking `or' at the end;

(G) in paragraph (7), by inserting `or' after the semicolon; and

(H) by inserting after paragraph (7) the following:

`(8) knowingly traffics in false authentication features for use in false identification documents, document-making implements, or means of identification;'.

(2) PENALTIES- Section 1028(b) of title 18, United States Code, is amended--

    (A) in paragraph (1)--

        (i) in subparagraph (A)--

            (I) by inserting `, authentication feature,' before `or false'; and

            (II) in clause (i), by inserting `or authentication feature' after `document'; and

        (ii) in subparagraph (B), by inserting `, authentication features,' before `or false'; and

    (B) in paragraph (2)(A), by inserting `, authentication feature,' before `or a false'.

(3) CIRCUMSTANCES- Section 1028(c)(1) of title 18, United States Code, is amended by inserting `, authentication feature,' before `or false' each place that term appears.

(4) DEFINITIONS- Section 1028(d) of title 18, United States Code, is amended--

    (A) by redesignating paragraphs (1), (2), (3), (4), (5), (6), (7), and (8) as paragraphs (2), (3), (4), (7), (8), (9), (10), and (11), respectively;

    (B) by inserting before paragraph (2), as redesignated, the following:

`(1) the term `authentication feature' means any hologram, watermark, certification, symbol, code, image, sequence of numbers or letters, or other feature that either individually or in combination with another feature is used by the issuing authority on an identification document, document-making implement, or means of identification to determine if the document is counterfeit, altered, or otherwise falsified;';

> (C) in paragraph (4)(A), as redesignated, by inserting `or was issued under the authority of a governmental entity but was subsequently altered for purposes of deceit' after `entity';
>
> (D) by inserting after paragraph (4), as redesignated, the following:

`(5) the term `false authentication feature' means an authentication feature that--

> `(A) is genuine in origin, but, without the authorization of the issuing authority, has been tampered with or altered for purposes of deceit;
>
> `(B) is genuine, but has been distributed, or is intended for distribution, without the authorization of the issuing authority and not in connection with a lawfully made identification document, document-making implement, or means of identification to which such authentication feature is intended to be affixed or embedded by the respective issuing authority; or
>
> `(C) appears to be genuine, but is not;

`(6) the term `issuing authority'--

> `(A) means any governmental entity or agency that is authorized to issue identification documents, means of identification, or authentication features; and
>
> `(B) includes the United States Government, a State, a political subdivision of a State, a foreign government, a political subdivision of a foreign

government, or an international government or quasi-governmental organization;';

(E) in paragraph (10), as redesignated, by striking `and' at the end;

(F) in paragraph (11), as redesignated, by striking the period at the end and inserting `; and'; and

(G) by adding at the end the following:

`(12) the term `traffic' means--

`(A) to transport, transfer, or otherwise dispose of, to another, as consideration for anything of value; or

`(B) to make or obtain control of with intent to so transport, transfer, or otherwise dispose of.'.

(5) ADDITIONAL PENALTIES- Section 1028 of title 18, United States Code, is amended--

(A) by redesignating subsection (h) as subsection (i); and

(B) by inserting after subsection (g) the following:

`(h) FORFEITURE; DISPOSITION- In the circumstance in which any person is convicted of a violation of subsection (a), the court shall order, in addition to the penalty prescribed, the forfeiture and destruction or other disposition of all illicit authentication features, identification documents, document-making implements, or means of identification.'.

(6) TECHNICAL AND CONFORMING AMENDMENT- Section 1028 of title 18, United States Code, is amended in the heading by inserting `, authentication features,' after `documents'.

SEC. 608. ILLICIT DRUG ANTI-PROLIFERATION ACT.

(a) SHORT TITLE- This section may be cited as the `Illicit Drug Anti-Proliferation Act of 2003'.

(b) OFFENSES-

    (1) IN GENERAL- Section 416(a) of the Controlled Substances Act (21 U.S.C. 856(a)) is amended--

        (A) in paragraph (1), by striking `open or maintain any place' and inserting `open, lease, rent, use, or maintain any place, whether permanently or temporarily,'; and

        (B) by striking paragraph (2) and inserting the following:

`(2) manage or control any place, whether permanently or temporarily, either as an owner, lessee, agent, employee, occupant, or mortgagee, and knowingly and intentionally rent, lease, profit from, or make available for use, with or without compensation, the place for the purpose of unlawfully manufacturing, storing, distributing, or using a controlled substance.'.

(2) TECHNICAL AMENDMENT- The heading to section 416 of the Controlled Substances Act (21 U.S.C. 856) is amended to read as follows:

`SEC. 416. MAINTAINING DRUG-INVOLVED PREMISES.'.

    (3) CONFORMING AMENDMENT- The table of contents to title II of the Comprehensive Drug Abuse and Prevention Act of 1970 is amended by striking the item relating to section 416 and inserting the following:

    `Sec. 416. Maintaining drug-involved premises.'.

(c) CIVIL PENALTY AND EQUITABLE RELIEF FOR MAINTAINING DRUG-INVOLVED PREMISES- Section 416 of the Controlled Substances Act (21 U.S.C. 856) is amended by adding at the end the following:

`(d)(1) Any person who violates subsection (a) shall be subject to a civil penalty of not more than the greater of--

 `(A) $250,000; or

 `(B) 2 times the gross receipts, either known or estimated, that were derived from each violation that is attributable to the person.

`(2) If a civil penalty is calculated under paragraph (1)(B), and there is more than 1 defendant, the court may apportion the penalty between multiple violators, but each violator shall be jointly and severally liable for the civil penalty under this subsection.

`(e) Any person who violates subsection (a) shall be subject to declaratory and injunctive remedies as set forth in section 403(f).'.

(d) DECLARATORY AND INJUNCTIVE REMEDIES- Section 403(f)(1) of the Controlled Substances Act (21 U.S.C. 843(f)(1)) is amended by striking `this section or section 402' and inserting `this section, section 402, or 416'.

(e) SENTENCING COMMISSION GUIDELINES- The United States Sentencing Commission shall--

 (1) review the Federal sentencing guidelines with respect to offenses involving gamma hydroxybutyric acid (GHB);

 (2) consider amending the Federal sentencing guidelines to provide for increased penalties such that those penalties reflect the seriousness of offenses involving GHB and the need to deter them; and

 (3) take any other action the Commission considers necessary to carry out this section.

(f) AUTHORIZATION OF APPROPRIATIONS FOR A DEMAND REDUCTION COORDINATOR- There is authorized to be appropriated $5,900,000 to the Drug Enforcement Administration of the Department of Justice for the hiring of a special agent in each State to serve as a Demand Reduction Coordinator.

(g) AUTHORIZATION OF APPROPRIATIONS FOR DRUG EDUCATION- There is authorized to be appropriated such sums as necessary to the Drug Enforcement Administration of the Department of Justice to educate youth, parents, and other interested adults about club drugs.

SEC. 609. DEFINITION OF VEHICLE.

Section 1993(c) of title 18, United States Code, is amended--

    (1) in paragraph (7), by striking `and' at the end;

    (2) in paragraph (8), by striking the period at the end and inserting `; and'; and

    (3) by adding at the end the following:

`(9) the term `vehicle' means any carriage or other contrivance used, or capable of being used, as a means of transportation on land, water, or through the air.'.

SEC. 610. AUTHORIZATION OF JOHN DOE DNA INDICTMENTS.

(a) LIMITATION- Section 3282 of title 18, United States Code, is amended--

    (1) by striking `Except' and inserting the following:

`(a) IN GENERAL- Except'; and

    (2) by adding at the end the following:

`(b) DNA PROFILE INDICTMENT-

    `(1) IN GENERAL- In any indictment for an offense under chapter 109A for which the identity of the accused is unknown, it shall be sufficient to describe the accused as an individual whose name is unknown, but who has a particular DNA profile.

`(2) EXCEPTION- Any indictment described under paragraph (1), which is found not later than 5 years after the offense under chapter 109A is committed, shall not be subject to

> `(A) the limitations period described under subsection (a); and
>
> `(B) the provisions of chapter 208 until the individual is arrested or served with a summons in connection with the charges contained in the indictment.

`(3) DEFINED TERM- For purposes of this subsection, the term `DNA profile' means a set of DNA identification characteristics.'.

(b) RULES OF CRIMINAL PROCEDURE- Rule 7(c)(1) of the Federal Rules of Criminal Procedure is amended by adding at the end the following: `For purposes of an indictment referred to in section 3282 of title 18, United States Code, for which the identity of the defendant is unknown, it shall be sufficient for the indictment to describe the defendant as an individual whose name is unknown, but who has a particular DNA profile, as that term is defined in that section 3282.'.

SEC. 611. TRANSITIONAL HOUSING ASSISTANCE GRANTS FOR CHILD VICTIMS OF DOMESTIC VIOLENCE, STALKING, OR SEXUAL ASSAULT.

Subtitle B of the Violence Against Women Act of 1994 (42 U.S.C. 13701 note; 108 Stat. 1925) is amended by adding at the end the following:

`CHAPTER 11--TRANSITIONAL HOUSING ASSISTANCE GRANTS FOR CHILD VICTIMS OF DOMESTIC VIOLENCE, STALKING, OR SEXUAL ASSAULT

`SEC. 40299. TRANSITIONAL HOUSING ASSISTANCE GRANTS FOR CHILD VICTIMS OF DOMESTIC VIOLENCE, STALKING, OR SEXUAL ASSAULT.

`(a) IN GENERAL- The Attorney General, acting in consultation with the Director of the Violence Against Women Office of the Department of Justice, shall award grants under this section to States, units of local government, Indian tribes, and other organizations (referred to in this section as the `recipient') to carry out programs to provide assistance to minors, adults, and their dependents--

> `(1) who are homeless, or in need of transitional housing or other housing assistance, as a result of fleeing a situation of domestic violence; and
>
> `(2) for whom emergency shelter services or other crisis intervention services are unavailable or insufficient.

`(b) GRANTS- Grants awarded under this section may be used for programs that provide--

> `(1) short-term housing assistance, including rental or utilities payments assistance and assistance with related expenses such as payment of security deposits and other costs incidental to relocation to transitional housing for persons described in subsection (a); and

`(2) support services designed to enable a minor, an adult, or a dependent of such minor or adult, who is fleeing a situation of domestic violence to--

>`(A) locate and secure permanent housing; and
>`(B) integrate into a community by providing that minor, adult, or dependent with services, such as transportation, counseling, child care services, case management, employment counseling, and other assistance.

`(c) DURATION-

>`(1) IN GENERAL- Except as provided in paragraph (2), a minor, an adult, or a dependent, who receives assistance under this section shall receive that assistance for not more than 18 months.

>`(2) WAIVER- The recipient of a grant under this section may waive the restriction under paragraph (1) for not more than an additional 6 month period with respect to any minor, adult, or dependent, who--

>>`(A) has made a good-faith effort to acquire permanent housing; and
>>`(B) has been unable to acquire permanent housing.

`(d) APPLICATION-

>`(1) IN GENERAL- Each eligible entity desiring a grant under this section shall submit an application to the Attorney General at such time, in such manner, and accompanied by such information as the Attorney General may reasonably require.

>`(2) CONTENTS- Each application submitted pursuant to paragraph (1) shall--

>>`(A) describe the activities for which assistance under this section is sought; and

`(B) provide such additional assurances as the Attorney General determines to be essential to ensure compliance with the requirements of this section.

`(3) APPLICATION- Nothing in this subsection shall be construed to require--

`(A) victims to participate in the criminal justice system in order to receive services; or

`(B) domestic violence advocates to breach client confidentiality.

`(e) REPORT TO THE ATTORNEY GENERAL-

`(1) IN GENERAL- A recipient of a grant under this section shall annually prepare and submit to the Attorney General a report describing--

`(A) the number of minors, adults, and dependents assisted under this section; and

`(B) the types of housing assistance and support services provided under this section.

`(2) CONTENTS- Each report prepared and submitted pursuant to paragraph (1) shall include information regarding--

`(A) the amount of housing assistance provided to each minor, adult, or dependent, assisted under this section and the reason for that assistance;

`(B) the number of months each minor, adult, or dependent, received assistance under this section;

`(C) the number of minors, adults, and dependents who--

`(i) were eligible to receive assistance under this section; and

`(ii) were not provided with assistance
under this section solely due to a lack of
available housing; and
`(D) the type of support services provided to each
minor, adult, or dependent, assisted under this
section.
`(f) REPORT TO CONGRESS-
`(1) REPORTING REQUIREMENT- The Attorney General,
with the Director of the Violence Against Women Office,
shall annually prepare and submit to the Committee on the
Judiciary of the House of Representatives and the
Committee on the Judiciary of the Senate a report that
contains a compilation of the information contained in the
report submitted under subsection (e).
`(2) AVAILABILITY OF REPORT- In order to coordinate
efforts to assist the victims of domestic violence, the
Attorney General, in coordination with the Director of the
Violence Against Women Office, shall transmit a copy of
the report submitted under paragraph (1) to--
`(A) the Office of Community Planning and
Development at the United States Department of
Housing and Urban Development; and
`(B) the Office of Women's Health at the United
States Department of Health and Human Services.
`(g) AUTHORIZATION OF APPROPRIATIONS-
`(1) IN GENERAL- There are authorized to be
appropriated to carry out this section $30,000,000 for each
of the fiscal years 2004 through 2008.
`(2) LIMITATIONS- Of the amount made available to carry
out this section in any fiscal year, not more than 3 percent

may be used by the Attorney General for salaries and administrative expenses.

`(3) MINIMUM AMOUNT-

`(A) IN GENERAL- Except as provided in subparagraph (B), unless all eligible applications submitted by any States, units of local government, Indian tribes, or organizations within a State for a grant under this section have been funded, that State, together with the grantees within the State (other than Indian tribes), shall be allocated in each fiscal year, not less than 0.75 percent of the total amount appropriated in the fiscal year for grants pursuant to this section.

`(B) EXCEPTION- The United States Virgin Islands, American Samoa, Guam, and the Northern Mariana Islands shall each be allocated not less than 0.25 percent of the total amount appropriated in the fiscal year for grants pursuant to this section.'.

Speaker of the House of Representatives.

Vice President of the United States and

President of the Senate.

The United States signed and ratified the Palermo Protocol on December 3, 2005 and became an official party to this agreement.

PROTOCOL TO PREVENT, SUPPRESS AND PUNISH TRAFFICKING IN PERSONS, ESPECIALLY WOMEN AND CHILDREN, SUPPLEMENTING THE UNITED NATIONS CONVENTION AGAINST TRANSNATIONAL ORGANIZED CRIME

UNITED NATIONS

2000

PROTOCOL TO PREVENT, SUPPRESS AND PUNISH TRAFFICKING IN PERSONS, ESPECIALLY WOMEN AND CHILDREN, SUPPLEMENTING THE UNITED NATIONS CONVENTION AGAINST TRANSNATIONALORGANIZED CRIME

Preamble

The States Parties to this Protocol,

Declaring that effective action to prevent and combat trafficking in persons, especially women and children, requires a comprehensive international approach in the countries of origin, transit and destination that includes measures to prevent such trafficking, to punish the traffickers and to protect the victims of such trafficking, including by protecting their internationally recognized human rights,

Taking into account the fact that, despite the existence of a variety of international instruments containing rules and practical measures to combat the exploitation of persons, especially women and children, there is no universal instrument that addresses all aspects of trafficking in persons,

Concerned that, in the absence of such an instrument, persons who are vulnerable to trafficking will not be sufficiently protected,

Recalling General Assembly resolution 53/111 of 9 December 1998, in which the Assembly decided to establish an open-ended intergovernmental ad hoc committee for the purpose of elaborating a comprehensive international convention against transnational organized crime and of discussing the elaboration of, inter alia, an international instrument addressing trafficking in women and children,

Convinced that supplementing the United Nations Convention against Transnational Organized Crime with an international instrument for the prevention, suppression and punishment of trafficking in persons, especially women and children, will be useful in preventing and combating that crime,

Have agreed as follows:

I. General provisions

Article 1

Relation with the United Nations Convention against Transnational Organized Crime

1. This Protocol supplements the United Nations Convention against Transnational Organized Crime. It shall be interpreted together with the Convention.

2. The provisions of the Convention shall apply, mutatis mutandis, to this Protocol unless otherwise provided herein.

3. The offences established in accordance with article 5 of this Protocol shall be regarded as offences established in accordance with the Convention.

Article 2
Statement of purpose

The purposes of this Protocol are:

(a) To prevent and combat trafficking in persons, paying particular attention to women and children;

(b) To protect and assist the victims of such trafficking, with full respect for their human rights; and

(c) To promote cooperation among States Parties in order to meet those objectives.

Article 3
Use of terms

For the purposes of this Protocol:

(a) "Trafficking in persons" shall mean the recruitment, transportation, transfer, harboring or receipt of persons, by means of the threat or use of force or other forms of coercion, of abduction, of fraud, of deception, of the abuse of power or of a position of vulnerability or of the giving or receiving of payments or benefits to achieve the consent of a person having control over another person, for the purpose of exploitation. Exploitation shall include, at a minimum, the exploitation of the prostitution of others or other forms of sexual exploitation, forced labor or services, slavery or practices similar to slavery, servitude or the removal of organs;

(b) The consent of a victim of trafficking in persons to the intended exploitation set forth in subparagraph (a) of this article shall be irrelevant where any of the means set forth in subparagraph (a) have been used;

(c) The recruitment, transportation, transfer, harboring or receipt of a child for the purpose of exploitation shall be considered "trafficking in persons" even if this does not involve any of the means set forth in subparagraph (a) of this article;

(d) "Child" shall mean any person under eighteen years of age.

Article 4
Scope of application

This Protocol shall apply, except as otherwise stated herein, to the prevention, investigation and prosecution of the offences established in accordance with article 5 of this Protocol, where those offences are transnational in nature and involve an organized criminal group, as well as to the protection of victims of such offences.

Article 5
Criminalization

1. Each State Party shall adopt such legislative and other measures as may be necessary to establish as criminal offences the conduct set forth in article 3 of this Protocol, when committed intentionally.

2. Each State Party shall also adopt such legislative and other measures as may be necessary to establish as criminal offences:

(a) Subject to the basic concepts of its legal system, attempting to commit an offence established in accordance with paragraph 1 of this article;

(b) Participating as an accomplice in an offence established in accordance with paragraph 1 of this article; and

(c) Organizing or directing other persons to commit an offence established in accordance with paragraph 1 of this article.

II. Protection of victims of trafficking in persons

Article 6
Assistance to and protection of victims of trafficking in persons

1. In appropriate cases and to the extent possible under its domestic law, each State Party shall protect the privacy and identity of victims of trafficking in persons, including, inter alia, by making legal proceedings relating to such trafficking confidential.

2. Each State Party shall ensure that its domestic legal or administrative system contains measures that provide to victims of trafficking in persons, in appropriate cases:

(a) Information on relevant court and administrative proceedings;

(b) Assistance to enable their views and concerns to be presented and considered at appropriate stages of criminal proceedings against offenders, in a manner not prejudicial to the rights of the defense.

3. Each State Party shall consider implementing measures to provide for the physical, psychological and social recovery of

victims of trafficking in persons, including, in appropriate cases, in cooperation with non-governmental organizations, other relevant organizations and other elements of civil society, and, in particular, the provision of:

(a) Appropriate housing;

(b) Counseling and information, in particular as regards their legal rights, in a language that the victims of trafficking in persons can understand;

(c) Medical, psychological and material assistance; and

(d) Employment, educational and training opportunities.

4. Each State Party shall take into account, in applying the provisions of this article, the age, gender and special needs of victims of trafficking in persons, in particular the special needs of children, including appropriate housing, education and care.

5. Each State Party shall endeavor to provide for the physical safety of victims of trafficking in persons while they are within its territory.

6. Each State Party shall ensure that its domestic legal system contains measures that offer victims of trafficking in persons the possibility of obtaining compensation for damage suffered.

Article 7
Status of victims of trafficking in persons in receiving States

1. In addition to taking measures pursuant to article 6 of this Protocol, each State Party shall consider adopting legislative or other appropriate measures that permit victims of trafficking in

persons to remain in its territory, temporarily or permanently, in appropriate cases.

2. In implementing the provision contained in paragraph 1 of this article, each State Party shall give appropriate consideration to humanitarian and compassionate factors.

Article 8
Repatriation of victims of trafficking in persons

1. The State Party of which a victim of trafficking in persons is a national or in which the person had the right of permanent residence at the time of entry into the territory of the receiving State Party shall facilitate and accept, with due regard for the safety of that person, the return of that person without undue or unreasonable delay.

2. When a State Party returns a victim of trafficking in persons to a State Party of which that person is a national or in which he or she had, at the time of entry into the territory of the receiving State Party, the right of permanent residence, such return shall be with due regard for the safety of that person and for the status of any legal proceedings related to the fact that the person is a victim of trafficking and shall preferably be voluntary.

3. At the request of a receiving State Party, a requested State Party shall, without undue or unreasonable delay, verify whether a person who is a victim of trafficking in persons is its national or had the right of permanent residence in its territory at the time of entry into the territory of the receiving State Party.

4. In order to facilitate the return of a victim of trafficking in persons who is without proper documentation, the State Party of which that person is a national or in which he or she had the right

of permanent residence at the time of entry into the territory of the receiving State Party shall agree to issue, at the request of the receiving State Party, such travel documents or other authorization as may be necessary to enable the person to travel to and re-enter its territory.

5. This article shall be without prejudice to any right afforded to victims of trafficking in persons by any domestic law of the receiving State Party.

6. This article shall be without prejudice to any applicable bilateral or multilateral agreement or arrangement that governs, in whole or in part, the return of victims of trafficking in persons.

III. Prevention, cooperation and other measures

Article 9
Prevention of trafficking in persons

1. States Parties shall establish comprehensive policies, programs and other measures:

(a) To prevent and combat trafficking in persons; and

(b) To protect victims of trafficking in persons, especially women and children, from revictimization.

2. States Parties shall endeavor to undertake measures such as research, information and mass media campaigns and social and economic initiatives to prevent and combat trafficking in persons.

3. Policies, programs and other measures established in accordance with this article shall, as appropriate, include cooperation with non-governmental organizations, other relevant organizations and other elements of civil society.

4. States Parties shall take or strengthen measures, including through bilateral or multilateral cooperation, to alleviate the factors that make persons, especially women and children, vulnerable to trafficking, such as poverty, underdevelopment and lack of equal opportunity.

5. States Parties shall adopt or strengthen legislative or other measures, such as educational, social or cultural measures, including through bilateral and multilateral cooperation, to discourage the demand that fosters all forms of exploitation of persons, especially women and children, that leads to trafficking.

Article 10
Information exchange and training

1. Law enforcement, immigration or other relevant authorities of States Parties shall, as appropriate, cooperate with one another by exchanging information, in accordance with their domestic law, to enable them to determine:

(a) Whether individuals crossing or attempting to cross an international border with travel documents belonging to other persons or without travel documents are perpetrators or victims of trafficking in persons;

(b) The types of travel document that individuals have used or attempted to use to cross an international border for the purpose of trafficking in persons; and

(c) The means and methods used by organized criminal groups for the purpose of trafficking in persons, including the recruitment and transportation of victims, routes and links between and among individuals and groups engaged in such trafficking, and possible measures for detecting them.

2. States Parties shall provide or strengthen training for law enforcement, immigration and other relevant officials in the prevention of trafficking in persons. The training should focus on methods used in preventing such trafficking, prosecuting the traffickers and protecting the rights of the victims, including protecting the victims from the traffickers. The training should also take into account the need to consider human rights and child- and gender-sensitive issues and it should encourage cooperation with non-governmental organizations, other relevant organizations and other elements of civil society.

3. A State Party that receives information shall comply with any request by the State Party that transmitted the information that places restrictions on its use.

Article 11
Border measures

1. Without prejudice to international commitments in relation to the free movement of people, States Parties shall strengthen, to the extent possible, such border controls as may be necessary to prevent and detect trafficking in persons.

2. Each State Party shall adopt legislative or other appropriate measures to prevent, to the extent possible, means of transport operated by commercial carriers from being used in the commission of offences established in accordance with article 5 of this Protocol.

3. Where appropriate, and without prejudice to applicable international conventions, such measures shall include establishing the obligation of commercial carriers, including any transportation company or the owner or operator of any means of

transport, to ascertain that all passengers are in possession of the travel documents required for entry into the receiving State.

4. Each State Party shall take the necessary measures, in accordance with its domestic law, to provide for sanctions in cases of violation of the obligation set forth in paragraph 3 of this article.

5. Each State Party shall consider taking measures that permit, in accordance with its domestic law, the denial of entry or revocation of visas of persons implicated in the commission of offences established in accordance with this Protocol.

6. Without prejudice to article 27 of the Convention, States Parties shall consider strengthening cooperation among border control agencies by, inter alia, establishing and maintaining direct channels of communication.

Article 12
Security and control of documents

Each State Party shall take such measures as may be necessary, within available means:

(a) To ensure that travel or identity documents issued by it are of such quality that they cannot easily be misused and cannot readily be falsified or unlawfully altered, replicated or issued; and

(b) To ensure the integrity and security of travel or identity documents issued by or on behalf of the State Party and to prevent their unlawful creation, issuance and use.

Article 13
Legitimacy and validity of documents

At the request of another State Party, a State Party shall, in accordance with its domestic law, verify within a reasonable time the legitimacy and validity of travel or identity documents issued or purported to have been issued in its name and suspected of being used for trafficking in persons.

IV. Final provisions

Article 14
Saving clause

1. Nothing in this Protocol shall affect the rights, obligations and responsibilities of States and individuals under international law, including international humanitarian law and international human rights law and, in particular, where applicable, the 1951 Convention and the 1967 Protocol relating to the Status of Refugees and the principle of non-refoulement as contained therein.

2. The measures set forth in this Protocol shall be interpreted and applied in a way that is not discriminatory to persons on the ground that they are victims of trafficking in persons. The interpretation and application of those measures shall be consistent with internationally recognized principles of non-discrimination.

Article 15
Settlement of disputes

1. State Parties shall endeavour to settle disputes concerning the interpretation or application of this Protocol through negotiation.

2. Any dispute between two or more States Parties concerning the interpretation or application of this Protocol that cannot be settled

through negotiation within a reasonable time shall, at the request of one of those States Parties, be submitted to arbitration. If, six months after the date of the request for arbitration, those States Parties are unable to agree on the organization of the arbitration, any one of those States Parties may refer the dispute to the International Court of Justice by request in accordance with the Statute of the Court.

3. Each State Party may, at the time of signature, ratification, acceptance or approval of or accession to this Protocol, declare that it does not consider itself bound by paragraph 2 of this article. The other States Parties shall not be bound by paragraph 2 of this article with respect to any State Party that has made such a reservation.

4. Any State Party that has made a reservation in accordance with paragraph 3 of this article may at any time withdraw that reservation by notification to the Secretary-General of the United Nations.

Article 16
Signature, ratification, acceptance, approval and accession

1. This Protocol shall be open to all States for signature from 12 to 15 December 2000 in Palermo, Italy, and thereafter at United Nations Headquarters in New York until 12 December 2002.

2. This Protocol shall also be open for signature by regional economic integration organizations provided that at least one member State of such organization has signed this Protocol in accordance with paragraph 1 of this article.

3. This Protocol is subject to ratification, acceptance or approval. Instruments of ratification, acceptance or approval shall be deposited with the Secretary-General of the United Nations. A

regional economic integration organization may deposit its instrument of ratification, acceptance or approval if at least one of its member States has done likewise. In that instrument of ratification, acceptance or approval, such organization shall declare the extent of its competence with respect to the matters governed by this Protocol. Such organization shall also inform the depositary of any relevant modification in the extent of its competence.

4. This Protocol is open for accession by any State or any regional economic integration organization of which at least one member State is a Party to this Protocol. Instruments of accession shall be deposited with the Secretary-General of the United Nations. At the time of its accession, a regional economic integration organization shall declare the extent of its competence with respect to matters governed by this Protocol. Such organization shall also inform the depositary of any relevant modification in the extent of its competence.

Article 17
Entry into force

1. This Protocol shall enter into force on the ninetieth day after the date of deposit of the fortieth instrument of ratification, acceptance, approval or accession, except that it shall not enter into force before the entry into force of the Convention. For the purpose of this paragraph, any instrument deposited by a regional economic integration organization shall not be counted as additional to those deposited by member States of such organization.

2. For each State or regional economic integration organization ratifying, accepting, approving or acceding to this Protocol after

the deposit of the fortieth instrument of such action, this Protocol shall enter into force on the thirtieth day after the date of deposit by such State or organization of the relevant instrument or on the date this Protocol enters into force pursuant to paragraph 1 of this article, whichever is the later.

Article 18
Amendment

1. After the expiry of five years from the entry into force of this Protocol, a State Party to the Protocol may propose an amendment and file it with the Secretary-General of the United Nations, who shall thereupon communicate the proposed amendment to the States Parties and to the Conference of the Parties to the Convention for the purpose of considering and deciding on the proposal. The States Parties to this Protocol meeting at the Conference of the Parties shall make every effort to achieve consensus on each amendment. If all efforts at consensus have been exhausted and no agreement has been reached, the amendment shall, as a last resort, require for its adoption a two-thirds majority vote of the States Parties to this Protocol present and voting at the meeting of the Conference of the Parties.

2. Regional economic integration organizations, in matters within their competence, shall exercise their right to vote under this article with a number of votes equal to the number of their member States that are Parties to this Protocol. Such organizations shall not exercise their right to vote if their member States exercise theirs and vice versa.

3. An amendment adopted in accordance with paragraph 1 of this article is subject to ratification, acceptance or approval by States Parties.

4. An amendment adopted in accordance with paragraph 1 of this article shall enter into force in respect of a State Party ninety days after the date of the deposit with the Secretary-General of the United Nations of an instrument of ratification, acceptance or approval of such amendment.

5. When an amendment enters into force, it shall be binding on those States Parties which have expressed their consent to be bound by it. Other States Parties shall still be bound by the provisions of this Protocol and any earlier amendments that they have ratified, accepted or approved.

Article 19
Denunciation

1. A State Party may denounce this Protocol by written notification to the Secretary-General of the United Nations. Such denunciation shall become effective one year after the date of receipt of the notification by the Secretary-General.

2. A regional economic integration organization shall cease to be a Party to this Protocol when all of its member States have denounced it.

Article 20
Depositary and languages

1. The Secretary-General of the United Nations is designated depositary of this Protocol.

2. The original of this Protocol, of which the Arabic, Chinese, English, French, Russian and Spanish texts are equally authentic, shall be deposited with the Secretary-General of the United Nations.

IN WITNESS WHEREOF, the undersigned plenipotentiaries, being duly authorized thereto by their respective Governments, have signed this Protocol.

Glossary of Acronyms

CACE – Campaign Against Child Exploitation
CIA – Central Intelligence Agency
CSEC – Commercial Sexual Exploitation of Children
CST – Child Sex Tourism
ECPAT – End Child Prostitution, Child Pornography, and Child Trafficking for Sexual Purpose
EU – European Union
FBI – Federal Bureau of Investigation
HIV/AIDS – Human Immunodeficiency Virus / Acquired Immune Deficiency Syndrome
ICE – Immigration & Customs Enforcement
ILO – International Labor Organization
ILO-IPEC – International Labor Organization, International Program on the Elimination of Child Labor
IOM – International Organization for Migration
NGO – Non-Governmental Organization
OSCE – Organization for Security and Cooperation in Europe
PROTECT Act – Prosecutorial Remedies and Other Tools to End the Exploitation of Children Today
TVPA – Trafficking Victim Protection Act

TVPRA 2005 – Trafficking Victim Protection Reauthorization Act
UN – United Nations
UNDP – UN Development Program
UNESCO – United Nations Educational, Scientific and Cultural Organization
UNHABITAT – United Nations Human Settlements Program
UNHCR – United Nations High Commissioner for Refugees
UNICEF – International Child Development Centre
UNICEF – United Nations Children Fund
UNIFEM – United Nations Development Fund for Women
WHO – World Health Organization

Afterword

Women In Need Network will continue to work towards eradicating human trafficking, assisting trafficking victims, and educating service providers, law enforcement, and the public. The support and friendship of a few key people has made this task easier, which is why I must thank Marguerite Cavanaugh, Kathy and Lewis Dinkins, and Maria Ramirez for all they have done to help the victims of trafficking.

Human Trafficking Program Kit

This essential kit includes:

Modern Day Slavery ~ Human Trafficking Revealed (hardcover)
PowerPoint CD-ROM
Study Guide
Case Management Guide
Human Trafficking First Responder / Victim Emergency Plan
Human Trafficking information cards
Resources
Newsletter
Poster
Partnership application & memorandum of understanding
much more

Guides included in kit
Recognizing human trafficking victims
Communicating with human trafficking victims
Building trust with human trafficking
Task force
Special needs of human trafficking

Kit available for only $449 - yearly updates only $99

Enclosed is my check for $449 for the Human Trafficking
Program Kit
Make checks payable to Catherine Paris

Name: _____

Address: _____

City: _____ **State** _____ **Zip Code** _____

Primary Phone: (___) _____ **Fax: (___)** _____

Email: _____

Mail to:
Catherine Paris * P.O. Box 773134 * Ocala, FL 34477-3134
www.ModernDaySlavery.org
www.CatherineParis.com

About the Author

Catherine Paris, founder of Women In Need Network, is an expert in the fields of domestic violence and human trafficking. She has created educational programs, written curricula, speaks, and trains on these topics. Catherine is available for speaking, training and as a consultant; please contact her for further information:

c_paris@WomenInNeedNetwork.org

Human Rights Experience:
* CEO & Founder of Women In Need Network
* WIN International Training Institute
* M.I.T./SloanSpace: Chair of Gender Issues & Human Rights Working Group
* Speaker
* Trainer
* Author
* Developer of Curricula

Writing Experience:
Books
Modern Slave Trade: Human Trafficking Revealed Information Every Woman Should: Domestic Violence Handbook

Curricula
Faith Based Community Response to Family Violence
Effects of Family Violence on Children
Family Violence: Justice For All
Human Trafficking: How Much Do You Know?
The Cost of Domestic Violence in the Workplace
Sexual Harassment in the Workplace
Helping Male Victims of Domestic Violence
Train the Trainer (3 day program)
Train the Jailor - Domestic Violence Programs for Prison Personnel

www.CatherineParis.com

www.ingramcontent.com/pod-product-compliance
Lightning Source LLC
Chambersburg PA
CBHW051726260326
41914CB00031B/1762/J